HIDING
FOR
MY LIFE

HIDING FOR MY LIFE

BEING GAY IN THE NAVY

KAREN SOLT

SHE WRITES PRESS

Published 2024
Printed in the United States of America

Print ISBN: 978-1-64742-672-9
E-ISBN: 978-1-64742-673-6
Library of Congress Control Number: 2023924304

For information, address:
She Writes Press
1569 Solano Ave #546
Berkeley, CA 94707

Interior design and typeset by Katherine Lloyd, The DESK
She Writes Press is a division of SparkPoint Studio, LLC.

To Mom,
for giving me your wicked sense of humor,
a tough spirit, and the uncanny ability
to always land on my feet.

And to Paco,
for bursting my heart wide open
and helping me remember my capacity for love.

AUTHOR'S NOTE

This book is a memoir. It reflects the author's present recollections of experiences over time. In an effort to protect the identity of some of the people who appear in this memoir, their names and characteristics have been changed.

CONTENTS

PART THREE

PART ONE

THIS TRUTH
WON'T SET ME FREE

I t's Monday, September 18, 1995, and today is my first day wearing the uniform of a chief petty officer (CPO)—starched and pressed khakis, one-inch gold United States Navy anchors on my collar points and one on my brushed gold belt buckle, my name tag centered over my right shirt pocket and my ribbons over my left, my warfare insignia directly above my ribbons, and my garrison cap with a gold chief's anchor pinned to its front left side tucked under my belt. Every enlisted Navy sailor strives to be a chief, and I've arrived. This is the biggest achievement of my life.

The sunrise is obscured by dark clouds and fine mist lands on my windshield as I approach the front gate at Naval Air Station Whidbey Island, Washington. I dim my headlights and hand the sentry my ID card.

"Good morning, Chief!" he says, then inspects both sides of my ID before handing it back.

"Good morning!" I reply, flying high on the sound of that word. *Chief.*

The gate guard steps back and waves me through and I

proceed to VP-1 (Patrol Squadron One), my aviation squadron on the Naval Air Station. For the first time ever, I park in CPO parking, just outside of the VP hangar. I place my garrison cap on my head and quicken my pace to enter the hangar through one of the open sliding doors as a gentle rain starts to fall.

The VP hangar at Whidbey Island is a massive structure capable of holding four large aircraft. The frame is constructed of large wooden beams resembling those found in old barns and is wrapped with ivory white metal siding. Huge double doors on each side can slide open to allow planes to be towed inside for maintenance (today, the crew is working on one of our four-propeller P-3C Orion airplanes). There are two decks, or levels, inside the hangar, each of which holds myriad offices utilized by command leadership, administrative, operational, and maintenance personnel.

Pride surges through me with each step; I hold my head a little higher as I stride across the great expanse of the hangar floor in my shiny new brown shoes. Wearing the uniform and embodying the traits of a chief petty officer is a dream come true.

Shipmates I have worked with for the past three years beam and greet me with my new honorific title. "Good morning, Chief!" repeatedly echoes through the huge chamber as I pass by.

"Good morning," I respond over and over, feeling the difference that rank makes.

My office, and all of the other offices besides Maintenance, are one deck up. Feeling weightless, I take the stairs with ease. When I arrive topside, I follow the hallways to the Admin Office, where the most amazing and tireless group of yeomen—Navy sailors whose specialty is clerical work—I know are gathered around Petty Officer Kimbrough's desk in the back of the spacious office, already hard at work. High bookshelves line the walls and hold every manual a yeoman needs to do the job.

Large windows look down on the squadron's seven other P-3C Orion airplanes.

"Hey, everyone!"

My team hops up from where they're seated to meet me in the middle of the office, and they all bombard me with high fives and hugs. "Chief!"

It truly cannot get any better.

Petty Officer Kimbrough, a second class yeoman whom I've been working with for the past year, is an absolute rock star. Now the leading petty officer (LPO), since I am a newly appointed chief, she launches into the tasks for the day as we situate ourselves around her desk. A bubbly, fun Filipino Caucasian powerhouse with round cheeks and a perpetual smile, Kimbrough is consistently two steps ahead of every single action item that comes across our desks. Her work ethic makes my life infinitely easier. She is hungry and thirsty for the responsibilities that come with increased leadership—a flashback to a version of me from just a few short years ago.

Like always, she has a handle on the day and I'm only in her way, so I leave my team and walk one room over to my desk, which is situated in an entryway just outside of the offices of our commanding officer (CO), executive officer (XO), and command master chief (CMC).

Seated at my desk, I've just begun my daily ritual of going through my inbox when the CMC walks in, stops, and looks down at me with a full smile. "Good morning, Karen."

He has never called me Karen before.

"Good morning, H," I hear myself say—timidly and for the first time, because chiefs and *only* chiefs can call him by his name (or, in this case, his initial).

"Do you have a minute?" he asks. "I'd like to see you in my office."

H's stature is formidable and his military presence natural without his even trying. He is the very epitome of who I am striving to become. The overhead light reflects off of his bald head, and the muscles ripple under the skin in his forearms. He is an incredibly strong man, though not especially tall at five foot nine. As the top enlisted person in my squadron and my mentor, Master Chief Halverson has made me rise to a new level. Without a doubt, he has made me a better person in the years I've served under his leadership.

"Absolutely." I grab my notebook and stand to follow him.

H's office is a spotless, bright, organized room with tan carpet. A large wooden desk and chair fill half the room and face the door. Two additional chairs are situated in front of where he sits, which are usually reserved for a sailor and that sailor's chief. Chief petty officer manuals, plaques, and some of his awards are neatly arranged on a tall wooden bookshelf that rises behind him.

He walks around his desk, turns, and smiles as he places his hands on his hips. I have always been secretly amazed by his exemplary personal appearance. His uniform is always sharp and crisp, and fits him like it was tailor-made for his wide shoulders and fit, trim waist. My chest expands as a single realization comes over me: for the first time in three years, I feel like I actually belong in this room with him.

He seems to be sizing me up as well. "You're a natural in that uniform," he says. "I am so proud of you."

Making H proud, but mostly hearing that he already is, means everything to me. "Thanks, H," I say, trying to keep my voice steady. "I really appreciate that. I can't believe I'm wearing khakis!"

H reaches down, opens the middle drawer in his desk, takes out a small red box, and holds it in his hands. The box is familiar; it's similar to the one I purchased a few weeks ago with gold chief anchors centered behind a clear plastic cover, the ones I'm now wearing on my collar points. He gazes at it for a moment.

"These were mine, Karen," he says, looking up, "the *nine* anchors that I was pinned with." He reaches across his desk and hands me the box. Sitting beneath the plastic cover is a set of well-worn and slightly tarnished master chief anchors, which are exactly like chief anchors but with two silver stars at the top, as master chiefs are two pay grades above E-7, the rank to which I have just been promoted. He studies me for a moment, then softly says, "They are now yours. I want you to have them for the day you make master chief."

I'm stunned. It's a common tradition for chiefs to pass down the anchors they were pinned with to someone they've groomed, but receiving H's personal master chief anchors is an honor I never saw coming. There are many incredible chiefs and senior chiefs in the squadron who would cherish this gift, but he chose me. Me. It's only my first day as chief, after all. My next goal is senior chief, however, and then, he's right, my ultimate goal is to fill his shoes and become a command master chief—which, at the earliest, could happen six years from now.

The gravity of this moment is not lost on me, and I'm mindful of the responsibility he is bestowing on me: he's asking me to carry on his legacy. His anchors firmly in my hand, I stand tall and meet his eyes. "Wow, H, this is incredibly gracious of you. I promise I'll wear them proudly someday."

"You're welcome, Karen," he says, seemingly pleased. "I have no doubt you'll get there in no time." Then his smile fades, his thinning eyebrows crease the bridge of his nose, and his face takes on a more serious expression. "Um . . ." He hesitates. "There's one other reason I needed to speak with you."

"Sure, H—what's up?" I say in a chipper tone, although the rapid change in his demeanor is troubling.

H is always one to cut straight to the chase. "My life at home has been unbearable," he says. "It's been like this for years, and I just can't do it any longer. I'm leaving my marriage and am getting a divorce." There is an awkward pause as he looks down. When his eyes rise to meet mine again, they look soft. "And I want to be with you. I'm in love with you, Karen. As soon as I retire, we can be together. Will you be with me?"

My heart drops and my insides sink. *Damn it. Damn it. Damn it.*

H is retiring soon. He is on the verge of completing the Navy maximum: thirty years of service. He asked to remain on active duty a little while longer, but his request was denied. So he already knows he is about to lose his Navy, which he loves more than anything. And now he is about to lose his marriage. And he is hoping I will be there to catch his fall.

I see the sense of this on one level. H and I have become close throughout our years working together—traveling, battling each other in endless games of cribbage, working out, killing time stationed in faraway places, ribbing each other with the ease of hardworking shipmates who have been put through their paces. H is Joe Navy, and since meeting him I have strived to be just like him.

But I don't want to be *with* him.

My previous high and excitement dissipate, as if the last hour was a beautiful dream that never occurred. My chest caves in, my shoulders sink, and the air leaves my lungs little by little until I am completely deflated. With no idea what to do or how to respond, I stand frozen and try to ease my breath. My mind reels as I look past him toward the now blurry items sitting on his bookshelf.

He does not release me from his gaze. He waits, the secret of his heart in the space between us, looking for just one positive sign.

And I can't give it to him.

In a single moment, the best day of my career has completely flipped upside down. I stand there, paralyzed by fear. I want to flee, stop feeling, and completely check out. But I can't. Not now. This is about survival.

The silence is deafening as H watches me for what feels like decades, his expression landing somewhere between hope and fear—hope that he will get the answer he longs for, and fear that he won't.

My feelings are exactly the same, only for much different reasons. My hope is that I will survive this encounter and we both walk away intact. But my fear is much more pronounced and palpable than his. Mine is a fear that my life could change in ways that will be horribly painful; a fear that I am about to hurt and anger a man whom I deeply respect; a fear that all I have accomplished in the Navy will be stripped away and I will lose everything I have built over the last eleven and a half years of my career if I say the wrong thing.

Like no other moment in my entire life, it is critical I make the right move.

My heart is pounding out of my chest, and my legs feel weak. I have to engage my military bearing, shut down my fear, and keep it together. I have to tell him my truth. But if I utter the words I am about say, there is no going back.

It is a huge risk. In the next few seconds, I will tell the most senior enlisted leader in my command, a man who has the power to instantly end my career, that I am gay.

And being gay in the Navy is a crime.

I am absolutely gutted.

My first day as a chief petty officer. Before I walked into this office, I was relishing the rewards of a career that is rapidly taking off; happily anticipating reuniting with my love, Sue, after too many years stationed apart; and delighting in the fact that I am now over halfway to my eligibility for retirement. But all of this could be gone in the next few seconds, because of a system that forces me to stay hidden if I am to continue to serve.

Will the truth set me free, or will it end everything I have worked so hard to achieve? I don't know. But I do know that once I speak these words, there is no going back.

"H," I begin, "there is something I need to tell you."

I fill my lungs with one more deep breath, exhale slowly, and venture into territory that scares me more than almost anything I can imagine.

Chapter 1

THE SLICKEST
OF NAVY RECRUITERS

It's the last class of the day, and a Navy recruiter strides back and forth in front of the huge chalkboard of my high school social studies class. He talks about the benefits of life in the Navy. It's spring of 1983, my senior year, but I'm not sure if my teachers will give me the grades I need for a diploma, as there are a few classes I mostly ditch in favor of partying. I'm failing more than one of them.

The recruiter is a large man, a submarine chief petty officer who wears a crisp khaki uniform with gold anchors on each of his lapels and a pewter submariner emblem centered over rows of colorful ribbons above his left shirt pocket. His wide khaki hat with a shiny black brim and a large gold anchor centered in front sits on the table before him. He rambles on and on about seeing the world while I daydream and nod off. Patriotic? I do love baseball and hot dogs and can recite the Pledge of Allegiance, but that's where my patriotism ends. My allegiance is to my recklessness. At seventeen, I am well versed in the fine art of rebellion and somehow always manage to land on my feet.

He finishes his spiel, and I am reaching for my backpack

when my teacher abruptly announces she's excusing most of the class—with the exception of a few students. She reads some names from a list, one of which is mine.

Annoyed, I drop my backpack, sit back, and look around, noting that none of the half dozen of my peers who have also been asked to remain have plans after high school. My smart buddies who are off to college in the fall grab their stuff and tease me as they exit the classroom—"Go get 'em, Navy girl."

"You all are going to personally meet with the Navy recruiter," my teacher announces. "He'd like to ask you a few questions." She looks straight at me and grins.

It's no secret I'm on a one-way track to a life headed nowhere. I'm sure she hopes I will do something positive with my life, like maybe join the Navy, before I end up in jail.

Not likely, I think.

When it's my turn, I slump down at a desk in front of the recruiter, drop my backpack on the ground next to me, and exhale loudly. I'm there by protest and am obviously irritated that this bullshit is interfering with my hangout time.

He ignores me and scans a sheet of paper. I stare at his huge hat, which now sits on the edge of the desk.

He eventually looks up. "So, Karen, you want to join the Navy?"

"Uh, not really . . ."

He doesn't flinch. "Well, you scored really well on the ASVAB. You could have a nice career in the Navy."

I have zero recollection of taking the ASVAB (Armed Services Vocational Aptitude Battery) earlier this year. Apparently it's used to help the armed forces ascertain abilities in certain areas, all of which count toward a score that determines if you're qualified to enlist in the US military. It appears I am qualified. Awesome.

I slouch back in my seat, roll my eyes, and watch him with unconcealed irritation.

Still not flinching and obviously very skilled at dealing with defiant teenagers, he looks back down at his paperwork. "Mind if I ask you a few questions?"

"Whatever," I say, though what I'm thinking is, *Yeah, actually, no thanks*—and then, for some unknown reason, I stay and let him ask his questions. Muttered answers tumble from my lips for a variety of routine questions until he asks his jackpot question.

"Have you done drugs in the last six months?"

This I answer clearly. "Yep."

His mouth was poised for the next mundane question; now he fumbles over his words, stops, and raises his wide eyes. I calmly relish his apparent discomfort. He's probably used to teenagers saying no to this question.

An impressive *I am now your father* look takes over his face. "Don't do any more drugs for the next six months, and I will contact you again."

My backpack in my hand quicker than quick, I throw a *later, suckaaaa* smirk and one last eye roll his way and book it out of there. Navy bullet dodged.

A petite, gray-haired woman sits behind the steering wheel of an old red Buick with dented silver hubcaps as I fill her car with premium gasoline. My breath makes clouds in the evening air as I swap the nozzle from one hand to the other and jog in place in my slip-on blue-and-yellow Vans with blue-and-white-checkered soles. An embarrassing red "TEXACO" patch is on the upper left side of my light gray recycled-and-smells-like-grease men's shirt, which I've lined with an off-white long-sleeve thermal that I wear tucked into my faded 501 jeans. Life on the outside, as if high school was some kind of prison, is not going quite as well as I had imagined, and every time I put on this Texaco shirt and leave home for the gas station, freedom doesn't seem so free.

It's been five months since I barely graduated (and I only managed that by sweet-talking one of my teachers into giving me a D instead of an F). I landed my first job at a car wash and had a few months of fun cleaning cars but mostly having water fights with my coworkers in shorts and T-shirts in the hot Arizona sun. That job became not so much fun once fall arrived and all 115 pounds of me started freezing her ass off. Quitting, however, led me to this full-service Texaco gas station, where I have no idea what I'm doing.

The Buick is full and I'm already walking back to the warmth of the station, where I will blow on my hands and count the seemingly never-ending minutes till I'm done with this hellhole for the day, when the woman cracks open her window. "Also, please clean my windshield and look under my hood, young lady."

Shit.

I'm an expert at cleaning and squeegeeing windows, and I'm moving as quickly as I can; her windshield looks amazing within seconds. But when I raise the hood, my confidence evaporates. I stare at the engine for a minute. I have no clue what I'm looking for—couldn't find a dipstick to save my life. So I just stand where she can't see a damn thing I'm doing, let a few clouds escape my lips, and "look under the hood," and after what seems like a reasonable amount of time to check things out, I slam the hood back down and smile.

"Everything looks good under here!"

I am not a good person.

She pays and drives off and I return to the station and sit on the metal swivel stool in front of the window, praying that not one more soul needs gas tonight.

My job at Texaco takes me through the rest of fall. I've just arrived home one evening after a god-awful shift, by now 100 percent sure this will not be my career, when the phone rings.

I answer, and a voice I was not expecting to hear again sounds through the receiver.

"Hey, Karen, it's Chief Shady!"

"Oh . . . hey," I hesitantly respond.

"I'm calling to follow up with you. Have you done any drugs in the last six months?"

"No," I say, and instantly regret it.

"Great! How about you and I go down to Phoenix on Thursday and talk to some people? I'll even drive."

"Sure, Chief Shady," I cautiously say. "I'll go to Phoenix with you to talk to some people."

If it gets him off my back, what can it hurt?

He picks me up Thursday morning and drives me to Phoenix, where—he was right—I do talk to some people. Actually, I talk to a *lot* of people. In a large, fluorescent-lit room with dark blue hotel carpet that's faded in the aisleways that pass between the dozens of desks packed inside, I sit and talk with one person while he asks me a bunch of questions and writes down my answers. Then I move to another desk and talk to another person. Then I move on again.

This goes on for what seems like hours, but time is an illusion, and it also goes a lot slower when you're young and hungover, so it might only be minutes. I'm just not sure.

After the talking-to-people phase is complete, I am led to an open room with a carpeted platform lined with tall flags stuck into large metal disks, including the American, Arizona State, and US Navy flags. A dozen other young people are standing on the platform in front of the flags, and I am told to join them. A tall, thin sailor in a white uniform stands in front of us and raises his right hand.

"Raise your right hand and repeat after me," he commands.

I'm puzzled, but everyone else raises their right hand so I slowly raise mine too, feeling very strange. *Who are these people?*

The sailor says, "I, state your name . . ."

"I, Karen Solt . . ." I repeat stiffly.

". . . do solemnly swear . . ."

". . . do solemnly swear . . ."

I repeat every word that sailor speaks with my right hand in the air, and as I do I slowly—and I do mean *slowly*—realize that the words I am speaking form the Oath of Enlistment.

"I, Karen Solt, do solemnly swear that I will support and defend the Constitution of the United States against all enemies, foreign and domestic; that I will bear true faith and allegiance to the same; and that I will obey the orders of the president of the United States and the orders of the officers appointed over me, according to regulations and the Uniform Code of Military Justice. So help me God."

So help me God is right . . .

Chief Shady hums along to country music and sometimes gives me a wide, shiny-toothed grin as he drives me home. I sit low in the passenger seat and say nothing, still not entirely sure what just happened. Did I enlist in the US Navy, or no? One thing I am sure about: I feel like I've been railroaded.

He ignores my sour mood all the way back to my hometown, a particular attitude written all over his happy, humming face: *Who's the sucka now?*

When he pulls up in front of my house, he turns to me with the biggest smile. "This was a good day, Karen. I'll be in touch soon."

I want to punch him in the face, but I already feel like an idiot, so I get out, shut the car door, and walk toward my front door.

My head is down as I enter the living room to find my mom doing what she loves more than anything: reading a book. A petite woman with short brown, frosted hair, she's in a light green button-up evening robe and warm, fluffy white socks and is peacefully sitting sideways under a floor lamp on her favorite yellow love seat in front of our gas fireplace.

She smiles at me and sets her book on her lap. "Hey, Square!" Mom made up this nickname when I was a child and would often sing, *Kare-Kare, my little Square, you are my little Square-er.* "How'd it go?"

My deer-in-headlights look gives her pause; she takes her legs off of the couch, puts her feet on the glass coffee table, and pats the seat next to her.

I flop down, put my feet up with hers, and stare at the fire dancing over the gas logs. "I think I just joined the Navy."

She takes a second to process this. "What do you mean you 'think'? Where's the paperwork?"

I sideways-hand her my folder, and she thumbs through the paperwork before letting out a heavy sigh.

I look down at the top sheet of paper. It says I am slated for boot camp on 20 February 1984. It is October of 1983. In exactly four months, I have to report for duty.

I am smart and bright and quick-witted, an expert at wiggling out of a jam. But I am in the sinkhole of realization that I can't lie, cheat, or manipulate my way out of the four years in the US Navy I have just committed to serve—an eternity to my eighteen-year-old self.

I have just signed my life away.

Mom's white fluffy socks fall against the edge of my foot as I lean my chin against my fist and try to make sense of what has just happened. She sits quietly beside me, also deep in her own thoughts.

Finally, she shakes her head and picks up her book. Mom is used to me getting into jams and knows I'm a bit of a wild child; in fact, that quality is something she not-so-secretly loves about me. She regularly validates my scrappiness, like she does with her next words: "I don't worry about you, Square. You always manage to land on your feet."

Regardless, there truly isn't anything either of us can do about this. Today, I became US Government property. This realization is just beginning to sink in.

Chapter 2

TIME TO
SEE THE WORLD

There are sixteen things about leaving the nest in February of 1984 and flying all the way across the country to start Navy boot camp in Orlando, Florida, that stick out most prominently in my memory. All right, seventeen if you count feeling hugely relieved that I'd gotten out of having sex with my boyfriend at the time. Maybe eighteen if you count the fact that there was absolutely nothing that made me feel good about enlisting in the Navy. Okay, nineteen—despite my reluctance, I knew it was time to grow up.

Here is the list: 1) Being put on the bus by my parents while crying; 2) Not remembering the flight to Florida. Was I drunk? Most likely; 3) Getting off of the bus in Orlando and feeling like crying; 4) Being too fucking scared to cry; 5) Having a bunch of Navy people yell and start making me and other scared shitless people move really quickly; 6) Getting all of my hair cut off, except one inch of perm on the top, and looking like an awkward boy; 7) Standing in a long line of other numb recruits to receive shots in my upper arm with a pneumatic gun full of tiny needles in a half-inch circle; 8) Calling home after a few days and sobbing uncontrollably, to the point where I was choking on my tears and my parents thought I was dying; 9) Making one new friend, only one; 10) Sitting in a room and panicking when it filled with tear gas; 11) Learning how to fold every piece of my clothing into little tiny squares; 12) Getting "twenty minutes and twenty minutes only!" to eat; 13) Jumping into a pool with my uniform on, then taking the pants off, tying the legs together, slamming them over my head, and being told this would be my flotation device should I ever fall off of a ship; 14) Trying not to create any waves, my rebellious spirit quashed; 15) Being scared all of the time, every single second; and 16) Wondering 100 percent of the time what the hell I had gotten myself into.

After getting yelled at in front of the bus and falling into complete overwhelm, I am herded into the beauty parlor, where my individuality is removed by cutting my hair. This takes less than a minute with electric clippers. I then line up in my civilian clothes behind others with fresh haircuts and am led to the uniform section, an enormous, bright room filled with white tables. I am first issued a large green duffel bag called a seabag that will carry my entire life in it, and I stencil my name and initials on it in one-inch black letters. My guide for stenciling is a thick brown piece of paper that has my name, initials, and social security number cut out of it. Everything I currently own—yes, even my underwear—I will stencil with either a white or a black stencil pen that requires me to press down with all my might until the little silver ball gets out of the way, allowing ink to flow.

The workers who process new recruits eyeball my body and hand me a variety of uniforms that I quickly roll up and stuff in my seabag: Cotton Summer Whites; Polyester Dress Whites; Winter Blues, which are not blue but black wool; Dress Blues, the fancy dress uniform, also black and wool. I am issued a dress black-and-white combination hat that looks like an upside-down bucket, black oxford shoes, and steel-toed, ankle-high, black chukka boots. Three sets of dungarees—the working uniform, and what I will wear the most—are handed to me. These remind me of the gas station. Dungarees consist of a long-sleeve, dark blue, fleece-lined windbreaker jacket; a light blue button-up shirt; and hideous, high-waisted, denim bell-bottom pants with two front and two back square pockets. They are accessorized with a black belt, silver belt buckle, steel-toed black chukka boots, black socks, and a black garrison cover—a soft, flat fabric hat that resembles a ripe banana and is adorned on its front left side with a pewter eagle. A large lady behind one of the tables bellows, "Hats in the Navy are called 'covers,' ladies, as they cover your head."

In charge of my boot camp company are two recruit company commanders (RCCs). They might as well be God in this moment, as everything I do is either approved of (almost never) or disapproved of (constantly) by them. One is a tall and lanky first class petty officer (E-6) with pasty white skin, short gray hair, large, clear-rimmed plastic glasses, and a deep, raspy voice. The other is a short Black second class petty officer (E-5) with a perfectly formed afro, a quick wit, and a bodybuilder's physique. They both have a toughness that scares the shit out of me and I never look either of them in the eye, even when they get inches from my face and try and goad me into it. The last thing I'm looking for these days is attention.

My company is comprised of about seventy women with similar haircuts. We live together in a "compartment," a huge open room as big as a football field. A spotless white linoleum floor spans the deck, which we wax and buff each day to maintain its sheen. Overhead bright fluorescent lighting is its own form of torture, and not only shines from the ceiling but also reflects off the polished deck. Big square structural beams run through the center of the compartment between dozens of bunk beds. Each bed has a small shelving unit on its outer edge, and this is where I neatly keep my few possessions.

Becoming a part of the military machine is intimidating, overwhelming, and scary, and alcohol withdrawal blindsides me in those grueling eight weeks. Without my liquid courage, a roller coaster of feelings and emotions bombards me, frightening the hell out of me. I am scared to stand out or be noticed, which is confounding, since I usually thrive on chaos. As I am confronted with my own insecurity and fragility, boot camp has its intended effect: out of necessity, I bond with and come to rely upon the shipmates in my company—I become a part of the team. Being independent, something I have always craved, is not useful here. Without my shipmates, I am nothing.

A typical day in boot camp is jam-packed with so much activity I quickly forget who "Karen" is. The day begins with "Reveille," a horrible roar of a bugle call that startles me upright in my lower bunk. It feels like I've been dead asleep for less than thirty minutes, but even though the windows are black, my RCCs say "Reveille" blows at sunrise.

When I realize where I am, my feet hit the deck and my nervous system goes into fight or flight. I meticulously make my bed with perfect 45-degree corners on my smoothly tucked-in sheets and fold my scratchy gray wool blanket into a square and place it at the foot of my bed. I then pull the top flap back from its corner, making it a square blanket with a diagonal line. As with much of boot camp, this only feels like a mind game and doesn't seem to have a purpose.

When I'm confident a quarter could be bounced off my sheets, I flip-flop my way to the head (bathroom), where I dissociate, avoid eye contact, and self-consciously shower with my fellow recruits next to a tall silver pole that has six shower heads attached to it.

I get dressed in my dungaree uniform and line up on the inside of my bunk and stand at attention next to my upper-rack bunky, vacantly facing my fellow recruits on the opposite side of the room. My RCCs inspect the room while I bite the inside of my lip and listen for yelling, commotion, or bedding to hit the deck—a telltale sign that someone didn't pass inspection—and pray I'm not the cause of it.

After the entire company passes bunk inspection, I head down the outside concrete stairwell, get into formation, and shiver at attention until I hear the magic words, "Forward, march!"—at which seventy women step out in unison with their left foot and march to chow using cadence: "Left, left, left-right-left."

It is still dark, which proves my sunrise point.

The formation is brought to a stop at the entrance of the chow hall. "And . . . halt!" We take one last step with our left foot and snap our right foot next to it, landing back at attention—heels touching, toes at a 45-degree angle.

A sailor emerges from the chow hall. "Company K046! You have twenty minutes, and twenty minutes only, to eat!"

We are let into the hall, and I cram as much food down my throat as quickly as possible (a habit I'll hold on to decades from now). This is one of the few ways to numb out during these eight weeks. Thank God for ice cream sandwiches smothered with peanut butter. Without eating one at every single meal, I'm not sure I would have gotten this far.

Back in formation after chow, our RCCs march us either to the barracks to clean, work on our uniforms, and endure more inspections, or subject us to whatever "unique" training is happening that day. Sometimes I sit on the floor and try to stay awake while we learn about basic military culture, such as saluting etiquette, legal issues, the pay system, or the Navy's officer and enlisted ranking and seniority structure. Enlisted personnel start at recruit (E-1) and rise to master chief petty officer (E-9). Officers start at ensign (O-1) and rise to four-star admiral (O-10). There are chief warrant officers, who were previously enlisted chief petty officers before getting commissioned. Commissioned officers outrank all enlisted personnel. As an E-1, everyone outranks me, which only reminds me I've made a huge mistake.

Other training sessions require me to jump into a freezing pool, go to medical for additional screenings, or visit the uniform shop for more tailored fittings. The scariest task is donning fire gear and holding a hose in a burning building while I put out a "compartment" fire, which we all have to learn to do because everyone is responsible for fighting fires onboard ships.

My uniform takes constant attention to perfect. There are multiple ironing boards in my compartment and each day we are required to work on our uniforms, so I pull one next to my bunk. Spray starch helps me press in single creases and avoid dreaded "railroad tracks." This is critical to my survival. Three sprays of starch aid me in a quick pressing of my shirtsleeves and collar. I iron five vertical creases—called military creases—into my shirts, one that splits the middle of each front pocket and three that travel down the back, one centered and two approximately six inches lateral from the middle. When I get dressed, I pinch my military creases, pull them laterally, and tuck the excess under the fold of my pinch, which makes my shirt neater and flatter. All of my dress pants have a center crease, but dungarees do not. They are ironed flat, which is the only thing I like about them.

I polish my boots using water and torn strips from a cut-up T-shirt. I stick my index and middle fingers in the strip, wrap the excess around my hand and hold it in my palm, then alternate polish and small amounts of water, making little circles over and over until I can see my reflection in the toe of the boot. Lastly, I polish my dull belt buckle using a substance in a skinny metal can called Brasso. My belt buckle never shines well, which gives my RCCs more opportunities to yell at me.

Uniform inspections happen daily. If one recruit doesn't pass inspection, none of us do, so these can take minutes or hours. My aching feet are a constant reminder of my new life, and I've learned two ways of standing. The first is at attention, which is not so hard, as long as I keep my knees a little soft so I don't pass out. The other is parade rest, which is neither a parade nor rest: my feet wide and arms placed behind my back with my hands palm-out, flat, and together. In both poses, I covertly flex my muscles and wiggle my toes while keeping my peripheral vision peeled for my very perceptive RCCs.

After uniform inspection, I endure drill time and the exhaustive repetitive practice of basic military movements—"Left, face!" "Right, face!" "About, face!" There are so many faces, and I can do all of them with absolute precision, while holding the butt of my fake rifle in my right hand, the trigger toward me and the barrel softly resting on my right clavicle, by the end of the first day. After I put my rifle away, I work on snapping my right arm into an exact 90-degree-angle salute that magically lands the first two fingers of my rigid hand on the edge of my garrison cover. This proves to be a clumsy exercise in futility. My RCCs relentlessly berate me. "Recruit Solt! You look like a goddamn idiot! Get this shit right! You will constantly be saluting officers and will not embarrass me in the Fleet!"

"Yes, Petty Officer!" I shout, and snap my right arm up again, only to hit myself in the forehead.

It's in these moments I have learned to look straight through my RCC who is yelling two inches in front of my face using a lifesaving skill set known as "military bearing," which is like turning on a silent force field. Emotions and vulnerability become the enemy and are quickly neutralized. Anxiety and fear are masked by standing a little straighter and, when allowed to, speaking more directly and in a deeper voice. Military bearing is a mind-over-matter tactic and will serve me in countless moments well beyond boot camp.

Once drill time is over, I join my fellow recruits outside in my dark blue short shorts and tucked-in white-with-blue-trim crewneck T-shirt—both with a big "N" on them. We march to the grinder for physical fitness, as if I'm not already worn the hell out. Along the way and during my workouts, I silently curse myself for being a smoker.

I stumble, out of breath, back into the compartment an hour later, quickly rinse off, get back into my dungarees, and march in formation to chow, where one last meal fills me up for the evening.

The day wraps up with some personal time, where I can either smoke in a large classroom with the smokers (which I do) or sit on my rack and write letters (which I don't). This is also when I put final touches on my uniform for the following day. Naps are against the law, so when Taps, a slower and more welcome bugle call, goes off in the late evening, for the first time all day my fight-or-flight responses relax.

Sleep arrives within seconds.

When boot camp graduation finally arrives, my parents and younger brother, Paul, drive from Arizona to see me graduate. Paul recently turned thirteen and is merely happy to see his big sister. My dad, an Army veteran, now has two children in the military—me and my older brother, Dave, who is in the Air Force and stationed in England—and he is over-the-moon proud. My mom is just grateful I'm not dead, as those phone calls home were touch-and-go. I would sometimes hear her whisper to my dad during our conversations, "Ron, she says she's dying! Do you think she's dying!?"

The Navy has various specialties, or "ratings," like hospital corpsman, engineman, yeoman, personnelman, aviation ordnanceman, and many more. Most of my boot camp peers will be heading directly from here to their "A" school, where they will receive training for the specialty rating they were guaranteed when they enlisted.

Then there are those of us who don't have a rating or a specific guarantee, like me. What I didn't know before I got here was that recruiters must enlist a certain number of undesignated, or non-rated, sailors so ships have enough workers to cover shipboard evolutions, upkeep, and basic seamanship. These skills are taught in seaman "apprenticeship training," also in Orlando; that's where I'm headed next. After I complete apprentice training to learn these basic skills, I will go to a command and learn a different skill, or rating, that interests me through on-the-job training. Only then will I be able to apply for an official rating. My ability to sign documents without understanding their true intent is biting me in the ass once again.

At the beginning of apprenticeship training, my instructor passes each of us a sheet of paper to "request" the type of command or place that interests us. "This is your dream sheet," she says. "Your official orders will be received in a few weeks, but you will use this sheet to request either where you want to be stationed or what kind of command you want to go to."

I fill out my dream sheet. As an E-1, or seaman recruit, I am fully aware I am as low as they go, so the only thing I write is "West Coast." I don't care what command I go to, as long as I'm closer to home.

Orders are written by the Bureau of Naval Personnel in Washington, DC, and are sent via electronic means, called message traffic, to the schoolhouse. During the final week of apprenticeship training, my instructor holds up a stack of flimsy inked carbon paper and announces, "Orders are in!"

She calls us up one by one, using our last names. When she finally shouts, "Solt!" I walk to the front of the room and take the sheet from her, excited to see where I'm going. San Francisco? San Diego? Alameda? Washington State?

I can't believe what I'm reading: I am to report to the USS *Frank Cable*, a submarine tender located in Charleston, *South Carolina*. Definitely not the West Coast.

A submarine tender does just as the name describes: tends to the submarines that pull up alongside and tie up to the ship. As its tender, the *Frank Cable* will provide that submarine's supplies and perform much of its maintenance. Submarine tenders don't go out to sea very often; their mission is to be stationary so it's easy for submarines to dock alongside them and get their needs met.

With my new orders I am now "Going to the Fleet," which everyone says as if that makes me cool. But when my school instructor passes by and looks over my shoulder, she laughs. "The Rank Frank! Who'd you piss off, Solt?"

I'm officially screwed.

Chapter 3

NAIVE GIRL
ON A BIG-ASS SHIP

It's Saturday, June 9, and I've just arrived in Charleston. The cab stops and the cabbie looks back over his right shoulder. "Here we are. This is Pier Mike. It'll be $12.50."

I stare out of my back seat window at a huge gray ship tied up on the left side of a long concrete pier. The cabbie has no intention of getting out, so I put my combination cover on my head, pay him, and discover the air-conditioned dry air in the cab is not my new reality as I step out into heat thick with humidity. The cabbie pulls the lever by his leg to open the trunk, and I hear it pop open; I walk over and lift my heavy seabag, the big green duffel bag that now holds my entire world inside of it, out of the back and shut the trunk. Before I take one step, he's off.

Directly in front of me is a tall rolling gate topped with barbed wire that separates the base from the pier. I'm insecure and scared. My Dress Blues—a wool black jacket and skirt, a long-sleeved white shirt, a little black tie, a black-and-white combination cover, two-inch shiny black pumps, and *nylons*— are already beginning to stick to my skin. I grab my stuffed seabag by the straps that make it a neck-to-upper-thigh back-pack and try not to fall over as I hurl it onto my back and walk toward the gate.

The pier sentry checks my ID card and allows me entry onto the pier that berths the USS *Frank Cable*.

Walking those few hundred yards feels like traveling miles. As I inch along with all of my belongings on my back, I try to look cool, but mostly I try to not be seen. *Trying* isn't working, though, as my seabag is heavy as hell. I take it off of my back, grab it by the straps, and carry it as far as I can before I have to set it down to catch my breath, and then I repeat the exercise over and over again. Sweat runs down my back, and I'm close to heatstroke in my wool jacket. My cover keeps slipping down to my nose, and I feel like a five-year-old clomping along in her mother's heels. It's a long walk down what feels like a runway with all eyes on me; I'm convinced everyone is thinking, *Wow, that new seaman recruit is a hot mess.*

I finally arrive at the brow, a metal staircase and walkway that wind their way up to the ship's quarterdeck, the point of entry and exit on all Navy ships. There are little holes in the steps of the brow that snag my heels. Amused eyes watch me, and I curse them in my head.

From the top of the staircase, I walk down the long plank of the gangway. My military bearing comes in handy for the first time in "the Fleet" as I set my seabag down, face and salute the American flag, and then turn, face, and salute the officer of the deck (OOD).

"Permission to come aboard?" I request, holding my salute. It's a request I will make countless times in the years to come.

He salutes back. "Permission granted!"

I exhale and drop my salute, and my cover slips down to my nose again.

■ ■ ■

The *Frank Cable* is an enormous gray metal floating city, longer than two football fields and approximately fifteen levels, or stories, tall. There are two sides to the ship: port, which is the left, and starboard, which is the right. Each passageway looks like the next, and I'm lost before I've even taken ten steps.

My first lesson is that women never wear skirts on ships. The reason for this is that shipboard ladders, which are everywhere, are made out of metal with little holes in the steps, just like the brow. The ladders have handrails on each side but are still narrow, super steep, and treacherous (a great place to fall and break your leg or hurt your back—the latter of which will happen to me and lead to lifelong back pain). Rumor has it they are also a great way for guys to look up your skirt. They're a total blast to slide down in pants, however—lightly holding the slick handrails, keeping your legs up, and allowing gravity to do the rest. At some point, most sailors develop knee, hip, and back problems from years of going up and down these steep stairwells.

The other huge obstacle in this damn skirt are the knee knockers, which are the bottom portion of an oblong watertight door. Watertight doors are also everywhere throughout the ship and have a long metal arm that is "dogged" down—pressed down—to close them. In the event of a fire or flooding, they give us the ability to seal off compromised spaces. This makes me happy, but these knee knockers, which stand about eighteen inches off the deck, do not, as I have semi-permanent bruises on my shins from hitting the lip when I misjudge its height.

The ship has a constant humming that makes me feel like I've just fallen into a computer processing unit. Air-conditioning, plumbing, electrical systems, and various sailors working throughout the spaces provide the white-noise background of a self-contained unit, a sound that will soon become my new normal. A quiet ship is not a good thing, as this means it has lost power, and a ship without power is a vulnerable ship. Both this noise and the smell I'm taking in will replicate itself on every ship I report to in the future. Pipes, fittings, and wires line the overhead of each passageway, and the ship has a metallic, oily odor that is only covered up by the pungent scent of the wax used to buff the deck of every indoor space. The ship is cleaned daily. When I was a child, field days were the days I got on a yellow school bus and went to see something cool. In the Navy, field day means I get to either wipe down bulkheads and large pieces of equipment or swab, wax, and buff a passageway or my office.

This damn skirt uniform only reconfirms my lifelong *being a girl* obstacle. When I was young, I was fearless and bold and what I wanted more than anything in the world was to be one of the boys.

At four years old, my mom found me in the closet sulking. "What's wrong, Square?"

Poking my lip out, I whined, "I hate dresses! I want to play with the boys!"

To my pure delight, I was allowed to hang out with my older brother and the neighborhood boys for the next half a dozen years, skateboarding, throwing a football and baseball, having BB gun wars, and riding my stripped-down BMX bike like the fiercest little tomboy ever.

My mile-high Arizona hometown was surrounded by natural granite landscape, and my stomping grounds were full of ponderosa pine trees that soared to the sky and massive granite boulders, some larger than a one-car garage, that looked like transformers invading the wooded areas. The large vertical gaps in the bark of a ponderosa pine were perfect for a small nose like mine to breathe in the scent of pure vanilla. You could mostly find me either in the woods or traversing boulders, jumping from one to another like I had natural springs in my legs. I had long blond hair, suntanned shoulders, and the toughest bare feet, and I felt invincible, strong, and free. That is, until the universe reminded everyone I was a girl.

Needless to say, between the ladders and cleaning and the knee knockers—and so much more—I will never wear a skirt on a ship again after today.

The messenger of the watch escorts me to my berthing, the shipboard living quarters that sometimes houses up to three hundred sailors. The more junior you are, the larger your berthing, and this is a large berthing. "You need to pick a rack," she says as I'm trying to catch my breath from carrying my seabag down all those ladders (with zero help, I might add).

There are multiple sections in here, each with six three-tier racks facing each other. All have royal-blue sliding curtains to allow for a small bit of privacy. Middle racks are the prime choice, as they're easy to get in and out of, but they are rarely available. Top racks are the hardest to get in and out of, but you can sit up in them and no one ever steps on them. The person in a top rack has to be extra careful getting down, because God forbid you step on someone else's rack. Bottom racks are easy to get in and out of but are always stepped on and are obviously the closest to the deck, making them more susceptible to dirt (plus, no one wants other people's feet in their face when they wake up).

Each rack is made out of heavy metal that opens up as the main storage area under a two-inch-thick, back-breaking, hip-piercing mattress. Middle racks are the easiest to open, as you can stand and just lift. Top racks are the hardest to open, because you have to stand somewhere—usually on the edge of the middle rack, balancing on your tippy-toes and hoping you don't overstep. Lifting a bottom rack is done while sitting on the deck, making you even more dirty. Opening a rack is like opening the hood of a car; they have a metal stick inside of them that you use to prop the top up so it doesn't slam down on your head, which would be a real bummer.

Everything in my seabag will have to fit in my rack and within a small upright locker that's the same size as my high school locker, which I could barely fit my books and backpack in. It's in this moment that I grasp why they taught *clothes folding* so meticulously in boot camp.

No middle racks are available, and I want some space to isolate.

"I guess I'll take that one," I say, pointing to a top rack.

She writes down my rack number and leaves, and the second she does the reality of just how far out of my element I am becomes crystal clear. *Fearless and bold* now elude me. I have no idea where they went, but they're gone. I unpack and stay in that berthing until Monday morning, so afraid to get lost that I don't even go to the mess decks to eat that weekend—I just cower and ration the few snacks I brought with me, desperately wanting to get drunk and too scared to go do it.

I wake up Monday morning, hungry and nervous, to find lots of commotion and dozens of women who were away from the ship over the weekend getting dressed and ready for morning quarters, where all hands muster in formation for roll call, instruction, and inspection. Three senior petty officers—the same ranks of my godlike RCCs—stand between the six racks. They glare up at me, and without saying one word I know I have invaded their territory. I avoid their glares and notice another section where other young seamen just like me are located. By the end of the day I have moved, dodging my first turf war, although they will continue to glare at me every single time they see me, solidifying my belief that *I am horrible at first impressions.*

After I get into my dungarees, I'm escorted to the Crane Division in Deck Department, my first assignment on the *Frank Cable.* Deck Department is where all undesignated seamen who went to apprenticeship training go until they find a rating and make their way out. After meeting my leading petty officer (LPO) and my chief, who looks at me like I'm naked and creeps me out, I'm handed a scraper, wire brush, and paintbrush and am taught how to chip paint, brush away rust, and repaint the spots I have chipped or brushed away with the standard color: haze gray. Every Navy ship is painted haze gray. "Haze gray and underway" is the first Navy rhyme I memorize, and I soon learn that it's one every sailor is familiar with.

I also start learning how to load and offload pallets of supplies or parts that are craned from the pier to the ship and then craned down to the submarines tied up alongside of us.

My early days on the ship are rough, as I have few friends and am very homesick. And there is an additional challenge that I didn't expect: It is 1984, and the Navy is in the early stages of integrating women onboard ships. Of the 1,400 sailors onboard, less than 70 of us are female, and I quickly determine there are three types of Navy men: professionals, sexists, and sexual harassers. My new work center is full of the two latter types, and I am constantly dodging comments and looks from my peers, my supervisors, and even my chief, who always winks at me and asks, "Hey, Seaman Solt, what are you doing later?" It is so much a part of my everyday Navy life that I never even think of putting in a complaint. I just ignore it and walk away.

I spend many nights on a small metal stool at the pay phone booths at the front of the pier crying to my mom, "I really messed up, Mom. I hate it here."

"Oh, Square," she soothes me, "it'll get better. You'll figure it out." But I suspect she secretly agrees with me.

After those phone calls, I go to the base club and drown my sorrows (the drinking age here is eighteen, so my fake ID card is no longer needed). On the weekends I spend the little wage I earn, $668 a month before taxes, on a hotel room; I need to get off of the ship at the end of each week or I'll lose my mind. Surrounded by dozens of young people away from home for the first time, it feels a bit like I am in college, without the homework or the ability to ditch classes. My new life is difficult and I am constantly being handed big life lessons, things that weren't so apparent in my small hometown where I knew almost everyone and had a friend in every corner.

Isolated, naive, alone, and stuck, I'm sure I have made the biggest mistake of my life.

Chapter 4

NOT THE KIND OF SPARKS
I WAS HOPING FOR

Dating men has never been my favorite thing up to this point, despite the fact that I dated the nicest guy in the entire universe for a little over a year in high school. Five foot eleven, with dark curly brown hair and a lean and fit body, Scott was the kindest and cutest corduroy-OP-shorts, slip-on-Vans-wearing Greek boy I'd ever known. Ditching school with him and cruising off in his yellow Chevy Luv, complete with roll bar and KC lights, to Sedona, Hassayampa Lake, or the Verde River (actually any body of water) was my life. We were great friends and had so much fun driving behind Thumb Butte and to bonfire parties held deep in the woods. But I was an alcoholic teenager afraid of commitment and desperate to keep my independence, so I ended the relationship. My friends thought I was crazy—*You let a good one go, Karen.* He then found a new, super cute and smart girlfriend, and I was completely jealous. But I just figured I simply hadn't found the right guy yet.

Last year, after graduating high school, I started dating Jim, an adorable Italian guy who, at five foot seven, was just an inch taller than me. He had curly dark brown hair, longer than

Scott's, and he wore his 501 jeans like no other. He would pick me up from the gas station and shoot pool with me at my parents' house. The more he wanted to make out, the more I wanted to shoot pool and hit the local bars on Whiskey Row with my fake ID. I wanted to be interested in men, but for some reason I couldn't understand, I cringed when Jim wanted to get intimate. He was far more sexually experienced than I was—which wasn't difficult to achieve since I'd dated the nicest guy in the universe before him, a guy who never pressured me. But not Jim. He wanted to take our relationship *to the next level* and all my friends were having sex, so I figured it was time to take the leap.

The weekend I lost my virginity, Jim took me away to a lovely cabin in the woods. He was kind and considerate and patient, and I was awkward and nervous as hell and had a few drinks before we got into bed. As we began to have sex, it was obvious he was having the better time. I was just hoping it would be over soon, thinking, *Maybe it's a first-time thing.*

The next morning, Jim was awake before I was. He smiled and wrapped his arms around me, his eyes and the bulge between his legs telling me everything I needed to know. *So soon?* But I wanted to be a good girlfriend, so we had another round. And I hated it.

Actually, hate is too strong a word—it was more like, *Why the hell do my friends enjoy this?* We stayed together until I left for boot camp, but sex never became my favorite activity.

Fine. The truth is, I hated it.

But now I am in the Navy. I'm in a different city with new people, feeling lonely and isolated. And one day as I'm sitting by myself on deck, chipping paint and brushing off rust, an attractive second class diver with short tapered brown hair, a tan body, and chiseled muscles walks over to me.

"Hi, I'm Eddie," he says. "Do you want to go out with me Saturday night? I can show you around Charleston if you like."

I glance around, thinking, *Surely he isn't talking to me!* But I'm the only person here. He's maybe five foot nine and not only is he super cute, he is also an E-5, which impresses the hell out of my puny E-1 self, still in my first few weeks on the ship. I point at my chest and give him the *You mean me?* look.

He grins and nods. I decide to go for it.

"Sure," I say. "I'd like that!"

Eddie is waiting as I walk down the pier Saturday evening. He smiles and we walk out of the gate together. Feeling a little nervous, I climb into his cute little VW Bug and to my enormous relief he hands me a pint of liquid courage in a paper bag. We leave the base and start driving around Charleston. My window is down, the music is up, and I have a drink in my hand. It feels good to be off the ship and away from the base, enjoying a little bit of freedom. It's been a while since I've felt this happy.

The moon reflects off of the water as we drive over the Cooper River Bridge an hour later. He turns down a few side roads before he parks in a secluded spot that he seems familiar with. We sit there, drinking and talking about the ship and life in the Navy. He's nice and easy to talk to, and I am relaxed and feeling no pain when he leans over and kisses me.

The stick shift between us is awkward and hard to maneuver around.

"Let's get into the back," he says.

We start to make out in the back seat, which verges on claustrophobically small. Then he presses into me in a way that makes my heartbeat elevate—but not out of passion, more out of fear. He then roughly grabs my breast with one of his hands.

I brace. "Hey . . . easy . . ." I say, and push his hand away.

The look on his face is an unnerving mix of confidence and irritation. He leans into me and grabs at my breast again, more forcefully this time. He's not a very large man, but he easily pins me down as I struggle against his weight.

"Don't worry," his hot breath slurs against my neck, "I won't get you pregnant." As if getting pregnant is the only thing to worry about.

I sober up quickly, but no matter how much I fight or how many times I say, "No!" or "Stop!" my strength is no match for his. A part of me disconnects as he takes something that doesn't belong to him.

The music blares as we drive back over the Cooper River Bridge to the ship. I lean against the passenger door with my legs together and my arms crossed over my chest. He is not driving a straight line, which barely registers, even though he drifts close enough to the side of the bridge that his sideview mirror scrapes the metal barrier and little sparks fly off in the darkness of the night. I watch the sparks as if they are a part of a dream, not flinching or caring if we wreck. Not caring about anything.

The Navy has its own judicial system. Most minor disciplinary issues are dealt with by a sailor's immediate supervisor with minimal form of punishment. For example, in my early career I was regularly given extra military instruction (EMI), which consisted of working or cleaning an extra two hours after normal working hours. Today, EMI can no longer be used as a form of punishment, as its intended purpose is to be used as "instruction."

For more serious cases, the Navy uses articles within the Uniform Code of Military Justice (UCMJ) to try and either acquit or punish accused sailors. The two ways the Navy carries out addressing and trying violations of the UCMJ are through non-judicial punishment (NJP) and court-martial.

The Navy calls NJP "Captain's Mast" because the commanding officer, or captain, of that unit can try and punish their sailors without that infraction becoming an official part of their civilian record. A few of these violations include disorderly conduct, disobeying a lawful order, unauthorized absence (UA), disrespect, and insubordination.

The violation is initiated on a form called a report chit, which is routed through the accused sailor's chain of command. A Disciplinary Review Board (DRB) is then conducted by the chief petty officers, and if it is beyond their level of resolution, they pass it up to the executive officer for an XO's Inquiry (XOI). The final step is Captain's Mast, where, if one is convicted, punishment can include loss of pay, reduction in rank, extra duty, and even time in the brig.

Court-martials are a step above NJPs, and there are three types: Summary (the lowest), Special, and General (the highest). Court-martials are similar to civilian courts and are usually reserved for felonies or other substantial infractions, such as murder, sexual assault, espionage, and desertion. Also, the accused can deny NJP and have their case tried at a court-martial for resolution. Being convicted at a court-martial can carry the weight of dishonorable discharge, imprisonment, and even death, in some cases.

Now knowing this, here's what should have happened after my coworker and friend heard the details of my "date" with Eddie through my tears Monday morning and reported my assault to my supervisor (who she also happened to be sleeping with, which is another story entirely): once my supervisor knew I was in trouble, his concern should have been for me and my well-being. He should have brought me in, asked if what my friend said was true, notified my chain of command, and then had me taken to Medical to get evaluated. He should have protected me and acted professionally.

He didn't.

Rather than check on me, he confronted Eddie—who, of course, denied everything.

Just to make sure I know he isn't intimidated by my accusation, Eddie and his diver buddies swarm me while I'm doing my usual on deck, chipping paint and removing rust, and he loudly announces, "You're a joke! It was consensual, and it's your word against mine!"

Rather than coming to my aid, my supervisor laughs—he's one of the boys, after all—and goes back to his work.

Everyone knows.

Assaulted and humiliated, I say nothing, put my head down, and return to chipping paint.

Like dysfunctional and alcoholic homes, Navy culture is a thing unto itself. Protecting the unit and keeping the family secrets are a silent part of the agreement. After having the priorities of teamwork and having each other's back drilled into me in boot camp, I understand that going against that grain is the quickest way to be ostracized. There is tremendous pressure not to make waves, even if those waves are cries for help, calls for justice, or reporting harassment and assault. Breaking ranks would make me an outcast, and I already feel so alone. So I swallow my shame and never speak about it again.

Nothing happens to Eddie. In the aftermath of his assault, I become angry and don't trust anyone, especially myself. This isn't a new feeling, though. It's just at a deeper level than I've experienced it before.

After crying in privacy for days on end, I swallow my tears and swear to myself that I will never let my guard down again.

Chapter 5

LESS LOST,
MORE FOUND

When I was ten, I took my final swing for equality in a world where equality felt impossible—I tried out for Little League baseball.

The phone rang at home that night, and my mother answered.

"Hello, Mrs. Solt," the commissioner said, "your son made the team. Uh . . . but your daughter . . . she can't play."

"Oh? She wasn't good enough?" Mom had a clever way of subtly not saying what she was very much saying. "I attended the tryouts, and she seemed as good or even better than many of the boys."

"We-ell, it's just that she's a girl," he stammered. "And girls don't play Little League."

"Oh, I see. That's a shame. I wonder why you let her try out if you already knew you wouldn't let her play?" Mom turned to me, and her tone let both me and the commissioner know how disappointing this was. "Square, they won't let you play. I'm so sorry."

Absolutely bummed, I crawled off to my room to nurse my disappointment.

The phone rang again later that evening. My mother answered again.

"Mrs. Solt, it's Faith Blair. I've agreed to coach one of the Little League teams this year but told the commissioner I would only do so if your daughter is allowed to play. I was at the tryouts and she's great. If she still wants to play, she has a place on my team."

My little kid heart was ecstatic and I couldn't wait to play. But the commissioner and some of the parents were not so thrilled a girl was breaking through barriers they were not ready to have broken. When I returned to the dugout each inning and sat on the bench to start taking off my catcher's gear and get ready to bat, I'd hear their comments stream down from the bleachers: *"They need to get that girl off the team. She's the reason they're losing."*

Coach Faith, one of the first amazing badass women in my life, would squat down in front of me, help me unclip my leg guards, and compassionately look into my eyes. "Don't you listen to them, Karen," she'd say. "You're doing great."

In spite of her encouragement, I knew the score. I had already spent years not fitting in with the girls and trying to fit in with the boys. I thought I was pretty successful with the latter until the day it was clear that I didn't belong with either group.

That's when I started to stuff my feelings down and escape my pain by following in my father's footsteps.

My dad was the best escape artist I've ever known. He was very loving. He was also very alcoholic. He and my mom ran the family business, a large clothing store, which supported not only our family but also my grandparents. My dad worked hard and he drank hard—a sloppy, affectionate kind of drunk. I'd slowly sneak by his downstairs office every night and up the stairs to avoid his goodnight kiss, and every time I'd nearly make it but then I'd hear, "Kaaarrrreeeennnn."

My shoulders would slump; I'd freeze and turn around.

While my mom giggled and my brothers ran up the stairs, my dad pulled me onto his lap in his tighty-whities and white ribbed tank top, booze seeping from his pores. I would quickly give him a hug and a peck on his whiskered face. He'd hold me close and I would stiffen. "That's my girl," he'd slur.

Just another reason I wanted to be anything but a girl.

You could usually find my dad downstairs in his office, where he kept small airplane-size bottles of booze hidden in his desk drawer. He wasn't always like that. He actually was my first drinking buddy. When I was five, he would hand me a small glass of beer poured from his. I'd look up at his thick, wavy, combed-back, jet-black hair and his glistening hazel eyes behind gold wire-rimmed glasses, and his proud smile would make me feel cool, special, and loved.

But one tragic night when I was six, I broke my arm while playing with him. It was a simple game of "horsie"—I rode on his back as he crawled the living room floor on all fours, trying to buck me off. The final ride of that evening, he reared up and I flipped off and landed on my arm, snapping both bones an inch above my wrist. I stood up, my arm dangling like a noodle, and said, "I think I broke my arm."

Not once did he ever play with me or my brothers again after that night. My dad was a sensitive man, and I can't say that I'll ever fully understand his reasoning, but I think he felt so bad about what had happened that he resorted to isolated drinking in his office, where he made only me give him goodnight kisses and where he remained for the rest of my childhood. And since my broken arm seemed to be the catalyst for his retreat, I felt responsible for all of the breaking in my family.

But I still tried to be myself. That is, until I was heckled by parents who weren't ready for a girl like me and the boys I used to trust suddenly began to see me as a girl. When that happened, they started trying to get me alone; I was no longer safe with them. These events all rolled into one giant disillusionment, and I became angry and lost. When the Little League season was over, I gave up on the gender equality gig and started stealing booze. Dad was right. It was a great way to disconnect.

Now, having been sexually assaulted and publicly humiliated, I simmer with near overwhelming amounts of anger, shame, and fear and resort to behavior that has served me since I quit Little League. If I'm not going to be protected, I will damn well figure out how to survive—by drinking, lying, cheating, and manipulating.

I spend most of my weekends drinking alone in hotel rooms. My bitterness toward the entire system, which feels rigged against me, soars to a whole new level. The game now is to play by MY rules.

I report one Sunday morning for duty after a particularly rough night to learn I have been assigned the 0800–1200 pier sentry watch. Most Navy commands have duty sections, where a percentage of the crew remains at the command for twenty-four hours to maintain a presence and stand watches. This is especially true onboard ships. The *Frank Cable* has six duty sections, so every six days I stay on the ship and stand whatever watch I am given by my section leader.

The pier sentry paces in front of the wheeled gate at the entry point of the pier with a 12-gauge shotgun slung over their shoulder and ensures no one enters without proper identification. I'm not sure how I am intended to stop anyone, because I don't have ammunition for the shotgun—maybe a quick *whack!* upside the head with the stock will do the trick if a problem arises.

The pier sentry this morning has one major problem: I'm horribly hungover. I can barely walk. The shotgun feels like it weighs a hundred pounds. My lame attempt at pacing in front of the gate lasts maybe thirty minutes before I decide that I will sit in the pier sentry booth and *keep an eye on things*. I place the shotgun on the ground between my feet, muzzle upward—it's not like it's loaded or anything—and fall asleep.

The next thing I know I'm bolted out of my dream state by my department head, the ship's first lieutenant (LT), shouting, "Get up, Seaman Solt!"

I'm not sure how long I have been asleep, but I can feel that I have a circular muzzle imprint centered an inch above my eyebrows.

I snap to attention and my right arm quickly salutes. "Yes, sir!"

He salutes back and glares at me with disgust. "Report to my office after your watch, and don't you fucking sit down again!"

Scared shitless, I respond, "Yes, sir!"

He stalks away.

I report to his office after my watch is over and stand at attention while he yells at me.

"You're an idiot! You could get in serious trouble! You could lose a lot by making such a stupid mistake!"

I nod, agree, show remorse, but mostly I engage my military bearing and dissociate until he's done reaming me out.

"Now get the fuck out of my office!"

"Yes, sir!" I say, and about-face my ass out of there.

This is the extent of my punishment. The first lieutenant yells at me. *Big whoop.* I walk away unscathed, adding another *I don't give a flying fuck* to my list.

I care less and less as the days grind on.

Mercy arrives in the form of a temporary transfer from the Crane Division, which means I can quit dodging my creepy chief and horrible supervisor. My new position is mess cranking.

Navy mess decks are where shipboard chow is served. For a junior sailor, mess cranking is a rite of passage. A stint in the shithouse. It's paying your dues. And it's not a blast. You work extremely long hours with very few days off, either assisting the cooks in food preparation, working in the scullery, serving food, cleaning the mess decks, or all of the above. Mess cranks can work in a variety of dining halls—in the Enlisted Mess, where the E-1s to E-6s eat their chow; in the Chief's Mess, where the E-7s to E-9s eat their delicious food; or in the Wardroom, where the officers eat their pretend fine cuisine. Navy structure works everywhere.

I am assigned to the Chief's Mess, where chief petty officers eat, have meetings, and go for privacy from their sailors and, more importantly, from the young ensign who won't shut the hell up with his stupid questions. Chiefs have the best food. Actually, chiefs have the best of everything.

The Chief's Mess is where I meet Tami, another mess crank. We work in the scullery, where we steal huge crab claws and fill our bellies, as she tells me the funniest stories about the trouble she evidently cannot avoid. Tami is five foot five and 115 pounds, with pale skin, doe-like brown eyes, rosy red thin lips, and short, wavy, dark brown hair that sticks in curls to her forehead in the heat. Proudly from *Wiscahhnson*, she has a deep yet subtle and distinct voice with just a tinge of an extended accent. A no-bullshitter, Tami always says what she means.

Each day we wobble with four large, heavy black bags full of wet trash tied together and slung over our shoulders down the pier to the dumpsters on the outside of the sliding gate. This is where we hide out, smoke cigarettes, and get to know each other.

During one such trip, we're sitting side by side out of sight on the concrete slab that supports the dumpster when Tami takes a drag on her cigarette, glances at me, and then looks away. Tiny little sweat bubbles start multiplying between her upper lip and the bottom of her nose, something that happens when she's either nervous or perspiring in the Charleston heat. She surveys the area, as if any other idiot would be hanging out by a dumpster, then whispers, "You do know I'm gay, right? I have a girlfriend and we have an apartment across town."

Growing up in my conservative little hometown, I never met one gay person, and gay people weren't very visible on television or in the movies in the '70s and early '80s, so before enlisting I didn't even know that being gay was an option. But there was talk amongst the other recruits in boot camp of a few women who were gay, so I now knew that it was a thing and was aware of a few lesbians on the ship.

I follow her lead—also glancing around and lowering my voice—as I say, "Yeah, I figured so. Doesn't it make your life in the Navy even harder?"

She nods and purses her lips. "It's just one more thing to deal with. I was stupid to enlist in the first place. I can't make a move without being picked apart, and it only adds pressure on top of everything else." She takes another drag off her cigarette and looks directly into my eyes. "You'll keep this between us, right?"

"Of course I will," I say, bumping my elbow against hers. As if I have anyone to talk to besides her anyway. "But what happens if they catch you?"

"They'll kick me out. My aunt got kicked out of the Army when I was a teenager. It happens all the time on the ship. Here one day, gone the next. It's just one more thing . . ." She shrugs, drops her cigarette, and crushes it with the toe of her boot. "Anyway, you ready to head back?"

I twist my cigarette against the side of the concrete slab and toss it in the dumpster. "Not really, but they're probably looking for us by now." We walk back around the dumpster, show our ID cards to the sentry, and slowly meander down the pier to the ship.

■ ■ ■

While working these super-long hours, Tami and I talk non-stop about life back home, mine in the mountains and her by lakes. She speaks in code about her girlfriend Mindy—smoothly changing Mindy's pronouns to "he" and "him" and her name to "Mike," which I find fascinating—and I tell her about my ex-boyfriends. Tami loves to fish and ice fish and trout fish and kayak fish and would choose freezing her ass off in Wisconsin over sweating to death in the heat and humidity of Charleston in a heartbeat.

We also talk about the constant sexual harassment (although I never tell her about Eddie, hoping to put the assault so far behind me that it will completely vanish from my memory). As an engineman and the only woman in her division in the Engineering Department, Tami is incessantly harassed by her senior chief. She tells me about the day she reported for duty: He called her into his office, pointed to a chair, and without looking at her said, "Take a seat." She sat down, and he swiveled his chair around and glared at her dead in her eyes. "Here's what you need to know, Fireman Ames. There's two places where women belong in this world, the bedroom and the kitchen." His scowling face looked her up and down. "Do we understand each other?"

Tami was petrified, wide-eyed, and frozen. "We do, Senior Chief."

"Good." He pointed at the door. "Now get the hell out of my office!" From that moment on, he's made it his personal mission to make her life pure hell.

Tami quickly becomes a close friend, but due to her *rules are made to be broken* attitude, our time together is cut short. She rolls her eyes behind her senior chief's back one day in the

Chief's Mess and he finds out, which gets her reassigned to the Enlisted Mess decks.

Between our twelve-hour shifts and opposite twelve-days-on two-days-off schedules, Tami and I don't catch up with each other again until a few months after her reassignment, when we are both placed back in our shitty divisions.

One Friday afternoon, Tami, dressed in gray parachute pants loaded with silver zippers and a black sleeveless shirt with a big white Pegasus printed on it, sits on her bottom rack as I pack my own clean civilian clothes in my blue backpack and stuff my dirty work clothes in my white mesh laundry bag to wash out in town.

"What are you doing this weekend?" she asks.

"The usual." I shrug. "Going to a hotel." As the ship rarely gets underway, except for a day or two to run the engines and do circles in the ocean or to chase after hurricanes, hotels remain my haven.

Tami rolls her eyes. "Wanna come hang with me and my *boyfriend*?" She quickly glances at the other half dozen women in the berthing. "I've told Mike all about you, and he'd love to meet you. We have an extra room with a bed. You can stay the weekend if you want."

I haven't trusted anyone since the assault and have mostly kept to myself. But I like Tami. She's kind, honest, and spunky, and her take-shit-from-no-one nature is refreshing. And I really need a friend.

"Thanks," I say. "I'd like that."

Tami smiles and gets up. "Cool, then let's get the hell out of here."

Her confident way is something I have come to love about her. We grab our backpacks and laundry bags and exit the berthing. After getting permission to go ashore from the OOD, we stride to the end of the pier and take a right toward the front gate. On the other side of that gate we are no longer on US Government property and the rules are different.

Tami clearly has a civilian routine, and it kicks in the moment we get off of the base. She turns to face the traffic and sticks out her thumb. My mouth drops open in amazement and I glance around, worried that someone might see us.

But I'm also thinking, *Damn, this girl is so badass.*

And before I know it my thumb is raised too, and I find myself hitchhiking for the first time in my life.

Chapter 6

A NEW WAY
OF LIFE

A lively woman about Tami's size with very curly, short chestnut-brown hair, deep brown eyes, and an explosion of personality greets us at the top of a flight of concrete stairs when we reach the apartment complex.

Mindy beams, throws her arms around Tami's neck, and kisses her. "Yay, babe! Happy weekend!" She then smiles at me and the bubbling-over, childlike joy on her face softens the perpetual lump in my chest.

Tami's mood instantly shifts; a big grin spreads across her face. "Babe, this is Karen. The girl I mess cranked with. She's going to hang with us this weekend."

"Karen!" Mindy exclaims, and pulls me into a warm embrace that makes me feel like she's my long-lost sister. "Welcome! I've heard so much about you!"

Tami strides off to the kitchen, returns with two beers, and hands me one. "Let's get you settled. Wanna see the apartment?"

The centerpiece of the entire apartment is a walnut chest-high full bar that sits in the far-left corner of the naturally lit living room. Upside-down glass tumblers hang from a circular stand on its surface. A woodsy picture of a lake rises on the wall behind it, and a plush maroon couch is on the back wall facing the door. I already feel at home.

"Wow," I say, "that bar is awesome."

Tami laughs. "That thing is my pride and joy. You just wait."

We walk past the kitchen on our left and down the hallway, where my room is the only door on the left, just across from a full bath. A twin-size bed is pushed against the right wall, across from an empty closet, and cheap, metal, mostly bent horizontal blinds cover a window that faces the doorway. Their room and a full master bath are at the end of the hallway.

We return to the living room and exit a sliding glass door on the right to the outside patio. Tami hands me a beer and grabs a seat on a wooden bench, and I plop down on a small black wrought iron chair. We place our feet on a matching wrought iron table, light cigarettes, and sip our beers.

Tami relaxes back on the bench. "What do you think?"

"It's amazing," I say. "I'd love to have a place like this to get away from the ship."

Mindy doesn't smoke, but she comes out to join us anyway. She sits next to Tami and settles into her side. She's the epitome of free—free with her affection, her joy, and her honesty. Tami rests her hand on Mindy's leg as I take long drags on my cigarette and learn more about them. I loosen up in their presence; I didn't realize how much tension I had been holding until now.

Tami talks about how much she hates the Navy and her struggles with how gays have to adapt by serving silently. "Do you remember the homosexuals lecture in boot camp?" she asks, putting her fingers up to air-quote the word "homosexuals." "The lecturer said, 'Gays can't be in the Navy, because you can't trust them. If they were captured in war, they couldn't keep a secret.'" She takes her feet off the table and leans forward. "I sat there thinking, *Are you fucking kidding me? I've been keeping a secret since I was sixteen years old. If anyone can keep a secret, it's a gay person.* It was ridiculous! Remember that?"

"Uh, well no," I say meekly. "I was detoxing in boot camp, to be honest. I remember very few lectures."

We all chuckle at this.

"Seriously, though, I don't know what I was thinking." Tami shakes her head. "My aunt told me that it was going to be hard, but I never expected this. Between dealing with the bullshit in my division and then constantly hiding that I'm gay, it's much worse than I expected."

Mindy puts her hand on Tami's back, caresses it in small circles, and turns to me. "I'd be perfectly fine if she got out. I hate how they treat her and can't believe they get away with it." She pulls Tami's chin toward her and gives her a small kiss. "We'll figure it out, babe. Now, no more Navy talk. Let's enjoy ourselves. Remember? It's the weekend."

Tami puts her feet back up, leans back, and smiles lovingly at Mindy. "All right, babe." She looks over at me. "See? I told you she's great."

Tami and Mindy's fun, wild, and adorable gay friends arrive Saturday night. Think of the 1980s hit movie *St. Elmo's Fire* and then remove everything, especially the straight women and men, except for the music and haircuts, and then add excessive partying. Mindy's ex-girlfriend, Ronda, her girlfriend, Stacy, and brother, Donnie (also gay, as is made clear by his blue-and-white-striped Speedo), are the first to arrive. Then Teresa, a tall, quiet woman with loose curls in her short dark hair, shows up. Teresa is also from the ship, and rumor has it she has a secret crush on Tami that everyone knows about. They welcome me into their fold, and we drink, laugh, and dance all evening. I'm enjoying every minute with my new friends.

By the end of the weekend, that extra room with a bed in it has become *my* room. I notice that this is the first time ever that I have felt natural and comfortable in my skin, and I start to put the pieces together. After growing up in a home where displays of affection weren't visibly expressed, I am experiencing playful and loving connection with amazing women—hugs, arms around my neck or waist, closeness on the couch, sideways sits on laps. And I feel safe to be myself.

After years of wandering and stumbling around, I have finally found my people. Deep in my belly, the place where all truth resides, I realize what I have been missing.

My truth—that I am gay.

Sitting on the deck one evening with Tami and Mindy a few weeks later, I turn to Tami and speak words that I never expected to say. I am not even trying them on for size; I am simply stating what has now become clear to me.

"How did you know that I'm gay?"

Tami nearly spits out her drink, and she and Mindy turn to each other and laugh.

"I knew it from the moment I met you," she says. "But coming out is very personal, and especially with the military witch-hunting us, you never want to ask anyone directly, because they could get offended, maybe even turn you in, and then you'd be done. After a while, I just knew that I could trust you and figured you hadn't realized it yet. The real question is, how did you *not* know?"

I shake my head and shrug. "I just didn't. Never even considered it because I didn't know anyone who was gay. Looking back, I had a huge crush on a neighborhood girl when I was about eight and another on a summer camp counselor when I was in my early teens. But I was already drinking a lot by then, and I was so lost . . . but now that stuff makes a lot more sense."

They both nod, tenderness in their eyes. Then Tami's tone gets more serious. "Just remember to always watch your back. You never know who's watching, and there are a lot of people who want to see us fail. Anyway . . ." She pauses and gives me a half-smile. "Enough about that shit." She takes Mindy's hand. "Ready for bed, babe?"

We give each other hugs. "Good night, Karen," they say.

"Night, you two."

As they head to their bedroom, I finish my cigarette and think about how my life is changing. I'm so much happier than I was just a few months ago, but a discernable tension between my personal life and my work life is beginning to form. I am relieved to know that I'm gay, but anxious knowing, as I'll have to carefully monitor my speech and actions onboard the ship going forward. It is a tension between being myself and intentionally *not* being myself. But this isn't exactly a new problem, as being myself has been an issue for as long as I can remember.

I snuff out my cigarette in the near-full ashtray on the table and consider my options: 1) Be myself and try to not get caught for being gay, or 2) Don't be myself and be miserable.

My choice is clear: I go with option #1. I choose me. And I'll do what Tami is doing and stay as hidden as possible.

The following evening, I decide to share my great news with someone who has always been supportive—my mom. I call her from my trusty pay phone at the end of the pier.

"Hey, Mom, I need to tell you something."

She lets out an audible exhale. "Oh. Hey, Square. Sure. What's up?"

Her exhale is not surprising, as I regularly call my parents from these same pay phones with some sort of drama. Our most difficult call was after the assault. I was sobbing, which was so hard for them to hear, and my dad wanted me to keep silent and put my head down—"Don't create any waves, Karen. I don't want it to get worse for you. Just keep trying to blend in."

My nerves are getting the better of me, and I am stumbling through all of this. I blurt out the words before I can stop myself: "Mom, I'm gay."

A silent *Good Lord* transmits as another heavy exhale through the line. "Honey, are you sure? Don't you think *THOSE* people are influencing you?"

I stiffen and join in on the audible exhale party. "*THOSE* people are my friends and are amazing and kind, and yes, Mom, I'm sure."

"But you've always liked boys. I think you're just confused, Square."

"Actually, I've always struggled with boys." My face gets hot, and I rise from the metal swivel stool. "Forget it, Mom. I'm sorry I brought it up." It's just too much. All I want is her support and for her to be happy for me. But her response feels like a rejection. "I'll call you later," I say, and then hang up the phone without saying goodbye, because this conversation is creating a tsunami-sized belief within me: if she won't accept me, no one will.

From the start, it is clear there is a reward and a risk to being gay.

The reward is so easy to feel in the deepest part of my soul. Realizing that I'm gay and being among people whom I absolutely adore liberates and realigns many things within me. For the first time in my life I have begun to feel comfortable in my own skin. When I'm not at work, I am with people who accept me for who I am, and I am finally able to let my guard down.

I have found a place where I can be me. My step is lighter. The enormous confusion and isolation is all but gone.

But the risk is enormous and intangible in so many ways. It lingers within me as questions not fully formed—*Who will accept me? Who will reject me? Who will still love me?* And those are the easy questions. The tougher questions, questions I will constantly have to face from now on, are: *Will I get caught? Will I be okay? Am I safe?*

Those are the questions that will keep me on edge for the remainder of my time in the military. Because it is 1984, I am US Government property, and being gay in the Navy is a crime.

Chapter 7

WITCH HUNTS

The US military had policies prohibiting homosexuals from serving starting at the beginning of World War II. In 1984, the Department of Defense's policy on homosexuality stated: "Homosexuality is incompatible with military service. The presence in the military environment of persons who engage in homosexual conduct or who, by their statements, demonstrate a propensity to engage in homosexual conduct, seriously impairs the accomplishment of the military mission. The presence of such members adversely affects the ability of the Military Services to maintain discipline, good order, and morale; to foster mutual trust and confidence among service members; to ensure the integrity of the system of rank and command; to facilitate assignment and worldwide deployment of service members who frequently must live and work under close conditions affording minimal privacy; to recruit and retain members of the Military Services; to maintain public acceptability of military service; and to prevent breaches of security." Also, according to DOD, a homosexual is "a person, regardless of sex, who engages in, desires to engage in, or intends to engage in homosexual acts."

With the policies written in their favor, the military used all means at their disposal to eliminate us from its ranks.

Approximately 1,500 homosexuals were annually expelled from military service between 1980 and 1990, and of the different branches within the military, the Navy had the highest rate of discharge—51 percent. For the Navy specifically, the Naval Criminal Investigative Service (NCIS) was the arm of the law. I don't know what they called their method.

We called it "witch hunts."

NCIS was notorious for calling one of us in and then intimidating that person into naming others. One interrogation could lead to many gay service members being found guilty and processed for separation. Their coercion was so fierce that friends turned in friends and partners even turned in their lovers. If NCIS was successful, and I never heard of one instance where a person walked away unscathed, the Navy would administratively separate gay service members with a "general" discharge. The administrative separation process is a streamlined and cost-effective way to discharge sailors for a variety of reasons, including failing fitness standards, a pattern of misconduct, or even drug abuse. Gay enlisted sailors would be administratively separated for "homosexual conduct" and officers would be separated for "conduct unbecoming," all of which would be noted on their DD-214, a form that every service member gets when separating from active duty.

Civilian employers ask veterans for their DD-214, so I knew I didn't want a general discharge with *homosexual conduct* on mine; it would stay with me and affect future employment opportunities from that point forward. Essentially, that form would "out" me to the world, whether I wanted to be outed or not.

From the moment I knew I was gay, everything changed. Mostly for the better, as it was a relief to know why I'd always felt so different from others. But while homophobia certainly wasn't new and the Navy wasn't the only place where I had to watch my back, the stigma and discrimination against the gay community were things I would have to adapt to. There wasn't a place where I didn't have to watch my back, and the added threat of my lifestyle being considered a crime in the Navy made the stakes that much higher.

The gay liberation movement started in 1969 during a week-long uprising that was kicked off after a botched police raid at the Stonewall Inn in New York City, a mafia-run bar that was mostly frequented by LGBTQ+ patrons. A bar could lose its liquor license for serving homosexual patrons and the mafia took advantage of this law, paying off New York police while raising their prices and serving watered-down drinks to their LGBTQ+ customers. But on June 28, 1969, a police raid was met with resistance, which turned into a weeklong, full-blown riot. Up to 2,000 LGBTQ+ rioters who had years of pent-up anger and frustration for the way they had been treated set to the streets in Greenwich Village, protesting against discrimination, police harassment, and brutality. One year later, on June 28, 1970, the first Christopher Street (the location of the Stonewall Inn) Liberation Day, considered the first gay pride march, was held. Similar gay liberation events in San Francisco, Chicago, and Los Angeles were also held that year. This was the beginning of what we now know as the annual LGBTQ+ Pride celebration.

Homosexuality has undergone many phases in the categorization of mental illness disorders as well. In the first edition of the American Psychiatric Association (APA) Diagnostic and Statistical Manual (DSM), published in 1952, homosexuality was listed as a sociopathic personality disturbance. In 1973, the APA removed the diagnosis of homosexuality from the second edition of its DSM, declassifying homosexuality as a disease or psychological disorder, but replacing it in the third addition as "ego-dystonic homosexuality." This diagnosis specifically labels people who express "persistent and marked distress" about their sexual orientation, which is essentially *internalized homophobia.*

Dealing with familial, religious, and societal stigma and a life of being treated as *other* is something that creates deep scars and can certainly create "persistent and marked distress." LGBTQ+ people get kicked out of families and religious communities, are disproportionately subjected to bullying, and have to engage in a constant fight for equal rights in a world where we are marginalized. Being othered and stigmatized is what ignites internalized homophobia, an internal shame about one's sexuality, especially in young LGBTQ+ people who are just finding their way in life. "Ego-dystonic homosexuality" is not a mental illness. It's an internalized reaction to discrimination. It's also what makes the suicide rate in the LGBTQ+ community significantly higher than average.

In 1984, the AIDS epidemic—considered by many to be a "gay disease," which created less support for homosexuals and even more stigma nationwide—was surging in the US. With this in mind, the almost nonexistent support from Ronald Reagan's administration resulted in no AIDS relief or funded research support at the federal level. Pat Buchanan, Reagan's communications director, even described AIDS as "nature's revenge on gay men." By 1987, the same year when all classifications of homosexuality were completely removed from the DSM, nearly 21,000 Americans had died from AIDS.

As a sailor in the Navy when being gay in the military was considered a crime, there was little to no mercy toward homosexuals by the US government—the same government I worked for and whose top leadership said that AIDS was nature's revenge on gays. The DOD's policy on homosexuals affected everything I did in the Navy. I quickly learned that if I wanted to keep serving—and I did—I would need to stay very closeted. As an addict and a misfit, hiding was already the most normal and predictable part of my life. All I had to do after coming out was cultivate a deeper form of hiding within a system that hunted me and my fellow gay shipmates.

As time went on, I would come to feel the same frustration and anger that Tami and my other gay friends regularly expressed over the injustice that we endured. Hiding who I was while loving who I was created exactly what the third version of the DSM would consider a psychiatric disorder: *ego-dystonic homosexuality*, an insidious internalized homophobia embedded within the depths of my soul.

Within my first year in the Navy, I learned to constantly look over both shoulders—one for sexual harassment and the other for witch hunts and NCIS. I constantly dodged sexual comments from all angles, including from my supervisors and chiefs. I eventually quit ignoring them and instead responded with looks of disgust, which they seemed to relish as there weren't any repercussions for their behavior.

But at least they were open with their harassment. Hiding my gayness was much trickier, as I never knew who was friend or foe. I didn't know if a shipmate would overhear a conversation, or if a male sailor might tell others I was a lesbian if I turned him down for a date. These were very real situations and threats that stayed in the back of my mind. Service unto itself was a commitment to put myself in danger, but not knowing who would react to my homosexuality in a dangerous or vindictive manner created more fear. *Who is the enemy here? Is it me, or is it the person trying to "catch" me for being myself?*

Being othered under a policy that turned love into criminality created a whole population of gay service members who were deprived of the liberty to be ourselves after giving up our freedom to serve our country.

Fortunately, I was never alone, as all my gay friends were in the same boat. They became my family. We loved, cared for, and watched out for each other within our beautiful community. We lived our lives as honestly as we could, always with a threat hanging over our heads, and hoped and prayed that the day would never come when one of us might be pulled into NCIS for interrogation.

Many of us were successful. And far too many of us weren't.

Chapter 8

FINDING MY NICHE

While in formation one day during morning quarters on the weather decks, my chief makes an announcement: "The first lieutenant [the guy who caught me with my head on a shotgun] needs someone to come work in his office and be his yeoman."

You could hear a pin drop.

His beady, bloodshot eyes scan the ranks. "Well? Any volunteers?"

Nobody makes a move. I, just like everyone else, stand at attention and avoid his eye contact. *Keep your head down, Solt.* Although I love typing and clerical work and would love to get out of chipping paint, I'm not taking the bait. I have learned by now that raising my hand is a trick.

"Well, it's going to be one of you, I can tell you that." He salutes. "You're dismissed."

Chief calls me into his office later that morning. My supervisor sits next to him. "Seaman Solt, you've been chosen as the first LT's yeoman. He's expecting you after lunch."

They watch for my reaction.

"Roger that," I say with a poker face. I'm sure they are as happy to get rid of me as I am to be done with them, as I have been a complete pain in their ass since my assault. "Anything else, Chief?"

"No. That'll be all."

I shrug and leave their office, hoping this is the last I ever see of either of them.

Just after lunch I arrive at the Deck Department Office, where the first LT and his yeoman work. A clean-cut seaman sits at a four-drawer, gray metal desk that's bolted to the deck. Large equipment onboard ships is either bolted or welded down, and anything that isn't secure is physically tied down when the ship gets underway so it's sure to stay in place.

To the right of this desk is a door that leads into the first LT's office.

The seaman looks up from his typewriter and smiles. "Hi, I'm Seaman Brady. I heard they picked you. You are going to love it here. It's *so* much better than being out on deck."

"God, I hope so—I frickin' hate it out there," I say, still unsure but now a tiny bit hopeful.

Seaman Brady is also undesignated but is being sent to YN "A" school in Meridian, Mississippi, where the Navy will train him to become YNSN Brady instead of SN Brady. I will take his place and work directly for the first LT, which scares me because he has a reputation for being a hard-ass and he really yelled at me that one time. These days, I assume that anything good in the Navy comes with a catch.

Seaman Brady slides a heavy gray metal chair with a padded seat over to me. "Take a seat," he says. "We have a lot to cover before I leave."

That day, we go over typing, reviewing paperwork, running to the ship's Admin Office for mail, creating and tracking evals and other correspondence, and all the other administrative tasks the first LT needs done. Fortunately, I'm already a good typist, and the rest of my new duties seem simple as long as I stay organized. This could be good after all.

Becoming the first LT's yeoman is so much better than I could have imagined. Within a week, I have settled into my new role.

"You seem good, so I'm going to Personnel to have them prepare my orders," Seaman Brady says on the morning of day five. He leaves the office to walk amidships to the starboard side and the Personnel Office, where he will sign his school contract and receive his written orders.

He returns an hour later, looking bummed, and walks behind me into the first LT's office. A few minutes later, they come out and Seaman Brady slumps down next to me.

"I'm not going to school after all," he explains. "They say I'll have to extend my enlistment for another year, and there's no way in hell I'm doing more than four years."

The first LT looks at me. "Since Seaman Brady isn't taking the school billet, I'd like to offer it to you. You're a natural, Seaman Solt, and I think you'd be a great yeoman. You will have to extend an additional year, but I think it's a good deal. What do you think?"

I'm stupefied. I can go to YN "A" school, get off of the ship for a few months, *and* get designated as a yeoman, a job I really like, just like that?

I realize that the first LT is still waiting for my response.

"Thank you, sir," I say quickly. "Yes. I'd definitely like to go to the school."

Seaman Brady looks down, clearly disappointed, but the first LT is pleased.

"Great!" he says with a smile. "Let's go see PNC and get you set up for school."

He and I walk to Personnel together, where he tells the personnelman chief, "Please change the name on those Yeoman "A" school orders to Seaman Solt."

A half hour later, I'm signing the documents, wondering where I would be without the first LT taking his third risk on me. He gave me a second chance when he caught me sleeping on a shell-less shotgun; then he pulled me out of a division where I was losing my mind. And now this—a new rate and a fresh start. He's the first one in the Navy who's seen something promising in me. I'm grateful for him; he's just single-handedly changed the trajectory of my career.

When Tami and I leave the ship that evening, I'm so giddy that I'm semi-skipping.

"Guess what?" I say after we step off the brow. "Seaman Brady didn't want to extend for a year, so I'm going to YN "A" school in two weeks! Can you believe it?"

She shakes her head and rolls her eyes at my apparent delight, then laughs. "That's awesome! How are you going to get there?"

"I'm going to drive, so we, and I do mean *we*, are going to go look at cars this weekend," I say. "I need to find one that will be cheap enough to finance but also won't break down on the way to Mississippi."

Now we both laugh, even though the thought of that does freak me out a bit.

The next day, we test-drive a truck that breaks down *during the test drive* before I land on a black Plymouth Champ with gold pinstripes running down its sides (the stripes do not help it go faster). It's ugly-cute and resembles a fishbowl on wheels. I name it the *Tramp Champ*. It has front-wheel drive, and when I slam it into first gear and peel out, the front of the car lifts and vibrates and the front wheels *screeeech*, which makes me giggle. I love it.

We drive it home and I engage my car wash background and wax it in the sun, even though Tami advises against it. I'm obviously the expert here, so I ignore her advice, but when I try to remove the wax I find that the South Carolina heat has melted it into the paint, which means my car is now black with gold pinstripes and embedded swirls.

When I go to tell Tami what I've done, I find her and Mindy sitting quietly on the couch, looking somber.

"What's up?" I flop down next to them.

Tami turns to face me. "We're moving into a small trailer to save money and be closer to the base. We're bummed, but you'll have to find another place to live when you get back."

My heart drops. They have made such a difference in my life. It scares me to even think of being alone again. I can't imagine not walking home with Tami each evening, hanging with her and Mindy on the deck, and sleeping in my empty room with a bed. The vulnerable little girl inside of me, the one who's finally found a home where she can be herself, wants to say, *Forget it, I won't go to school.* But the part of me who knows how to stuff down her feelings and press forward looks through her friends and engages her military bearing. "Oh. Hey. Of course. I totally get it." I look down. "But we'll still hang out when I get back, right?" Sadness wells up inside of my chest.

Mindy moves next to me and wraps me in her natural bear hug, then ruffles my hair until I'm squirming and blushing. "Hell yes, we'll still hang out when you get back, silly!"

She releases me and I turn to my first gay friend, the person I trust more than anyone these days, and await her response.

"You can't get rid of me that easily," Tami says. "You're family. Always will be." She puts her arm around my shoulder and leads me outside to the deck. "Come on, bud. Let's go burn one."

We exit the slider, light up cigarettes, and sit in silence, both in our own thoughts. Things are changing rapidly. I'm finally getting a break and am enjoying my work in the Navy, but it's coming with a loss that I sure wasn't expecting.

Chapter 9

THE CHAMELEON LIFE

After completing Yeoman "A" school, I report back to the *Frank Cable* and am assigned to the Admin Office. No more Deck Department, cranes, or chipping paint, and no more chief or supervisor hitting on me. Time to put my training to use and settle in as a fledgling yeoman.

My good luck continues as it appears I've hit another jackpot: the yeomen in my office are all women, and three out of the six of us are gay! Deeply closeted, of course, but still gay. My new supervisor (gay) is YN2 Peggy Quinlan. I got to know Peggy a little bit when I picked up the first LT's mail from Admin before leaving for school. As she's giving me the rundown of the office, she subtly informs me that the discreet captain's yeoman, YN2 Dean, is also gay.

Our department head is a fun-loving and playful dude who works out of his stateroom, the place where officers sleep. Anytime he comes into the office we give him hell—"Chicks only! Get out!"—and he laughs, drops off and picks up paperwork, and promptly exits. It is my first Navy experience filled with fun and bonding, which is definitely a welcome change.

My chief, YNC Roll, is a tall, skinny woman with straight red hair that lands just above the bottom of her collar, which is the longest a female sailor's hair can be without putting it up and still be within regulation. She runs a tight Admin Office, has a dry sense of humor and a nasally voice, and is open to any kind of shenanigans, as long as the work gets done.

YN2 Quinlan is a tough supervisor who pushes and expects the most out of me, but she also teaches me that I can work hard and have fun at the same time. She wears her curly, honey-brown hair pulled back into a ponytail and pinned up with a plastic barrette, wears large brown plastic-rimmed glasses, and has a fast walk. A huge set of work keys dangles from her front belt loop, and because of her quick pace those things are noisier than the ship's whistle, so I always hear her coming. She calls me Sloopslot, imitating the ship's postal clerk chief (PCC), who absolutely cannot pronounce my simple four-letter last name during morning quarters.

The captain's yeoman, YN2 Dean, is the other gay yeoman. As his personal yeoman, she spends more time with the captain than most people on the ship and has her own small office behind our desks so she can shut her windowed door and focus. She is quiet and professional and has a settled life with a partner she adores, which is nice for me to see.

Two other yeomen complete my new coworkers. The first is YN2 Thurston, a very skilled and fun Black yeoman we call Ginneeeee (it's short for something—maybe Virginia?). She teaches me many things about being a good yeoman and also makes me her accomplice in covert operations to catch Peggy and the chief off guard. Last but not least is YN3 Smith, a tall, quiet blond girl who simply thinks we're all crazy and constantly shakes her head at our antics.

I am welcomed into the fold and Chief Roll assigns me as the correspondence YN. I've loved to type since learning how to do it properly in high school typing class, one of the few that I actually attended. My gray, metal, welded-to-the-deck desk sits at the far right in the front of the office behind a tall counter that has a waist-high swinging door to keep customers from entering the main office. Peggy is on my left and Ginneeeee is on her left. Smith and Chief sit behind us, and Dean is in the far back.

My new gray chair has a padded seat and armrests. It also has wheels. I immediately unscrew the spring underneath the seat so it rocks and I can recline when I want to. It is also a blast to roll around the office, though when we're underway I have to tie it down so I don't crash into everything and get nothing accomplished. Sometimes I put my feet up and do that anyway, when Chief isn't in the office—and when I'm not sleeping under my desk. Being at sea is like being rocked to sleep and weightless at the same time, which sometimes makes it impossible for me to stay awake. When that feeling overcomes me, I crawl beneath my desk for a little shut-eye.

My first true love is a Xerox 860. It is one of the first word processors ever made and stores data on an 8-inch floppy disk, a new capability in the administrative world. I type letters, awards, endorsements, instructions, situational reports, and evaluations. But my daily absolutely-have-to-get-done task is the preparation of the Plan of the Day (POD)—a 14-inch sheet containing the ship's schedule, duty section information, and announcements that is passed out at morning quarters.

My motivating and fun-filled days in Admin fly by, as opposed to my grueling, never-ending days chipping paint and brushing away rust in the Deck Department.

While I was at Yeoman "A" school, I reached two very important life milestones. The first was a spot promotion to third class petty officer—YN3 or E-4—because I loved that school and did really well. The other was my first tattoo. I'll spare you most of the details of that story, but I'll tell you this much: it involved an excursion to a little white trailer situated on a very dark dirt road and getting tattooed by a drunk and not at all hygienic guy with a tattoo on his penis, and I'm lucky I got out of that one alive.

Now that I've been promoted to YN3, I have a black emblem of an eagle with one chevron—called a "crow," it looks like a wide V—ironed on the upper portion of my left sleeve. To make sure that a new E-4's crow doesn't "mysteriously" fall off by, say, getting reduced in rank at NJP for a disciplinary infraction, Navy tradition is that all E-4 to E-6s *tack it on* you, which is a fancy term for *punching you in the arm*, which is another way of saying *hazing*. (Within a couple of decades, hazing will no longer be tolerated in the Navy, but we haven't arrived there yet.)

Soon after returning to the ship, I moved in with Peggy and her partner Robin on the other side of Charleston by the weapons base. Robin is also on the ship, a third class torpedoman's mate, and is a tiny, five-foot-two, ultra-freckled, pale-skinned redhead. She is a big kid who is forever dancing or driving around singing to Madonna or other popular '80s songs, but she also has a passion for torpedoes and weapons and is very proud of her big-ass silver nine-millimeter pistol.

One night I couldn't find my key and she and Peggy didn't hear my knocks, so I crawled through the bathroom window—only to find a very sleepy but very committed Robin standing in the shower with the barrel of that gun pointed at my head.

"Goddamn it, Kern!" she exploded, clearly not too mad to use her nickname for me. "I coulda killed ya!"

Just like at Tami and Mindy's, our apartment is a makeshift gay bar where I feel free to hug, laugh, drink, dance, and just be myself. We rarely go to actual gay bars because gay bars are sometimes raided by the police, especially here in the South, and one bad interaction with the police could get back to my command. I don't know how I'd explain that one away. So we create incognito "bars" in our homes with other Navy lesbians. My gay community gives me a sense of normalcy and freedom. Leaving work and going home feels like changing into a different mental uniform, from silent and closeted to out and free.

Because the party's always on at my gay-bar home, I am typically hungover and late for morning quarters. The PCC continues to completely bastardize my name during roll call, and as I'm usually not there, he tries one after another—"Petty Officer Slot! Petty Officer Sloop! Petty Officer Slut!"—with no response. Even when I am there I wait, just like everyone else, to see what words fly out of his mouth until one of us finally puts him out of his misery with a "Here, Chief!"

When I'm not there, Peggy usually covers for me, since it is her fault for living so damn far from the ship in the first place—"I have her doing some work in the office, Chief!"

One day I stumble in at 0745, fifteen minutes late for quarters and out of breath. Peggy exhales, rolls her eyes, and calls out, "Hey Sloopslot! Great you could join us! Guess what you have tonight?"

My chief lets out a little snort behind us.

I roll my eyes and head for my desk. "I know, I know, EMI . . ." When everyone else departs the ship at knock-off time, or 1600, I will stay on the ship for two hours of *extra military instruction*—swabbing, waxing, and buffing the passageway outside of the Admin Office. This happens almost daily, so my passageway always looks amazing.

I actually don't mind waxing and buffing. The key to quality buffing is to let the buffer do the work for you. If you hold it too tight, it will fight you and keep slamming into the bulkhead, which is exhausting and not cool. However, if you keep your grip light, just barely holding on, it will glide back and forth with ease. There is a certain satisfaction in handling it properly and making passageways shine like glass.

What I do mind is spending two extra hours on the ship when I know my friends are off having fun without me.

At 1800, the passageway before me spotless, I finally set off to meet up with Peggy, Robin, Teresa, Tami, and Mindy and the rest of the gang, who I know are already three sheets to the wind. I arrive to find Robin dancing by herself in the living room, eyes redder than her red hair, and singing to the Mary Jane Girls. She whips her head around and yells out, "Kern!"—then stumbles and almost falls over.

"Hey, Robbie!" I yell over the music. I head to the kitchen to grab a Milwaukee's Best, because that shit is cheap and I am broke. When I get back to the living room, I shout, "Let's play bottle rocket wars! Who's in?"

Everyone is in, except for Tami. "Someone could get an eye poked out," she warns, which absolutely blows my mind coming from *Miss Hitchhiker* herself.

The rest of us head outside, split up, and shoot at each other with bottle rockets. After diving behind some bushes in my camouflage pants, I momentarily stop to watch my group of wonderful friends giggling and having the time of their life. A bottle rocket then zooms by my head, and I shriek and fall to the ground.

I lie there laughing and feeling the love I have for these women. This is the only place in my life where I can freely be myself, and I can't imagine anything more perfect.

Tami and I remain in the same duty section, so she comes to my office as often as possible. We shut the door, put our feet on my desk, and talk about life. With the exception of duty days and the times when she joins parties at my house, we see each other a lot less these days. I miss her—our long walks down the pier, hitchhiking together, our smoke breaks on the deck.

One weekend duty day, I'm typing an award when I hear the door open and find Tami standing on the other side of the tall counter, her face a mix of relief, panic, and anger.

"Hey, bud!" I say. "Come in!" I grab Peggy's chair-recliner and roll it next to mine.

She stomps through the swinging door, flops down, and puts her feet on my desk. She's fuming. "My section leader has been on my ass all day. I just finished my watch, and now he wants me to go field day the office. I told him that I needed to eat because I didn't even get lunch, and he said that was my problem."

"Are you fucking kidding me? He can't do that!" I exclaim. I open my desk, pull out a package of Oreos, and hand them to her. She grabs a few and puts one in her mouth.

I don't know how she deals with the relentless abuse, and I also don't understand why he's got it out for her. She's the nicest person. I assume that it's because she's the only female in her division. That and her wicked eye rolls.

"Well, he did and I can't do shit about it. Who would I go to? No one gives a crap about me." She lowers her voice, and her eyes shine with tears she refuses to shed. "I'm seriously thinking about turning myself in, Karen. I see people getting out all the time. I'm not sure I can do this anymore."

NCIS occasionally rounds up lesbians on the ship, and they get immediately discharged. So far, none have been my close friends, but each time I worry about them being coerced into giving up more names, as each name could eventually lead to me. I finally like the Navy and don't want to get caught and kicked out—but I know Tami would welcome it. I wish she could catch the break I have.

I tap her boot with mine but don't know what to say. Her dark mood scares me, and so does its potential consequence. If she gets kicked out, she'll no longer be on the ship with me. While we don't see each other as much as we used to these days, it's comforting that she's right around the corner. I don't want to lose her.

"Well, if you do turn yourself in," I finally say, "I'll understand—but I don't know what I'll do without you."

Just then the phone rings. I pick up.

"Admin. Petty Officer Solt speaking. This is a non-secure line. Can I help you?"

"You seen Ames!?" The voice on the other end is demanding.

"Nope. Who's this?" I give Tami the *you better get the fuck back to work* look. She takes one heavy foot at a time off the desk, sighs, and slowly lumbers out of my office.

"It's her section leader. If you see her, tell her to get to her shop ASAP."

Click.

Tami's work battles are constant, and she's been tested since day one. In many ways, I'm surprised she's lasted this long.

Chapter 10

THE SOUTHERN BELLE

On a sunny, hot, and humid summer night in Charleston, I sit outside Ronda and Stacy's apartment on a brick wall. I'm side by side with a sweet southern girl named Savannah who is stationed onboard the USS *Canopus*, another submarine tender located just a few piers over from the *Frank Cable*. We've been partying all afternoon with the crew and Savannah and I have been talking, laughing, and flirting with each other for hours. Now, as the sun sets and my legs dangle below me, Savannah cries, distraught over her recent breakup with her straight married girlfriend, who is also on the *Canopus*. The smell of freshly cut grass mixes with evening heat as she sobs and I lean into her, occasionally giving her a gentle nudge.

The small world of lesbianism is what has brought Savannah and me together. She came to Ronda and Stacy's party to be a "buffer" for her friend who has a crush on me. This friend is Stacy's ex-girlfriend, and she also went to Engineman "A" school with Tami. If you'll remember, Ronda, Stacy's girlfriend, is also Mindy's ex-girlfriend. (I know it's hard to follow. It's not easy for me either, if that helps.)

I'm just grateful that Savannah's friend brought her as a buffer, because she is very cute and her accent is adorable. Although alcohol has sent her into a state of bummed-outness, she is my first crush, and I'm just happy I get to sit next to her on this wall.

"I ruined everything," she says, tears streaming down her freckled cheeks.

"I'm sure you didn't ruin everything," I say, softly bumping her elbow. "Have you tried to talk to her?"

She gulps in a labored breath and cries some more. I'm not helping.

Savannah is from a small town in Central Georgia, is three weeks older than me, stands five feet, four inches tall, y'alls me to heaven and back, and has beautiful blue-gray eyes, highlighted wavy blond hair, loads of pale freckles, and a strong, toned, sexy body.

I thank my lucky stars when, in the coming weeks, she starts joining the parties at my place every weekend.

"Hey, *girlllll*," she always says when she arrives and sees me. Her eyes twinkle and she wraps her arms around my neck. It takes us no time to grab our beers and head to the couch, where we curl up with each other and, our limbs intertwined, flirt and joke and laugh and talk for hours. Occasionally she leans in and gives me a small kiss—sometimes on the lips, but usually on my cheek.

After a few short weeks, I know more about Savannah than I ever did about either of my previous boyfriends. Her favorite color is blue, she loves country music, especially Reba McEntire, and her favorite aunt is her aunt Louise, but she calls her "Weezy." She tells me about her family, her small hometown, and how much she loves to fish. I tell her about my family, tubing down the Salt River, and romping through the pines in Northern Arizona. My heart melts when I'm with her, and I could talk to her for days. But inevitably, after one too many beers, Savannah regresses into remorse about her ex-girlfriend and I become her sounding board.

One Saturday afternoon, Savannah arrives and leads me by my hand to the couch, where she sits down with her right leg bent underneath her and her left foot still on the floor. She holds both of my hands in hers as a serious expression comes over her face. "I don't know how to tell you this, Karen, but the *Canopus* is changing homeports to Kings Bay, Georgia. We leave next month."

My mouth drops open; I feel like I've been socked in the gut. The USS *Canopus* is leaving Charleston?

When a command does a homeport change, they take all of their people, pieces, and parts to that new location. *Everything* moves, including the ship, the crew, and the crew's family. Many sailors with dependents don't want to make these moves, because it disrupts their family unit—perhaps their spouses have good jobs, or their children are established in their schools. These sailors can look for orders to another command in their current homeport, and the Navy will work with them to make as many accommodations as possible without hurting the integrity of the mission.

Gay sailors don't get this option. We go where we're told to go, even those of us in committed relationships, because our relationships are a secret. We're automatically assumed to be single, which means when we find out about a homeport change we either learn to move mountains to stay co-located with our partners, get out of the Navy altogether (when our commitment is up), or spend years apart and try to eventually find our way back to each other.

Savannah gently squeezes my hands and glumly looks up to see how I've taken her news.

Not well. She's leaving and there is nothing I can do to stop it. It feels like a missed opportunity.

"Damn . . . I can't believe it," I mutter. "I feel like I'm just getting to know you."

"I know, girl. Me too." She sighs and pulls me into her arms. "I'm so bummed."

My feelings for Savannah are a bizarre and tangled mess—lovely, intense, and emotional. Now I realize why I was never fully invested in my relationships with men: it's a completely different experience to fall for a woman. I've been waiting for her to get over her ex-girlfriend, but now I see that she has feelings for me too and we're about to be homeported two hundred miles apart. It will be nearly impossible to manage a closeted relationship with that distance between us.

Savannah and I spend every moment we can together before her ship leaves Charleston. When the dreaded day finally arrives, Tami and I stand on the weather decks of the *Frank Cable* and watch the *Canopus* untie her lines from the dock and set sail for Georgia. Savannah and I haven't made any commitment to each other, and as her ship sails away, I wonder if I'll ever see her again.

When the *Canopus* is finally out of sight, Tami tries to make me feel better. "It's gonna be okay, bud," she says.

I sigh and put my head down, and we walk back through the skin of the ship to our work centers.

A few days later, Peggy and Robin are in the kitchen making dinner and I'm drinking a beer and watching TV in the living room when the phone rings.

Robin answers, then yells out, "Kern! You can pick your damn lip up now! Your girl is on the line!"

I quickly rise from the couch and hustle to the kitchen, my face hot and red, elbow Robin, and snatch the phone out of her hands. "Hello?"

"Hey, girllll, I thought about you the whole way down here

and I already miss you," Savannah drawls. "Can I come see you this weekend?"

"Heck yeah, you can come see me!" I exclaim.

Robin rolls her eyes and walks over to stir the spaghetti sauce on the stove.

Savannah arrives Friday evening when a full-on party is going down at my place. She falls into my arms and kisses me at the door. "Hey, girllll . . ."

Without another word, she leads me to my bedroom.

We shut the door and sit on my bed, and she puts her hands on my cheeks. "The moment we left, you have no idea how much I missed you. I want to try and make it work between us." She looks into my eyes. "I love you, Karen."

I've been waiting my entire life to feel what is so special about the words "I love you." In this instant, hearing them from a woman for the first time, I finally understand.

I am loved. As myself.

My outer and inner world finally connect in truth, and a warmth fills my body. "I love you too, Savannah."

As we giggle and kiss, we also make plans for how we can possibly make this work, including committing to one of us driving the two hundred miles between us every weekend. It's nothing, we decide, when you're this in love.

The months fly by, and I count my days through each workweek to the weekend when I get to see Savannah. My friends think I've lost my mind and we will eventually burn out. I'm convinced that is not possible.

One Friday in September, I'm wrapping up my day and getting ready to drive to Georgia when a gay personnelman friend stops me in the passageway. She takes my upper arm in her hand, pulls me close, and whispers, "Tami turned herself in. She's in Legal right now."

I step back and blurt out, "Seriously? Fuck!" then stand frozen in the passageway, immediately self-conscious. As I dart quick glances to my left and right, I try to figure out what to do. My instincts tell me to go to Legal and tell them she was just joking. That her temper got the best of her. That she'd like a do-over. But of course I can't do that, and it's too late anyway. She already said the magic words: *I'm gay.*

I go into my office and whisper to Peggy, "Tami turned herself in."

Peggy keeps her head down, scribbles her initials in the chop block of a long blue folder, and slides it into Chief's inbox. "Hey, Chief, Sloopslot and I are gonna go burn one."

Chief squints her eyes and tilts her head, because nothing gets past her, but nods. Peggy and I put on our ballcaps, wind our way through the passageways and up a few ladders, and exit to the weather decks. We pull up our pant legs, remove our cigarette packs out of our socks, and light up.

My mind is whirling. It's hard to believe that Tami has turned herself in, even though she constantly threatened it. I feel horrible. I wish she had come to me, let me talk some sense into her. But I haven't been here. I've been in Georgia.

I lean against the railing and stare out over the water.

Peggy slides in next to me. "She's doing what she needs to do, Karen. If she thought she had another choice, she would have taken it. This is the easiest out you could get."

"I know. But damn, Peg," I sigh, "I feel like shit. She's my bud."

Peggy leans in closer. "I know. It's such a drag. It really is. But there isn't anything you could have done to make things better for her. Her division is the worst. She needs to be out and living her life. The Navy isn't for her. She'll be happier. Just trust that."

By knock-off time, Tami has already been escorted off of the ship, and I know that we won't get to say goodbye. I have been lectured repeatedly by her and many others: *If you ever get caught, don't contact any of us, not even in town. There will be a spotlight on you, and you'll put us all in jeopardy.* Because of that fear, I know Tami won't contact me. She'll do everything she can to protect me, which means staying away. And it isn't wise for me to try and see her either, badly as I want to.

I've just lost my best friend.

I drive the two hundred miles south that night to be with Savannah. She greets me at the door and instantly notes the look on my face. "What's wrong, babe?"

"Tami turned herself in today," I say, my face crumpling. "She's already gone. I didn't even get to say goodbye to her."

She puts her arms around me and holds me before leading me to the couch, where we talk about Tami and how awesome she is and how much I'll miss her. I can't imagine being on the *Frank Cable* without her—which, combined with how much I want to be with Savannah, is all adding up to some fast math. And I've done some research.

"I think I've found a way that I could be with you on the *Canopus*." I venture into this territory cautiously. "Would you want that?"

"Oh my God, girl—I would love that!" she squeals. "But how?"

One of my roles as a yeoman is to be familiar with the Navy's administrative and personnel regulations. As a combat misfit, I'm also a firm believer in *where there's a will, there's a way.* As soon as the *Canopus* left Charleston, I researched ways Savannah and I might be co-located and I found one possibility—one slim chance to move the mountain that's between us.

"I would have to do a hull swap to the *Canopus*," I explain.

"A what, babe?" she asks with her sweet accent, which instantly makes me melt.

A "hull" is the body of the ship, and each Navy ship has a hull number. The *Frank Cable*'s hull number is AS-40, and the *Canopus*'s is AS-34. Same exact type of ship, mission, and purpose—*AS* means "submarine tender"—but different numbers, and the higher the number, the newer the ship. A "hull swap" is when two sailors of the same rate and pay grade swap positions on the same type of ship at no cost to the government—meaning no travel pay will be issued and no household goods will be shipped at the government's expense. Its intent is a seamless swap of duty. If approved, I will fill the billet of an already-assigned YN3 on the *Canopus* and a YN3 from the *Canopus* would fill my billet on the *Frank Cable*. (An extremely rare occurrence. In my entire career, I will never meet another sailor that has completed a one-for-one hull swap like this.)

Savannah and I agree that no one in their right mind would want to transfer to Kings Bay from Charleston (except me), so her job is to find a YN3 on the *Canopus* who wants to return to Charleston. We put our plan in motion the following week, after she easily finds that YN3 and gives me his name and information. He and I both put in our hull swap requests in short order, and all there is to do now is wait.

Other than Peggy, who knows what I am doing and thinks I'm batshit crazy, my leadership is confused.

"I don't get it, Petty Officer Solt," my chief says when I nervously hand her my request. "You're doing so well. I thought you loved it here."

"I do love it here, Chief," I reply honestly. "It's the best place I've ever worked. But I just want to go to the *Canopus*." Unable to look her in the eyes, I put my head down. "I just do, Chief."

She stares at me, clearly aware that there's more to the story, but it's one I can't tell her: *I want to be with my amazing new girlfriend who I love with all of my heart and am losing my mind without. Please don't tell NCIS.*

She sees that I'm determined, so, being the awesome and supportive chief she is, she signs my request and routes it up to my commanding officer, who approves it. It is then sent to the bigwigs in DC for final approval—or disapproval—while I sit on crossed fingers.

Chief walks into the office a few weeks later holding a piece of paper and wearing a sour look.

"Petty Officer Solt, your hull swap has come back. It's been approved."

Peggy spins in her chair and turns to face me. I avoid her smirk as my face turns beet red and I try to not look as thrilled as I am.

"Wow," I manage. "Thanks, Chief. I sure appreciate your support."

She walks by and gives me the *I hope you know what you're doing* look. I am simultaneously stoked and scared to leave my comfort zone with my great all-woman office and misfit gay family. But for love, I have to give it a shot.

All my friends think I am making a mistake, but I pay them no mind. After making a decision, I typically move forward; I always land on my feet, after all.

I head to my trusty pay phone and call Savannah that evening. "Babe, it's approved! I'll be there in January!"

"Really!?" she says, and her excitement tells me I've made the right decision. "Awww, that's awesome! I love you, girllll."

Chapter 11

MOVING MOUNTAINS

Savannah and I start our budding relationship in a one-bedroom trailer in Woodbine, Georgia, which translates to "the middle of nowhere." Our brand-new simple white trailer, which isn't much but is at least something, sits on a long dirt road at the end of a row of barely-hanging-on but mostly-falling-apart trailers. We are together, happy, and proud. Woodbine is just a dash northeast of the Kings Bay Submarine Base, which is just a smidgen north of the Georgia–Florida border. It also might be the birthplace of the slow and simply impossible-not-to-hit armadillo, as they are a constant obstacle on my drive home each evening.

Each day after work, after turning right off of Armadillo Boulevard and driving down the long, dusty dirt road full of other trailers, I smile when I see Savannah's tan Ford Ranger pickup truck. I pull in next to it, wait for the dust to settle, then get out, walk up the two wooden steps to the paper-thin front door, and step onto freshly carpeted floors that echo over a canyon of emptiness with a "Hey, babe!"

Savannah greets me with a kiss, a hug, and a "Hey, girlllllll."

I go to the kitchen and grab a beer, and she follows me down the hallway to the left to our bedroom and sits on the bed as I get out of my uniform and we catch up on our days.

Things at work aren't quite as great as I had hoped for, but I love coming home to my sweet girl in our new trailer. Every night as I'm falling asleep and holding her tight as the big spoon, I'm as happy as I've ever been.

The new Admin Office I've been assigned to on the *Canopus* is the pits, especially after my amazing half-gay, all-chick office on the *Frank Cable*. The other yeomen are cold and impersonable, and I'm walking on eggshells trying to find my way in the uptight, rigid office—so not me. Luckily, the tall, quiet, blond-headed admin officer dude sees my challenge and very quickly determines that I am not suited for noiseless office spaces. He transfers me to work for the ship's chief engineer, aptly shortened into the contraction the "cheng."

Ships have many departments—Engineering, Deck, Repair, Weapons, Admin, Intel, Supply, and Operations, and, on some ships, such as aircraft carriers, Aviation. Each department has one department head and subordinate divisions that are led by division officers.

The Engineering Department is responsible for shipboard lighting, electricity, boiler rooms, sewer systems, and the engines. If the ship can't get underway or if the power goes out, it is the cheng's responsibility. With this move I will be our cheng's personal yeoman, working solo in the ship's Logroom.

The Logroom is similar to the Deck Department office on the *Frank Cable*. My gray desk and chair and office equipment are in the front room and the cheng's office is directly behind me, with a door he can shut so that he can yell at the division officer responsible for the latest screwup. My desk faces the door, so I can see sailors walking through the passageway while I'm working and even wave to a cute freckled third class engineman, my little spoon, as she passes by with a huge, shocked smile on her face: *I can't believe you're actually here.*

The cheng is simply the greatest guy. A lieutenant commander (LCDR—O-4), he is rough and tough and as crusty as they get. Not at all consumed with his personal appearance, he has a round, scruffy face, unkempt and thinning gray hair, and wears a wrinkled khaki working uniform that's only pressed around his plump belly. The epitome of an engineer, he is highly intelligent but dirty, smells like oil, and doesn't give a shit. He and I make a perfect team.

The cheng absolutely loves me because at such a young age I am independent and take care of my work without bothering him. But his mind is blown when I take the initiative to edit, rewrite, and smooth up sixty E-5 evaluations without his help.

Evaluations are either annual or bi-annual reports that each sailor receives as a report of their performance. All members of a peer group are ranked against one another. The rough-draft input starts in the shop level, then gets routed to the division officer, and finally to the department head, usually for signature. If the reports are for first class petty officers, chief petty officers, or officers, they keep going up the chain of command to the commanding officer for signature.

The cheng is so impressed that I have the skills to edit and smooth his evals well enough that all he has to do is sign them or pass them to the commanding officer that he gives me a 4.0 evaluation—the highest marks one can receive.

From that moment on, I spend most of my time at work in his stateroom, the place where he has his bunk, a desk, a chair, and two large stand-up lockers, which gives me privacy while I rewrite every evaluation for each peer group. I am doing a part of his job that he can't stand, and I don't want to hang out in the engineroom with him and smell like oil, so our arrangement works well for both of us.

"Babe, let's go dancing tomorrow night," Savannah says one Friday evening. She loves to dance in gay bars, and so do I—so, even though being in one comes at a huge risk, we occasionally accept that risk and drive forty-five miles south to a super cool one we know in Jacksonville, Florida. Between the lights, the music, the drag queens, and the women—mostly the women—there is nothing more fun than a night out enjoying the gay life with our people.

"All right, babe," I say. "Let's do it."

The next night, after a few hours of dancing and drinking with my girl, she is still on the dance floor, now dancing with the same chick over and over, which is irritating the shit out of me. I figure if Savannah can flirt with someone, so can I, so I start chatting it up with a cute woman at the bar.

Apparently my calculations are wrong, because a few minutes later my sweaty girlfriend walks off the dance floor, glaring at me, and pulls me aside by my elbow.

"It's time to go," she snaps.

"Why? I'm having a good time," I say. "And it looks like you're doing *just fine* out there."

"Karen, we are not going to do this shit here," she hisses. "Let's go."

She stomps away. I go after her and try to smooth things over, because I hate it when we fight. "I was just talking to her, babe, c'mon . . ."

"I'm leaving," she throws over her shoulder. "If you want a ride home, you'd better come now!"

I stop talking and follow her out.

She's silent and fuming and I'm silent and shut down and the forty-five-minute drive home feels like three hours.

As a child I learned that the best way to fight was to avoid fighting. My family didn't speak about the tough stuff or talk anything through. When my parents got angry at each other, they went silent and in separate directions, my dad to booze and my mom to busyness.

Whenever I got into trouble, which was rare, I would get one of two responses. The most common response was silence, which I interpreted as, *If we don't acknowledge it, it will go away*— which it always did. The other, more serious response I got, only from my mom, was *The Look*—no words, just a solid, direct stare that pierced whatever bullshit I was slinging and stopped me in my tracks.

But now I'm with my first love, and fighting with her is a true test of standing up for myself in a relationship. She grew up in a physically abusive family, so she is not one to back down, and when she's mad her anger scares me. I don't know how to argue like she does; I prefer silence over confrontation. And what I am finding out is that I don't always get what I want.

We finally arrive back home after the not-so-fun long drive back from the usually fun gay bar. We walk into the living room and Savannah says, "Don't do that shit again, babe."

"Fine, then don't you do that shit either," I respond.

We look at each other and sheepishly smile, because we know that we have a good thing, even with our occasional spats.

She takes my hand in hers and pulls me toward her. "C'mon, girl. You know I love you, even when you're a pain in my butt. Let's go to bed."

Because Savannah loves one person (me) and three things (*campin'*, *fishin'*, and *walkin' on the beach*), a few weekends later we load up her truck and head to Hanna Park, east of Jacksonville, where we find a nice semi-secluded spot by the beach. *Campin'* is safer for us than a gay bar, and Hanna Park is the perfect place to do everything we love.

Sporting my true colors in my blue-and-white *Frank Cable* baseball shirt, I set up the tent while she finds a private spot and ties our hammock under soaring southern pine trees. Then she grabs her *fishin'* pole, and we head to the nearby pond.

Savannah could fish for days and I could watch her for days, as I'm not a pull-the-horrible-hook-out-of-the-fish-while-one-eye-is-staring-at-me-and-it's-distressingly-flopping-in-my-hand kind of girl. I'm more of a hold-her-beer-kill-my-beer-and-watch-it-painlessly-die-in-my-hand kind of girl.

After *fishin'* we return to camp, where she gets the now-dead fish ready to cook on the campfire. Then we go lie in the hammock.

For the first few minutes, my body is tense; I find myself worrying who might be around us, unsure if we're safe. I hold her and try to relax and rid my mind of those thoughts. Then I hear a sweet and gentle, "I love you, Karen," and my tension melts and my concerns momentarily fade.

I wrap her tighter in my arms, take a deep breath, and feel the breeze coming off the water. "I love you too, babe."

On our way home, we stop at the beach, roll up our pant legs, and walk along the shore. At one point, Savannah leaves my side and heads to the water's edge, where she stares toward the horizon like there's something out there only she can see, a secret between her and the universe.

As I stand back and watch my sweet southern belle, I feel like the luckiest girl alive.

Chapter 12

AND . . . HALT!

Savannah's truck is in the drive when I get home from work one evening, a sweet reality I have gotten used to, but when I walk through the paper-thin door expecting her standard "Hey, girllll," accompanied by a kiss and a hug, I instead find her crying on the couch.

I sit down next to her. "What's wrong, babe?"

"Dawn is in the hospital," she sobs. "Her husband threw her through a window."

"That's horrible!" I place my hand gently on her back. "Is she going to be okay?"

Savannah looks down, slowly shakes her head, and continues to cry.

Dawn is Savannah's ex, a woman who is also on the ship with us. I was pretty sure that candle hadn't totally burned out, but now I see it clearly in her eyes. Savannah still loves her.

There is no "Hey, girllll" at the door when I come home for the next few days. Every night it is written all over her face. She is thinking about Dawn.

My heart knows that she is leaving. It's obvious. Emotionally, she is already gone.

The inevitable question comes a few days later: "Do you mind if I go see her in the hospital, babe? There's nothing going on. I just need to see if she's okay. I want to help her."

Stopping her would only make things worse. "Sure, babe. Go see her."

Savannah sees Dawn in the hospital and comes home sad. She goes again the next day while I stay home and get drunk. Of course, I don't want to lose her, but the writing is on the wall. I've already given up. We are both sad, but for different reasons.

A week later, it's late evening and I've been sitting on the couch for hours, drinking one beer after another. My drinking has escalated rapidly since the first day Savannah went to see Dawn.

Savannah is typically home by dusk, so my mind is spinning out of control. Finally, I hear a car approaching and then see headlights shine through the living room window as her truck pulls up to the trailer.

A moment later, she comes through the front door. I don't get up. She walks over and sits next to me on the couch without looking at me. I know what she's going to say before she even speaks the words.

"Karen, I need to talk to you," she begins in a hushed tone. "I am so sorry, but I'm still in love with Dawn. I want to try again with her."

I vacantly watch the perspiration stream down the outside of my beer can. "Have you been with her?" As if fooling around is more important than her being in love with someone else.

She keeps her head down. "Yes." This comes out as more of a whisper.

"I can't believe I left everything and moved down here," I say under my breath. "I should have known this was going to happen." I get up, walk out, and slam the paper-thin door behind me, softly muttering, "Fuck you."

She hates when I slam doors, which is why I slammed it—I knew it would make her come for me.

"Fuck you too!" She pushes me so hard I fall to the ground, which ironically gives me a moment of reprieve.

Fight over. Relationship over.

I go to the bedroom and furiously half-pack my suitcase while she sits silently in the living room, seemingly trying to avoid any more confrontation. My heart is broken, and I can't get out of there fast enough. I blow by her on the couch without one glance her way and leave that night, never to return to our trailer.

Not ever, not even to pick up the rest of my clothes.

I toss my few things into the back of the Tramp Champ and peel out. *Fuck this bullshit.* A cloud of dust billows behind me as I fly past the row of trailers all the way back out Armadillo Drive.

The lesbian network kicks into high gear, and after a phone call or two, which includes drunken sobbing over my breakup, I find a new place to live in no time flat.

My new roommate is Pam, a straight, tough, Irish ginger who plays softball as well as any tough lesbian. She's as wild as the rest of us, a cool, spunky, and fierce yeoman, and is also a total mother bear who will kick anyone's ass if they mess with me. This is a good thing, because heartbreak has made my anger—and my need to live life in the extremes, the best way I know to numb out—return with a vengeance. I need someone to look out for me.

Work hours are brutal because I see Savannah every day; every time she passes by my office it's like a knife to my heart. So I do what makes infinite sense to a twenty-year-old with a broken heart: I ask the cheng if I can be moved to another department.

He doesn't understand. "I don't get it, YN3. Why would you want to work somewhere else?"

It's déjà vu—the same conversation as before, a year and a half later.

"I just want to go to another department for my versatility and growth, sir," I lie through my teeth. "I've loved working for you, and I'm grateful." That part is true.

Because the cheng is simply the best, he respects my request and I become the Weapons Department YN.

There's a smattering of lesbians from the ship that rounds out my new underground gay network, but Alex and Sherah (both nicknames), a lovestruck duo, become my main running mates. We either shoot pool and drink beer at a local dive, the Cumberland Bar, on the weekends, or the three of us cruise all over Kings Bay in the Tramp Champ from one party to the next. They call me Fred (long story) and are having an affair, as Alex is already in a relationship with another woman I've nicknamed Elvira, because she has black hair, is twenty years older than Alex, has teenage kids, and seems angry. (She always gives me *The Look*, which makes me like her even less.)

Elvira tries to catch Alex and Sherah and I am their accomplice, driving like a madwoman and peeling out with my front wheel drive that now makes all of us giggle.

Alex is my closest friend on the ship. She is a second class hull technician who works in the Repair Department and spends most of her time performing maintenance onboard the submarines that are tied up alongside the *Canopus*. She is five foot four and has long, curly, light brown hair that poofs into a wild, uncontainable mess when she doesn't have it tied up.

Alex is a legend. In her short career, she has already been to one court-martial and four Captain's Masts (NJPs), the form of discipline afforded to Navy commanding officers. Her biggest offense was a fifteen-month desertion from the Navy when she was stationed in San Diego. If a sailor is absent from their command less than thirty days—even one hour—it is considered unauthorized absence. But more than thirty days is desertion and is a federal offense. Alex was already a deserter from the Navy for over a year and was working at a restaurant when her gay brother, who was living with her in San Diego, jumped from the Coronado Bridge and died by suicide. After his death, she was a wreck and left San Diego for Washington State; federal agents eventually tracked her there, knocked on her door, and arrested her for being a deserter.

Alex was returned to San Diego and went to a court-martial. She was reduced from E-5 to E-3, awarded sixty days of restriction and ninety days extra duty, and fined two-thirds of her pay for three months. The judge then gave her the choice of a bad conduct discharge or finishing out her enlistment and getting a fresh start. She chose the latter and started turning her life around—if living in Kings Bay, Georgia, drinking with me, having an affair with Sherah, and avoiding Elvira can be categorized as turning your life around.

Sherah is a seaman in the Deck Department. She is young and pretty and has long, brown curly hair that she skillfully puts up in a bun. She is independent as hell and mentally and physically strong. Even as a young seaman, Sherah takes shit from no one. She gives the best hugs and has the biggest heart and sweetest spirit. Her laugh is high-pitched, spontaneous, and contagious, and she and my bud are extremely smitten with each other. Driving the getaway Tramp Champ and ditching Elvira for these two lovebirds is a pleasure.

It's a weekend night and I am at the Cumberland Bar, shooting pool with Alex, Sherah, and a few other lesbians from the ship, including Savannah. She and Dawn didn't work out—again—so she is re-bummed, and though I can now stand to be in a room with Savannah again, I am still reeling with anger that never fails to come out when I am out drinking, like tonight.

Three of us are sitting at the bar on tall barstools, where we leave our beers when it's our turn to shoot pool. I'm racking the pool table when a woman around our age, a dude, and an older woman walk over, glare at us, and then sit on our barstools.

I walk the ten paces back to the bar to confront them.

"Uh, these are our seats," I say using my firm voice, standing eye-to-eye with the older woman.

She doesn't budge.

I turn to my friends and loudly declare, "Hey, guys, the bitch, the bastard, and her momma won't move."

That doesn't go over so well.

The younger one, the "bitch," jolts up from her barstool and gets in my face. "You want to take this outside?"

My pool cue still in my hand, I stand taller and say, "Damn right I do!"

We start heading toward the back door. The bar goes silent for a beat; then the entire bar clears out, many with pool cues in hand, to join the fight.

This is when I remember—*I'm not a fighter; I just have a big mouth.* But I am still reckless and angry, so I dive onto Her Momma just as she ducks. My momentum propels me over her and she and I both fall, but it also drives my forehead into the concrete parking lot ground. Everyone swings at each other for another minute; then someone yells, "Cops!" and twenty people start scrambling.

A few of us dash into the Tramp Champ and I peel out—hood raising, front wheels screeching, and my middle finger flying out of the window.

■ ■ ■

My master chief freezes as he enters the office that Monday morning and sees my black eyes and swollen forehead. He then shakes his head, chuckles, and says nothing.

I love working for the weapons officer. It's as rewarding as working for the cheng was, and my master chief is amazing. His desk is in the large, long front office with mine, so he's aware that I'm a bit of a train wreck outside of work, but he always tells me, "YN3, you've got something special and could really go places. Trust me. I've been around a long time. Reenlist. Stick around for another tour. You'll see."

Although I trust him and his compliments are nice, I'm just not sure about staying in the Navy another four years. His suggestion is emphasizing the fact that I have reached a crucial decision point, however. My two options are: 1) stay on the *Canopus* for another year and a half and then separate from the Navy, or 2) reenlist, get new orders, and get the hell out of Georgia.

I'm in another great planning moment—reminiscent of high school, when I had zero future in the works. My logic goes something like this: If I leave the Navy, then what? Back home? There's a total of 0.5 lesbians in my hometown. Of that, I feel certain. In the Navy, meanwhile, there are about a gazillion lesbians—closeted, of course, but I'm going to be closeted regardless of where I am, and so far I've figured out how to do it in the Navy and survive. Why not keep it going?

Master Chief rolls his chair over next to mine and tries not to gawk at my black eyes. "YN3, I have great news. When the ship is in the Bahamas next month, there will be a big reenlistment ceremony on the main stage at one of the casinos. What do you think? Want to be a part of it? I can get your name on the list, but we have to act quick."

Reenlisting? On a casino stage? Now that sounds like a blast! And hell, what's another four years?

"All right, Master Chief, I'm in!" I say, matching his enthusiasm. Then, more serious, I add, "But I want to go back to the West Coast. Will you help me call my detailer and see if I can get orders closer to home first?"

We go to his desk and dial my detailer, the person in DC who is responsible for assigning sailors within the yeoman rating Navy-wide. Fortunately, he cannot see my eyes.

Master Chief puts his phone on speaker and, sitting next to me, smooths the way for me.

"Hey, Chief, this is Master Chief Harper from the USS *Canopus*. I'm sitting here with my favorite yeoman. Please do me a favor and help her get good orders so she'll reenlist next month."

"Roger that, Master Chief. I'll certainly do what I can."

Master Chief leans back and gestures for me to talk.

"Hey, Chief," I say eagerly, "do you have anything on the West Coast?"

"There's nothing on the West Coast, YN3," he says. "But I do have a two-year tour on Antigua, an island in the Caribbean. How does that sound?"

The Caribbean? Are you kidding me!? "Sounds great, Chief!"

Master Chief high-fives me—a little too strongly, which kind of makes my head hurt and reminds me of the bar fight all over again. But I recover quickly. The Caribbean—a fresh start. I can't wait.

On September 1, 1987, I reenlist with many others on that casino stage in the Bahamas. My commanding officer is escorted to the stage by showgirls in sparkly purple bikinis with soaring pink feathers in their hair. Showgirl music is blaring and if someone were to start stripping right now, it would not surprise me in the least.

My favorite weapons officer—LT Mettle, a short, gray-haired prior-enlisted officer—reenlists me on that stage as we both raise our right hands. No trickery this time. I know what I'm doing . . . sort of.

Of course, I am possibly a tad bit drunk. We all are. It's the Bahamas!

Savannah watches me reenlist from the seats, this time holding my beer. I smile down at her. We've managed to become friends over time, and I will always love and be grateful for her, my first true love. She broke my heart, but I learned a lot from our relationship. And now I'm ready to move on.

PART TWO

Chapter 13

THE RAINBOW STATE

The next two years on Antigua are a mixed blessing. I learn about the beauty of island living, with its go-with-the-flow rhythm. My days are spent plummeting into endless potholes while driving on the left side of the road to one of the island's 365 white-sand beaches in my shitty white Pinto, which has holes in its muffler and makes me deeply regret letting go of the Tramp Champ.

Antigua is a whirlwind: I dodge more sexual harassment (you knew that); survive Hurricane Hugo; am promoted to YN2—E-5; make great new friends; am given a new nickname, Paco; and, of course, find my people, a handful of fun-loving lesbians.

In seemingly no time, my two years there are up and I find myself on the phone with my detailer again.

"Hey, Chief, do you have anything out West?" I ask him once again.

"The closest I have is a three-year staff duty tour in Hawaii," he says.

I can't believe my good luck. Hawaii is more West than even I envisioned. "I'll take it!"

The only downside of my new assignment is leaving behind a heartbroken, young, sweet girlfriend. She wants to stay together and make it work between Antigua and Hawaii; I do not. To make myself feel less guilty, instead of simply being honest with her (I hate it when she cries), I leave her my shitty white Pinto.

This does not, it turns out, make me feel any less guilty.

I finally land in Hawaii, which is a little sketchy, as the runway is very close to the ocean. As I exit the gate, I take my first inhale of Hawaiian air and immediately think, *This is what heaven smells like.*

I stroll down the open-air concrete walkway toward baggage claim escorted by a gentle breeze, swaying palm trees, and smiling Hawaiian people in aloha attire. I gawk at the lush, green, chiseled mountain ranges in the distance as I go.

I retrieve my luggage from the carousel just as a female chief in her khakis enters the baggage claim area. This must be my sponsor.

I grab my bags and walk over to her. "Are you Chief Walker?"

She nods. "Yes. You must be Petty Officer Solt."

I size her up as she shakes my hand. She is petite, with long, auburn, pinned-up hair, but she walks so damn fast—even in her skirt and one-inch black pumps—that I can barely keep up in my shorts and tennis shoes.

We load my luggage in the back of her tan minivan, and I get in the passenger seat. The moment she hits the gas pedal, small cockroaches scurry across the floorboards. My breath catches in my throat; I lift my feet three inches off the floor, make myself stay still, and try not to scream.

Chief Walker is one of the few Navy women I've ever known who wears a skirt to work every day. (Since we aren't on a ship, skirts are technically back on the uniform menu for me as well, but I've scratched them off mine—anytime I can help it, anyway.) She talks nonstop on the drive to the base, while I dissociate and stare at the floorboards. When we pull into the barracks, I practically jump out of her car. I stomp my feet for good measure, and once I grab my bags I tap them on the ground a few times too, just in case.

It can only get better from here, right? I think as I follow Chief Walker into the barracks.

My new assignment is the four-star admiral's command in Pearl Harbor, Commander in Chief, US Pacific Fleet. The abbreviation, CINCPACFLT, sounds out as "sink-pack-fleet." This is a high-visibility staff job and one that I had to screen and qualify for. Now with six years in the Navy under my belt, almost a third of the way to the pension-eligible twenty years, this command will help me determine whether or not I will become a career sailor.

After Antigua, Hawaii is as big as all of America as far as I am concerned. Its variety of food choices, malls and movie theaters, and roads that don't make my head snap around like a puppet are all instant benefits. The beaches in Hawaii are also amazing, comparable to the Caribbean. The water is warm, clear, and cleansing.

Mauka (island) showers are a daily occurrence—sometimes a small shower, other times days and days of downpour. Heavy rains make the red mud sticky and slippery but also keep Hawaii lush, beautiful, and laden with just the right amount of humidity. Rainbows always follow mauka showers, and all good gay girls love a colorful rainbow.

On Monday morning, I start my check-in process and am given a security badge that gives me access to buildings and rooms that I'm assigned to. I swipe, the door clicks, and I enter. If I don't have access to that space, the swipe won't work. This badge also depicts my level of security clearance. I have been granted access to Sensitive Compartmented Information (SCI), which is above Top Secret. This makes no sense, I know; the top should be the top. But this is the government, and we make up rules when we need to.

Chief Walker is a chief yeoman (YNC). She is my direct supervisor in a division within the Operations Department, which is located in a windowless, four-story building just inside Halawa Gate. Operations is where big decisions are made about the biggest of shit, a place where precision and proficiency are necessities, and I am excited to get a front-row seat to this part of the Navy.

Within the Operations Department are five divisions, and each of these divisions has a few yeomen and a captain (O-6) as the division officer. These captains report to my bosses, the assistant chief of staff (ACOS) for Operations and his assistant, the fleet operations officer, also captains. Most of these officers have been commanding officers of either ships, squadrons, or submarines, and all of them find it challenging to report to someone else after having tasted the privilege that comes with being the HMFDIC (Head Mother Fucker Directly in Charge, which is not a real Navy term but is used by everyone anyway).

One of my bosses is Captain Barkley, the ACOS for Operations and a former commodore of a destroyer squadron. He is 100 percent badass. His name is appropriate, as he barks more than any officer I've ever met. At everyone. One wrong step and he'll rip into you. But I think he is amazing, and he brings out my absolute best because anything below that results in an ass chewing. He is as tough and consistent as they get.

My other boss is Captain Robertson, the fleet operations officer, an aviator. He is the nicest guy. Aviators are known for being more chill than surface guys, and it's a stereotype I've found to be true.

The Navy has perceived levels of professionalism. The surface forces are the strictest; those guys will eat their young. The submarine forces seem more lackadaisical, as they have sloppy uniforms, but you wouldn't care either if you never saw the light of day. The aviation community is more chill and aviation officers all have nicknames, or call signs. Think *Top Gun*, then remove Tom Cruise but keep the sunglasses and the cockiness, and that's the aviation community. There are a few smaller communities, like Navy SEALs and the Seabees, who are all about their specific mission and have their own flow. All officers and chiefs wear black shoes, except aviators, who wear brown shoes. Hence Captain Barkley is a tough black-shoe surface man and Captain Robertson is a chill brown-shoe aviation dude.

My two bosses each have their own large office with big wooden desks behind a smaller front office reception area with a couch. This is where Chief Walker has her desk. Captain Barkley constantly berates her with no mercy—

"Don't you think that would be smarter, Chief!?"

"Yes, sir."

"Then do it that way, goddamn it!"

"Yes, Captain!"

I overhear these conversations from the reception area, and see her tight-lipped look as she quickly exits his office. As I am certainly no dummy, I don't say a word.

Two of my new responsibilities are opening the office on weekdays and relieving Chief Walker for breaks. Captain Barkley arrives between 0530 and 0600, so I arrive no later than 0430 to have his office ready for him. Captain Robertson arrives whenever the hell he wants to and is definitely not my main concern. Chief arrives at 0700, so the office is mine until then.

My days of all-night partying and being late to work are over because I am scared to death of being yelled at by Captain Barkley. Until he arrives I am stressed out of my mind, running around like a madwoman getting everything in place. One of my peers told me the captain once hurled a large brass anchor mounted on wood at him and yelled, "Get the fuck out of my office!" when he failed to perform a task to his standards. This will never be me. I'm determined to always be ready.

Captain Barkley's morning setup: The coffee pot sits on the left side of his desk, with his coffee mug and saucer directly in front of the spout. I wear rubber thumbs to sort the five-inch stack (or more) of morning message traffic into security classifications—Secret, Confidential, Unclassified—and then again into "Action" and "Info" categories. Once everything is sorted, I stack it in diagonal piles, like a fan, so that each pile is differentiated from the other. I place the completed stack in the middle of his desk, then go back to mine and nervously wait.

When he arrives, I bolt upright to attention. "Morning, Captain Barkley!"

He always rushes by, eager to get his day started, but he does send a small grin my way. "Morning, Solt!" I hold my breath as he arrives at his desk and scans everything.

When he smiles, sits, and pours his first cup of coffee, relief floods my body and I exhale.

I set up Captain Robertson's office in the same way, minus the coffee spout requirement, and I'm not afraid for my life with him. When he casually strolls in, between 0600 and 0700, I rise to greet him. "Good morning, Captain Robertson."

As smooth as they get, he flashes a full smile. "Good morning, Petty Officer Solt."

And so it goes.

A few weeks after I start working there, Captain Barkley gets really upset with the chief. "I don't want you at that desk anymore, Chief. Put Solt out there! She won't fuck it up!"

Chief is not happy about this new arrangement—nor does this help her to like me, which is kind of important when you work for someone—but Captain Barkley is the HMFDIC and I'm not about to argue with him. His temper doesn't intimidate me anymore either. Not only have I gotten used to him, but I actually relate to him. We're both driven by rage. The difference is that his is an external rage that he is free to express, and mine is an internal rage that I am required to swallow.

Unless I'm drinking, in which case the express train is lit.

Soon after my arrival on Oahu, another lesbian in the barracks invites me to a pool party in Aiea.

Local makeshift gay bar, located.

I meet Laura, a yeoman in the Coast Guard and the master tenant of the house, at the party, and she and I totally hit it off. By the end of the day, she's invited me to rent the house's empty third bedroom. I happily accept.

Our three-bedroom, one-story house sits at the top of Aiea and has a spectacular view of Pearl Harbor and the entire southern part of Oahu. The living room is just inside the front door, with an open kitchen directly behind it. A sliding glass door is on the far-left wall of the kitchen and takes us to the place we spend most of our time, the "lanai," where a light blue–cushioned wicker couch and two chairs are nicely arranged on a covered concrete slab. Laura's master bedroom with its king-size waterbed is at the end of a hallway, just to the right of the living room. My bedroom, a small, cozy space that holds my new twin waterbed, and has a small closet and a window that looks out onto the driveway, is next to Laura's. Melissa, our other roommate, is across the hall from me, and she and I share a full bath.

Laura is my first ever Coast Guard—Coastie—friend. She has big, loving energy and a robust laugh that can be heard throughout the house (and, most likely, throughout the neighborhood). She spikes the top of her shoulder-length straight blond hair, and her greenish-blue eyes change colors depending on what she's wearing. With ginormous shoulders and arms, she looks like a firefighter, but she's actually a *paddla* on a local outrigger canoe team, a team full of friends she's known for years. Her wooden paddle is her pride and joy, and it stands upright against a wall in the living room. A mother hen with a big heart and a generous spirit, Laura is very protective of me—of all of her friends, really, but I like to think she especially looks out for me. She loves the sun and the beach, but her two favorite things are paddling and throwing pool parties at our house for all our friends.

Melissa is a drinker and a rabble-rouser and is mostly aloof. She has pale skin that burns easily in the Hawaiian sun and shoulder-length brown hair that drapes out of the large hole at the top of the white golf visor she wears every day. She and Laura have an on-again, off-again relationship; I make it my business to stay out of it completely. I'm digging my new living arrangement and have no plans to make a mess of things.

Laura has been on the island for two years, so lesbians galore show up at our house every weekend to party all day and all night. We don't have an actual pool, but we fill a tiny rubber baby pool, the kind with two puffy rings, on the grass in our front yard, and I park my truck on the lawn to create a privacy barrier between the road and the house. Fortunately, the yard is much higher than the street, because in no time tops are off and three or four women are lying in that tiny pool, redistributing water all over the grass. Cecilio & Kapono's "Goodtimes Together" blares from the stand-up speakers inside the house, and everyone sings along with the chill island music.

Where all these women come from, I have no idea, but our house is a lesbian revolving door and I'm happy. Life on Hawaii couldn't be off to a better start with my challenging job, new friends, and awesome digs.

Chapter 14

SUE

I f you take a right out of my office and two more rights at the end of each long, bright, and white linoleum hallway, you'll find a storeroom called 301. This is where we store supplies and where incoming correspondence is distributed. Each day, Chief Walker relieves me at my desk and I walk to CINCPACFLT's main building, pick up Operations Department mail, and bring it back to 301 in a wide brown carrying case. I log classified material for signature and distribute the rest of the mail into metal boxes attached to the wall for the divisional yeomen.

This is where I meet Sue.

Chief Walker is explaining these duties to me when I hear a *click* and the security door opens.

"Morning, Chief!" says a very short, smiley yeoman with big cheeks, sky-blue eyes, and short curly brown hair. She heads to the mailboxes.

"Morning, Petty Officer Ramsey!" Chief says. She gestures in my direction. "This is Petty Officer Solt. She just reported and will be working with me in 301."

Like me, Sue is in her Summer Whites, a requirement at CINCPACFLT for all E-6 and below. As she walks over to shake my hand, I note how good her deep tan looks with the white uniform. "Welcome aboard! Call me Sue. If you need anything, I work upstairs in Fleet Warfare."

Her stunning blue eyes and sweet smile catch me off guard—so I engage my horrible first impression ritual and deflect my insecurity with a joke. "Thanks! I'm Karen. Hey, did you stand on your tippy-toes to trick your recruiter?"

Her eyes get wide, and she freezes for a beat. Then she relaxes. "I might have." She winks. "See you later." She offers us both a smile before walking out.

Sue stands at four foot eleven and a half but defiantly claims to be five feet tall. She is a sharp YN1 and is the lead yeoman in her division. Her captain, another super nice brown-shoe aviator, works for my captains, so her bringing correspondence to my desk soon becomes a regular part of my everyday work life.

I've never really believed in love at first sight, but if it exists, I experience it with Sue. Her mere presence turns me into a teenage schoolgirl—my heart beats faster, I get flustered, my face turns red, and I fumble over my words. But I keep my crush to myself, as I'm not even positive she's gay, and she's kind of a Goody Two-Shoes. It would be a huge risk to approach her.

One day in February, Sue enters my office and says, "Hey, I'm going to Woods's party tomorrow afternoon. Are you?"

This is my chance to finally figure out where she stands; without hesitation, I blow off tomorrow's pool party at my house. "I wasn't planning on it," I say boldly, "but I can meet you there if you want."

"Great!" she says. "See you there." She flashes me a huge smile before exiting my office.

I arrive at Woods's house the next day and note that Sue's always-spotless, dark gray, two-door Pontiac Grand Am isn't parked outside. The door is open and I can hear the party, so I walk through the house to the backyard lanai, where four of my coworkers are sitting in the hot tub. I'm trying to look good for Sue, so I have on a polo shirt and black jeans.

My coworkers are already fairly drunk.

"Hey, why don't you and your black jeans get in the hot tub with us?" one of them heckles me.

"There's no way in hell I'm getting in—"

I'm mid-sentence when two of them grab me by the back of my polo shirt and pull me headfirst over the edge.

Sue walks in just as I come up for air. That look on her face . . . Let's just say I'm not very good at second impressions either.

I crawl out soaking wet. "Uh, well, that was interesting. It looks like I have to go home and change." I turn to Sue. "Wanna come with me?"

I hold my breath.

She shakes her head in disbelief and laughs. "Sure. Sounds like a great idea."

I exhale, grinning.

We walk back through the house and reach the entryway, where, as soon as my wet feet meet the ceramic tile, I slip and land on my ass with a *thud*.

Sue's mouth drops open and her eyes widen; then she bends over and roars with laughter. "Good God! Are you okay?"

I cautiously get back on my feet. "Jesus, I really need to get the hell out of this house."

I look into her beautiful sky-blue eyes, and they tell me everything I've been waiting to know.

We drive to my house so I can change, and then we head to a bar in Pearl City, where we sit on barstools at a tall table and talk for hours. We quickly establish nicknames: I am "K" and she is "Q," short for Suzy-Q. She is amazing and interesting and adorable and tells me she has feelings for me too. She also informs me that she is not single—and her girlfriend is an officer, which is why she's extra private. Relationships between officers and enlisted personnel is called *fraternization* and is an article of infraction within the UCMJ, so their relationship is doubly illegal in the Navy's eyes.

Sue and her girlfriend live together in Makakilo, a twenty-minute drive west of Pearl Harbor. My heart sinks as she shares this information. But then she offers me a glimmer of hope: she plans to end her relationship.

"When?" I ask.

"I don't know." She shakes her head. "It's not going to be easy."

For her, I can wait.

Sue and I begin to see each other secretly in the coming weeks, during which time I learn so much. First, one minute away from Sue is one minute too long, so I start attending night classes with her. Yes, me, the one who barely graduated from high school—although, full disclosure, I do go to the car during the break, where I remain and drink from a cooler full of beer until class is over.

Baby steps.

I also learn that Sue is originally from Michigan, a short distance from Lake Michigan, and is the second-oldest child and the oldest girl in a large Catholic family of six siblings—three boys and three girls. She has more cousins, aunts, and uncles than anyone I've ever known. She loves and is loved and cherished by her entire family. She joined the Navy when she was eighteen and spent four years in San Diego before getting out. She returned home to Michigan but had difficulty finding a job, so she rejoined the Navy eleven months later.

SUE

Her first assignment upon reentry was at Naval Air Facility, Midway Island, a small island about a thousand miles northwest of Hawaii. During World War II, Midway was attacked by the Japanese on the same day as Pearl Harbor—December 7, 1941—and was also the site of the infamous Battle of Midway, six months later. Sue was stationed there for two years and loved it; while she was there, she developed a passion for scuba diving, snorkeling, fishing, and golfing on the island's small par-3 course. She also got into beachcombing—mostly searching for Japanese floating fish balls, hollow green glass balls used to keep fishing nets afloat. Her enthusiasm for those things is contagious.

Sue is unlike anyone I have ever been with—tough and competitive, tender and soft, smart and wise, fun and playful. She has an amazing sense of humor and a spontaneous laugh that makes her stomp her feet, like a full-body exclamation point. Her laughter fills a room. Her laughter lights up my entire world. And she is so not me. She rarely drinks, and she's attending college night classes because she wants to.

Sue is also afraid of confrontation and silence is her form of fighting, so she has yet to gather the courage to break up with her girlfriend, Donna.

After our one-month mark (which is forever in lesbian time, as we usually bring a loaded U-Haul on the second date), Sue and I sit on my couch. I'm frustrated.

"Come on, babe. Tell her. Enough already."

Sue looks away sheepishly, so I soften my tone, put my hand on her cheek, and turn her face toward me so I can look into her eyes. "Look, babe, I love you. I want to live with you. I want to come home to you every evening and wake up with you every morning."

"I want that too, K. I really do. But I'm scared to tell Donna. She's going to be crushed, and I don't want to hurt her."

"She's going to be crushed whether you do it today or a month from now," I plead. "But please do it soon, because Laura's lease is almost up and we have to find another place to live."

I'm trying to be strong and assertive, even though there's no way in hell I'm letting her go.

Soon after that conversation, the college leaves a message on Sue's home answering machine, notifying Sue and me that *our* paperwork for *our* next course is ready. Donna comes home from work, hears the message on the answering machine, and puts two and two together just as Sue is picking me and my cooler up for class.

The phone rings at my house as Sue walks in the door and pulls me into her arms. Laura answers it; after a second, her deadpan face turns to us and she puts her hand over the receiver. "Ummmm, whoever this is said, 'Put Sue on the phone right now!'"

Shit.

Sue's eyes widen and Laura hands her the phone. Sue puts the receiver to her ear, says, "Uh-huh," and "I know," and "Okay," over and over, and then hangs up.

I wait, looking at her. Her eyes are as big as half-dollars.

"Well," she says slowly, "it looks like I don't have to tell Donna anymore."

For the first time in my entire life, I have an appreciation for school.

Sue and I become the first renters of a tiny two-bedroom, second-floor apartment built on top of a house that Laura and Melissa will rent. We can barely fit the few scraps of furniture we have in our apartment, but this is new love—hell, we happily sleep together on my twin-size waterbed, where we roll to the middle and lovingly suffocate each other all night—and I am stoked that my friends and I will all still be together. Sue also brings her sweet yellow cockatiel, Ipu, who blows kisses and says "pretty bird" in a scratchy voice, to join our family.

Our new place doesn't have room for big pool parties, so we spend our weekends at our favorite beach, Makaha Beach, on the western part of Oahu. We load chairs, boogie boards, and a cooler full of beer into the bed of my truck and caravan there with Laura, Melissa, and some of our other friends.

Our ritual is the same every time: we find the perfect spot, I grab a beer and get settled in my chair, and Sue and some others head out to ride the waves.

Sue constantly tries to cajole me into getting in with them— "I'm going out, K. Want to come?"

I ain't no dummy. "Uh, no thanks, babe. I'll keep an eye on our stuff."

She rolls her eyes, fully aware that I'm more interested in drinking than getting pummeled by the surf.

My choice is of course always immediately validated as I watch them get their asses kicked by the whitewater. Sue occasionally comes up for air just as another wave takes her down again, and I stay put on my chair, laughing hysterically. They eventually roll up onto the shore, rearranging their bikini tops, spitting out water, and breathing hard. Sue stumbles toward me with sand in every crevice and shoots me an exasperated, silent, *Why the fuck didn't you save me!?* look.

I raise my eyebrows, curl my lip, and shake my head—*You got the wrong girl. I'm not getting in that shit.*

She holds her stare, still breathing hard, then violently shakes her head to one side to expel water from her ear and plucks more sand out of her bikini top. I giggle a little more.

She then exhales, flops down, smiles, and cracks open a beer.

■ ■ ■

In April we add another member to our family: a sweet, tiny, mixed-breed kitten with Himalayan blue eyes, a gray body and face, and a tail that is 100 percent striped alley cat. I hold him in the palm of my hand, instantly fall in love, and give him a name that is very meaningful to me—6-Pac. He is more like a cat-dog than a cat: he loves to ride in my truck with me, where he wraps his body around my shoulders and neck and lies down. He and I share a bond that I never expected.

The day Ipu soars through the living room and is nearly nabbed by a perfectly timed 6-Pac jump, we know we have a problem. Sue is sure that it will only be a matter of time before we come home to a pile of feathers. Of course, I know she's right, but I don't know what to do about it: I love Ipu, but I love 6-Pac more.

I say nothing as she pokes out her bottom lip and holds Ipu in the palm of her hand.

Then she has an idea.

"I know someone at work who already has a cockatiel." Her eyes brighten. "Let me see if she wants another one."

As fate has it, the woman is looking for another bird, so we say goodbye to Ipu and he goes to a new home with another real pretty bird he can blow kisses to.

And with that, my new family is set: me, Sue, and our boy 6-Pac.

Chapter 15

FORBIDDEN LOVE

New love is an incredible gift from the universe, a time of excitement, passion, and bliss. Sue and I spend every moment we can together—at work, at home, driving, in the evenings, on the weekends. Our chemistry is amazing, and we have an ability to read each other that's unlike anything I've ever experienced. Because we have to hide our relationship from the outside world, we have developed a unique language that is mostly conveyed through our expressions or subtle body movements. Her communicative eyes reach from across the room and grab me, and I instantly know where she stands, how she feels, and what she wants. Ours is an intuitive thing. Truly. It's as if I've always loved Sue.

Sometimes she'll unexpectedly slide by my office door when I'm smack in the middle of a pile of paperwork, her arms out wide, a silent "ta-da!" emanating from her glowing face, and my heart will leap. In those moments, a love-filled *Hey babe!* bubbles up from the butterflies in my stomach, but I smash the urge to say it. Instead, I fight my joy and stay professional, keep my talk impersonal, watch my eye contact, and pretend that she's simply a great friend—because *I just know that others will see it* if I let down my guard for even one second. Anyone who's ever been in love knows what it looks like, and no one at work can know about ours. For as much as we are in love, we are also deeply committed to a life of service; we're not ready to lose our careers over this.

When I first discovered that I was gay, I was young and reckless and had less to lose. But now that I have been in the Navy for six years and Sue for eight, the stakes are higher. We don't take unnecessary risks that might jeopardize our careers. We don't go to the gay bars, we never attend Pride parades or events, and we mostly socialize within our community of also-closeted and loving gay women, where we are safe to express ourselves.

In public our displays of affection are nearly nonexistent, with the exception of sweet smiles and loving gazes, none of which I take for granted. Those looks from Sue send a warmth through my body as powerful as if she had actually pulled me into her arms and kissed me. I stand clear across our favorite surf shop as she tries on clothes, and a forbidden part of me wants to walk over and tell her how beautiful she is. But I swallow that desire, anchor my feet in place, and watch her from a habitual distance that keeps us safe. Something as innocent as our hands brushing together while we're walking in public makes me momentarily tense up and glance around with paranoia. I feel it in my bones and remain hypervigilant, ready to dial it back or turn off the switch completely, if necessary.

Not expressing my love for Sue is like being robbed of a basic human right. Being in love with her is so easy. Pretending that I don't love her is excruciating.

Our anonymity is our top priority, however, and we become skillful chameleons, ready to change shade at the first sign of danger. In my truck at night, Sue's body is next to mine, her hand on my leg, her laughter rocking my side, a natural, comforting, and loving presence. But in the daytime she moves to the passenger seat and reaches across the valley of space between us, interlacing her fingers with mine on the seat. Movie theaters are another great place for cautious touches: when the lights go down, my hand finds hers and stays on her lap. But even in a dark theater, in that moment of freedom in a world where I can't be free, I remain observant of who's around us and especially who's sitting behind us. My guard is never completely down.

Our home is the only truly safe place. Only there can I fully be with her, let go of my defenses, and make up for lost time. The stolen glances, the times I couldn't kiss her or hold her hand or tell her how much I love her, all those times that I had to withhold my affection.

These small but enormous moments of freedom at home have never felt so good or been so clear to me, and it shows. I'm always beaming.

"Girl, you have lost your mind over this one," Laura tells me all the time.

And it's true. I can't help myself. I totally have.

Within a few months of our living together, I discover that there will be times when I have to hide at home—namely, when Sue's family comes to visit. She has not and will not come out to anyone in her family, many of whom love visiting her in Hawaii. This becomes our biggest issue.

One evening, as we're cleaning up after dinner, I decide to broach the topic again. Her mom and aunt are arriving for a weeklong visit in just a few days, and after prior visits from a few of her cousins, I already know how this is going to play out—and I hate it. So I gather my courage and, feeling my heartbeat elevate, form words that I am certain will start a fight: "Babe, can we talk about your mom and aunt coming?"

Sue is in the middle of drying a plate, her bronze shoulders glowing under the straps of her white tank top, but the second I voice my question the towel stops moving and she stiffens.

"K," she says, her tone crisp. "If this is what I think it is, I don't want to talk about it again."

My initial reaction is to instantly concede and deal with it. But I dread every visit, am resentful, and know it won't mysteriously disappear by ignoring it. "You never want to discuss it, Q. My family knows you're my partner. They know I love you and where you stand in my life. It isn't the same with yours, and I hate being treated like your roommate."

Sue puts the plate in the cabinet and turns around, her defenses up and her irritation high. Through clenched teeth, she says, "That was your decision to tell them, K. This one is mine, and my family won't understand! I'll tell them if and when I'm ready to!"

Her fear is obvious, and her eyes avoid mine as she searches for a way out of this confrontation. I can certainly empathize. Coming out is incredibly difficult, and Sue's family is very important to her; the possibility of being rejected is something she has witnessed firsthand and isn't willing to risk. She has a gay uncle who was disowned and ostracized by many in her family when she was a child. After observing that and also hearing the way that some of her family members speak about him behind his back, she naturally believes that she will be subjected to the same treatment if she comes out to them. But it's painful to watch her struggle. She's the most amazing person I know, and I can't believe that anyone who loves her wouldn't keep loving her if they knew the truth.

My coming-out process has had its share of ups and downs. My mom's "I think you're confused" response was hard to hear, but that was nothing compared to my older brother's reaction. He visited me on his way back to Arizona from England, where he served in the Air Force and became a born-again Christian. When I came out to him, he lectured me, Tami, and Mindy—"Living like this is an abomination, Karen. It's not biblical. It's not what God wants for you."

His words hurt and I didn't know how to respond, so I just retreated. This type of rhetoric and judgment about homosexuality was not new. It was everywhere. But I was very fragile and had been told my whole life that being myself was not okay. Being told that I was living in sin by people who I loved and who I thought loved me took my shame to a whole new level.

When I was on leave in my hometown after joining the Navy, I came out to some of my closest friends. A few were very accepting. Others weren't. One told me, "I don't have a problem with it . . . but my husband does." Naturally, we lost touch. Those times were hard and painful, but also important, as I only want friends who can love me just as I am.

So of course I understand Sue's fear, but for me, being honest with the people I love is vital. This honesty has resulted in judgment by some and abandonment by others—and that hurts, but it is hard enough to relentlessly hide who I am in the Navy. I can't do it for everyone else too. It is crucial for me to have a place in the world where I can exist freely rather than having to continually adapt, transform, or hide.

Her cheeks flushed, jawline fixed, and fists clenched at her sides, Sue is staring at me with a look of utter betrayal. This is the point when I typically give up, shut the windows so no can hear us, and smooth things over. But I stand firm this time, hoping that she will truly know how this makes me feel.

"You tell them they're sleeping in *my* room, the spare bedroom, and it's ridiculous!" I grit my teeth. "Why don't you tell them it's *your* bedroom if you're going to keep lying? It's awkward, embarrassing, and demeaning, and I feel like you're ashamed of me . . . that their opinion means more to you than mine."

I stop and wait. Then I see the look on her face and realize

I've said enough. I'm terrified she's going to feel so pushed into a corner that she will say something that can't be taken back, like, *If you don't like it, we can end this right now.*

She stares through me a moment longer, then turns her back and continues putting the dishes away. "I'm not doing it, K. I'm not telling them. You're just going to have to deal with it."

I want to scream. Instead, I take a deep breath and give up, knowing that this is the extent of my fight.

I throw one final jab—"It's ridiculous, Q"—then grab a beer and crack it open. "I'm going to see Laura."

I leave her in the kitchen, grateful Laura's still only a flight of stairs away so that she can talk me down.

Sue's mom and aunt arrive a few days later. Her car pulls into the carport, and I put on my best attitude and head downstairs to greet them.

Sue's mom, whom I've never met before, is a tiny, sixtyish woman with silver pixie-cut hair. She gets out of the car looking disoriented and tired. Sue's aunt then awkwardly scrambles out of the back seat, her short, wavy dark gray hair disheveled, and mutters under her breath that it would sure be nice if Sue had a four-door vehicle.

Sue helps her aunt, and I softly chuckle in amusement when she finally gets her feet on the ground. For the first time since I've known her, Sue is the tallest one in the crowd.

"Mom and Aunt Gladys, this is Karen, my roommate," Sue says, a tense smile on her face.

They smile and nod as I greet them. "It's nice to meet you both, and welcome to Hawaii! You go in. Don't worry about your luggage. I'll bring it up."

They seem relieved and thank me, and Sue leads them through the door and up the stairs to our tiny apartment.

I bring up the final suitcase, only to be thanked by Sue's mom for my "generosity."

"It's really nice of you to let us stay in your room, Karen. Thank you."

Sue stands behind her mom with a sheepish look, knowing that this absolutely makes me nuts.

I'm frozen and filled with shame but give my best phony smile and turn on my military bearing. "Of course! Just want you to be comfortable."

Sue won't even look at me.

Sue loves being with her family, and I fall into the shadows as the three of them catch up, laugh, and tell stories about folks back at home. They connect and bond, and I watch Sue light up in their presence. I try to learn as much as I can about her family. I want her mom to like me, to know how important I am to Sue. If Sue ever gets injured, I want to be by her side, to sit with her and hold her hand and be involved in her care, and the only way that will ever happen is if her family knows and accepts me as her partner. Mostly, I want her mom to know how much I love Sue. But those are empty wants, so I retreat, drink another beer, crack a joke, or make 6-Pac chase the feather on the end of a long clear plastic stick. I become a silent outsider, slipping into the kind of dissociated hiding that happens when you don't belong.

The day finally arrives when I carry their suitcases back down the stairs and load them into the trunk of Sue's car. I say goodbye to her aunt Gladys and watch, amused, as she shimmies into the back seat—something that has entertained me all week.

Sue's mom gives me a quick hug. "Karen, thank you again for letting us stay in your room. It was so kind of you."

"It was my pleasure," I say, exhausted and grateful to be at the end of this facade.

They drive away and I wave and then exhale, relieved that I can be myself again. Living a lie is already a constant in my life, but doing so in my home is the worst, and after Sue has prioritized them over me like this, reconnecting in their absence will not be easy. Small bits of trust have broken down, and my defensive walls have gone up.

As the years and visits pile up, so will my loss of trust.

But on this night, when we can't possibly know that this will grow into a near-insurmountable issue, I hold Sue in bed and reflect on our love—a love that is more than I ever imagined was possible, a love that much of our world is not ready for. Sure, we are well-versed in the reality of hiding, but there is a silent ache to be normal, a longing for a time when I won't have to hide, that I can't ignore.

I remain conflicted—love her as much as I can; hide my love for her as much as I need to. Sue has the same struggle, and I don't blame her for being afraid of losing her family's love and acceptance. Family rejection is common for gay people, and that kind of rejection is a spiritual wound, more than many can take. It would break my heart if that happened to her.

My arm wedged under her neck, I snuggle in closer and remind myself that we're okay and that I'm blessed. I get to catch this beautiful woman's blue eyes sparkling at me from across the room, laugh as she repeatedly comes up for air at the beach, and sit close to her in my truck, as long as it's nighttime and no one can see us. Most importantly, I get to hold her close every night.

The rhythm of our breath synchronizes and I drift off to sleep, reminding myself that I am living my life with a woman who lights up my world—and that's worth paying almost any price, isn't it?

Chapter 16

PROTECTORS AND PERSECUTORS

Throughout my career I will have countless straight friends and shipmates who will not only keep my secret but also love me just as I am, giving me hope within a system that is a constant silent threat. Some will be great friends who I'll confide in; many will be peers or seniors who will figure out that I'm gay without my telling them and watch out for me.

Unbeknownst to me, at least at first, Captain Barkley will be one of my silent protectors. He and I have that kind of unspoken mutual agreement—he looks out for me, and I gladly return the favor. Working under his leadership makes me more confident as I grow in my knowledge and solidify myself as a sharp second class yeoman who can handle whatever comes my way. He and Captain Robertson rely on me to keep their calendars and screen everything that comes into their inboxes for typos and clarity, but also to be their buffer and say no to anyone who wants to infringe on their valuable time. Think of me as an unpaid and very scrawny bodyguard.

"Solt!" Captain Barkley's deep voice bellows from his office one day. "Office hours are closed. No visitors!"

"Got it, sir!" This is a new order that regularly flies out of both of the captains' offices these days. It is now 1991 and Desert Shield and Desert Storm—together dubbed the Gulf War—have just ended after the surrender of Saddam Hussein's Republican Guard and Iraqi generals. Since the beginning of Desert Shield, the building has been abuzz with every senior staff officer shuffling in and out of the Fleet Command Center, a large room with screen after screen of active military operations. It is the first time in my career that I have been privy to true strategic operations, and watching Captain Barkley and his team of senior officers skillfully direct these efforts is an experience to behold—the mood is intense, the pace rapid, and the workload enormous. My top responsibilities are keeping up with and prioritizing the taskings and protecting both captains' availability.

Within minutes of Captain Barkley's order, another captain walks into the office. He sees both captains at their desks and starts to walk past me.

I stand to address him. "Sorry, Captain," I say with respect. "They're currently not available."

An incredulous look appears on this senior officer's face. "Excuse me, YN2?" He points behind me with ice in his eyes. "They're sitting right there."

"Yes, sir. But they're closed for office hours. Can I make you an appointment?"

He gives me *The Look* and turns on his heels. I glance back at Captain Barkley, nervous that I did the wrong thing, and he momentarily looks up and gives me a closed-lip slight nod before returning to the open folder on his desk.

Learning the fine art of Navy protocol is tricky, because I'm not a fancy person and these are fancy rules. But I am a good bodyguard, and I become skilled at ensuring that anyone junior to either captain is waiting either in person or on the phone before either of my captains makes themselves available. Not having junior officers lined up and ready is Captain Barkley's biggest pet peeve, so I hold my ground to ensure this happens.

Just after the spurned captain walks out of the office, Captain Barkley yells, "Solt! Get Bigelow on the phone."

"Yes, sir!"

Who the fuck is Bigelow? I thumb through the Navy Register, a large periodical with officer lineal numbers that notes their Navy-wide seniority. The lower the number, the more senior the officer, so numbers 1 through 10 would all be four-star admirals.

I find Bigelow and write down his lineal number. Then I dial Captain Bigelow's office, knowing that my captain is the senior ranking officer.

When a yeoman answers, I say, "Good afternoon. Captain Barkley calling for Captain Bigelow."

"Sure," he says. "Please put the captain on."

"Thank you, but Captain Barkley is senior to Captain Bigelow," I say. "Please put the captain on and I will connect them."

This can sometimes go on for an exhausting few minutes until I convince the other yeoman that I've done my research. Senior officers work hard to be treated with the respect they've earned. The systems of rank and privilege are intricate and detailed, and having an inside seat at the table of very respected and powerful Naval officers is not something I take for granted.

After a beat, he sighs loudly. "Fine. Stand by."

I'm placed on hold as he gets his captain on the line.

"Bigelow here!"

"Thank you, sir. Please stand by for Captain Barkley."

I connect them and then exhale.

■ ■ ■

Chief Walker glides into my office later that year, sporting her khaki skirt and her black one-inch heels. "Petty Officer Solt, you're to report immediately to NCIS."

My mouth drops open, shock surges through my veins, and the blood drains from my face. These are the words I have been dreading for the past seven years.

"Uhhh, okay, Chief," I say carefully. "Do you know why?"

"Nope. They just called and said that you're to report to them for questioning. I'll take the desk. Go." She smirks and starts rifling through my inbox while she waits for me to exit.

I grab my combination cover and leave the building in utter disbelief. With the extra workload from the Gulf War, NCIS and witch hunts have been the furthest from my mind. I try to steady my breath as I walk, knowing I need to appear calm. Actually, I need to appear innocent. But of what? Love? How can I pull that one off? How will I be able to control the shade of red that will likely rise to my face when they ask me about Sue? Of course they'll see that I'm gay. If they don't, either I'm a better liar than I thought I was or they need to find a new line of work.

NCIS witch hunts were more prevalent on the ships; my impression—until now, anyway—has been that they're less intense on shore duty. I'm always mindful of the threat and never fully let down my guard, but things have always felt more relaxed to me at this assignment. Maybe I just haven't noticed because sailors are more dispersed on shore duty than we are on a ship. Regardless, I'm angry I've let myself get into this position.

I arrive at NCIS and check in with a civilian receptionist who sits at a desk behind an open window. She has me sit in an outer office. After a few excruciating minutes, she escorts me to a stuffy, drab room where two agents sit on the other side of a white table.

They are exactly how I imagine cold-blooded witch-hunters would look: dark suits, pale and grim faces, meticulous haircuts, and intimidating eyes. Tight and serious. They stand as I enter and lock me in place with twin penetrating glares. Then the taller of the two motions with his open hand to a white folding chair in front of me.

"Please. Take a seat."

I sit and try to look cool and composed, but I'm mostly petrified and my body tells me that I'm losing my shit. Sweat runs down my back, my chest is pounding, and my right foot is in full fight-or-flight twitch mode under the table.

"Hello, Petty Officer Solt." The tall one must be the lead agent. "I'm Special Agent Jones and this is Special Agent Wiley. Do you know why we've called you in today?"

This is probably a normal first question, but I am certainly not giving up my cards that easily. "Uh, no. I don't." I try to keep my speech steady and look stupefied that I'm even here in the first place.

They glance at each other and then back at me before Jones places his forearms on the table, clasps his hands together, and leans in toward me. "Well, there was a cocaine bust in Antigua, and some of your friends were caught. They have been discharged from the Navy." His eyes light up as he delivers the next bit of information. "During the investigation, you were named as also being involved."

Suddenly I am many things—floored, confused, and baffled. I'm not at all prepared for *this* news. The interrogation I prepared myself for went something like this: "We have a picture of you with your girlfriend, so we know you're gay. We're calling her in next. The legal team is preparing the paperwork for your separation, and today is your last day in the Navy. We'll go easier on you if you cooperate and give us names of other homosexual sailors."

But that interrogation isn't happening.

I snap back to the reality of this unexpected situation and don't say a word, mainly because I'm dumbfounded and trying to make sense of what I've just heard. *There was a cocaine bust in Antigua, and some of your friends were caught.* My head is spinning. I can't believe I'm not here because I'm gay.

They watch for my reaction, not taking their eyes off me, and then one of them starts speaking again. I'm not hearing a thing, too busy drinking in the wave of relief that's just washed over me. This is territory I have no clue how to traverse, but for some reason I'm feeling a hell of a lot more confident than I was thirty minutes ago. Apparently, I have determined that being gay is a worse crime than getting busted for drug use.

"Do you have anything to say?" Wiley asks, now taking the lead.

A quick "nope" slides out of my mouth.

They glare at me.

"Are you willing to submit to a polygraph to prove your innocence?" he asks.

"Absolutely."

They look at each other and smile, which makes me instantly regret what I have just said. They can use that polygraph to ask me anything they want to, including if I have either engaged in "homosexual conduct" or had "homosexual tendencies." It doesn't matter that my being gay isn't what I was dragged in here for. These guys are notorious for screwing over sailors.

"Actually, no." Anger and defiance control me now. "I won't submit to a polygraph."

Delighted looks turn cross, and we glare at each other for a long moment.

"Is there anything else?" I ask.

One last scowl shoots my way before Jones loudly exhales, puts his hands on the edge of the table, and pushes himself back. "No. You can go."

It takes everything I have to steadily walk out of the NCIS office. I want to run directly to Sue to tell her what happened, have her hold me and calm me down. But obviously I can't, so I head to my office.

As I approach the office, I hear Captain Barkley's voice booming through the hallway. He is losing his shit at someone.

"Solt!" he roars when he sees me. "Get your ass in here!"

"Yes, sir!" I quickly walk into his office, feeling scared all over again.

Chief Walker scurries past me, and I have a feeling she just had her ass handed to her.

His face is beet red and beads of sweat cover his forehead. "What did NCIS want with you?" he demands.

"There was a drug bust at my last duty station, sir. They tried to interrogate me about it."

He glares at me like a father who just found out his teen-age daughter was called into the principal's office. He points his finger at me. "Never, ever, *ever* go see NCIS! If they call you in again, you come to me. Got it!?"

"Yes, sir, I got it," I say, grateful for his fatherly protection.

"That'll be all." He looks away, snatches a folder from his inbox, and sits down, still obviously furious.

"Yes, sir."

I return to my desk. Chief scampers out without giving me another look. I settle into my seat, take a deep breath, and wait until the blood pumping through my veins slows to a rate where I'm no longer hearing it throb in my head.

■ ■ ■

In March of 1992, Captain Barkley gives me my best 4.0 evaluation to date. Coming from a man who is a true hero and has been serving in the Navy longer than I've been alive, I am honored to read his comments. *My number one of twenty-five second class petty officers in the Operations Division. . . . Her knowledge and performance as a yeoman and petty officer are far superior to any other second class that I have known in twenty-eight years of Naval service.*

He will be retiring, as he wasn't selected to admiral—a snub that no one saw coming. He's really done it all and has given so much of himself and his life to the Navy. Now the spark in his eyes and the swiftness of his stride both diminish a little more each day; he is heartbroken. What a way for him to finish his distinguished thirty-year Naval career.

I want to make a phone call—"Hey, Navy. Solt here. Captain Barkley's biggest fan. You're making a huge mistake. He's the absolute best. Trust me." But I'm just a tadpole in a big pond full of wide-mouth bass.

After I finish reading his glowing evaluation, I turn around in my chair. He sits at his desk, topped with a stack of folders and messages and a full pot of coffee, working as hard as he always does.

I'm so grateful for this amazing man—how much I've learned from him, and how solid he's always been with me. I can't be 100 percent positive, because even one discussion about my gayness with him would compromise both of our careers, but my belly tells me that he has always known that I am gay and has protected me and my secret as if I were his own daughter. He knew that a trip to NCIS was my worst-case scenario, and I believe it would devastate him if I were caught. With all the people in the Navy who want to find me and kick me out for being gay, I consider myself blessed to have someone like him in my corner.

Chapter 17

IMPENDING DOOM

A searing pain shoots through my two-thousand-pound head the moment I attempt to crack my eyes open. I snap them shut and take a few labored breaths, trying to calm my panic and hoping for a different result the next go-around. That doesn't happen, so I silently beg my head to temporarily disconnect from my body.

The natural light filling up the room is not helping one bit. I realize that I'm not at home, and an involuntary groan escapes my mouth.

Sue is the only one in the room who's awake and she sits in the bed next to me, a worried look on her face, her hand on my ribcage. Watching me closely, she whispers, "You don't look good, babe. Are you okay?"

Sure, babe . . . I'm fine is not what's happening. I'm not fine. The last time I remember hurting like this was when I was nine years old, my first real drunk and a night I probably should have gone to the hospital. Instead, I deliriously threw up for hours while my parents stood by my bedside, asking me over and over, "Square, what did you take?"

Since moving my head will undoubtedly trigger another stabbing pain through my skull, I stare at Sue's leg. "I don't know, babe. My head is killing me . . . it hurts to move."

She gently starts to massage the back of my neck. After a few more minutes, she helps me sit. The pain is horrific; my nausea is just on the edge. I glance around the room and slowly begin to recall why I'm here and what went down last night.

I'm in a stunning one-bedroom suite that sits on the beach at the North Shore's Turtle Bay Hilton. A sea of women entangled in white sheets are sprawled around the suite. Balloons, bottles, and cans are scattered all over the floor. Laura, Melissa, and another woman are still asleep in the other queen-size bed, and two other friends are cuddled up on the pullout couch in the living room, directly in view of the open bedroom door. But it's the empty green Tanqueray bottle on my nightstand and the cake splattered on the walls that brings a few of last night's blurry events back into focus and validates the reason for my stabbing head pain.

All indications point to my survival of another *lesbians gone absolutely wild* party.

The night started innocently, a combined birthday party for one of the women on the pullout couch and going-away celebration for the rest of these women, as all of them, including Sue, are either leaving the island for new duty stations or are getting out of the service. The evening progressed just like all our other parties, with music, drinking, dancing, and laughter. At some point, I put down my beer and started drinking T&Ts—Tanqueray gin and tonic with lime—a drink I love, but one that detonates "nice me" and activates "absolute bitch" me. A few of my friends became so wild that birthday cake flew over my head and stuck to the walls. I joined in—and that's when I heard a knock at the door.

I opened it to find two security guards standing outside, which sent me into a gin-induced, confrontational rage. My friends pulled me back as I stuck out the chest I don't have and hissed, "What the fuck do you want!?"

The guards, two hundred pounds each, just stood there and looked at me like I'd lost my mind.

A calm and never-too-drunk Sue faced and backed me away. As she did, one of the guards said, "Look, ladies. We need you all to quiet down. The other guests are complaining. We don't want to have to call the police."

"Call the fucking police!" I yelled from the other side of the room, where Sue was trying to block me, push me into the bedroom, shut the door, and get me to chill the hell out.

Somehow, we didn't get kicked out.

By early afternoon, Sue and I are driving back from the North Shore to our new home in Aiea, a two-bedroom townhome with hideous orange shag carpet in the bedrooms and just as grotesque orange linoleum everywhere else.

I gaze through the passenger window at the Pacific Ocean as it rises to the horizon beyond the white sand and swaying palm trees and contemplate my dreary future.

Always intuitive, Sue says nothing and gives me space to lick my wounds.

The pain surging through my head is still getting the best of me, but I'm also ashamed of and embarrassed about my rage, which has been increasingly worse the last few months. My drinking has verged on reckless since I was a kid, but this is different. Lately, my drinking is less and less manageable, and it feels like all my stuffed-down pain, shame, and grief are catching up to me. My controlled emotions rapidly turn to a zero-filter rage when I'm drunk, especially when authorities try to contain me. Never getting hauled off and charged with being a complete idiot by an officer of the law as the result of one of these outbursts is the definition of privilege. I've been lucky so far.

My apprehension and sadness about what lies ahead is a two-fold impending doom and is heavily contributing to my dark mood swings. Laura and the rest of my gay friends are leaving Hawaii, and due to the Navy's policy of fairly rotating sailors between sea and shore duty, it's also time for Sue to transfer to sea duty. She has been given overseas orders and will depart in May. For more than two years she and I have spent every possible moment together; now we will be apart for the entire next year. I will certainly miss my friends, but I'm shattered by the reality of being separated from Sue. She is my world.

I gaze at her from the passenger seat and try not to cry, remembering the phone call we made a few months ago to her detailer.

Sue placed the phone on our octagonal glass dining room table and gave me a sweet smile as we sat across from each other, both of us hoping that she would get orders to stay in Hawaii.

"Well, here goes," she said, and pushed the speaker button before dialing.

A man's voice came through the speaker. "Yeoman Detailer, Chief Johnson speaking."

Sue leaned in. "Hi, Chief. This is YN1 Susan Ramsey." She gave him her social security number. "I'm up for orders in May and I'd love to stay in Hawaii. Is there a squadron or a ship available here?"

"Hey there, YN1. Let me check my system. Wait one."

I nervously stared at Sue, my heartbeat in my throat, while we waited for him to return.

When he came back on, he said, "Well, I don't show any open billets in Hawaii. How about San Diego?"

Sue's eyes widened in shock and then her eyebrows lifted, her face a virtual question mark.

My inability to speak in that moment was unbearable. All I could do was shake my head no.

"Um, not San Diego, Chief. Do you have anything else?"

"Let me check." A few more clicks on his keyboard and then, "Well, it looks like there's a one-year tour on Diego Garcia. If you go there, you will have the duty station of your choice when your year is up. You can go back to Hawaii then if you want to."

Sue's face sank into compliant resignation. Diego Garcia. In the middle of the Indian Ocean. All the way on the other side of the world. But it was our best option; one year was certainly better than three. My palms up, I nodded at Sue.

"Sure, Chief," she said. "I'll go to Diego Garcia."

We sat immobile after she hung up the phone, each wanting to console the other but neither of us knowing what to say or do. Neither of us had anticipated that a long separation would actually happen.

Sue quietly drives as I look out of the window. Sugarcane fields line the road, and the ocean is now behind us while I ponder the other half of my two-fold impending doom. Even scarier than losing Sue is my awareness that my drinking is *a thing*—one that will take me to a depth I might not survive if I don't face up to it. I don't know what to do or where to turn, as alcohol is as natural to my body as air is to my lungs and stopping drinking seems so far out of my reach. The absolute worst part is that drinking isn't the fun it used to be. It no longer takes off the edge; it now forces me *to* the edge. It's been my protector, my go-to, my way to numb out. But problems are catching up to me—horrific hangovers that make me feel close to death, bad memory and constant blackouts, and out-of-control anger. I'm going to get my ass in a lot of trouble if I keep trying to fight people. Without my loving relationship with Sue and my surprisingly successful career, I'm not sure where I'd be.

Sue glances over. "How are you, babe?"

Tears well up in my eyes, and I shake my head and look

toward the floorboard. The bridge of my nose burns, and my throat constricts as I fight to maintain control. Then I turn to her and softly eke out words that have never before escaped my lips.

"Babe, do you think I have a drinking problem?"

Sue is never one to speak too quickly; she takes a few breaths before she responds. "I don't know, K. You drink like the rest of your friends."

I stare at her sadly for a moment. "That I do," I say, and look back down.

Sue doesn't need to tell me something I already know. I am an alcoholic. My belly is simply never wrong. And an end, whatever that may be, is heading my way.

I put my head in my hands and massage my temples as I let this realization sink in and wait for the flood of emotions I'm feeling to pass through and dry up. I close my eyes, lean back against the seat, and try to fight my despair.

Life without Sue *and* without alcohol? I'm not sure I'll be okay without either one of them.

Chapter 18

THE INEVITABLE GOODBYE

The day I am dreading is rapidly approaching. Soon, I will drive Sue to the airport, where she will board a commercial flight that will take her halfway around the globe to Diego Garcia. For the first time ever since we moved in together, I will say goodbye to my love, my world, my person, knowing that I won't see her again in a few short hours. The person I cuddle up to at night, the one I can't wait to see when I open my eyes each morning, the one who holds me, smiles at me, laughs, and shares her life with me is leaving.

I will stay behind with 6-Pac, sleep in our bed, and live in our home. All of the components of our life together will still be at my fingertips. But little of that will matter without her to share it with.

I have already decided that in order to avoid constant worry and grief, I will need to make work my focus. I will stay busy outside of work too, becoming the financial manager, the house-keeper, the *take care of all the shit at home* person. All of that will occupy my time and my heart until I can be with her again.

Sue, meanwhile, has a difficult journey ahead of her. She'll sit on airplanes for nearly a day, making small talk with the person next to her, and try to repress her sadness and put the goodbye she just had with me out of her mind. When she arrives in Diego Garcia, she won't know anyone. She'll be without me and 6-Pac, without the comforts of her home and the life that is so familiar to her. She will spend the next year living, working, and bonding with a new group of people, relying on them as her family, for companionship, for laughter, as the people who have her back. She will find new gay friends, those she can relate to and who will know her truth. Her connection with me will be difficult to maintain, as phone calls are limited and are also monitored, and snail mail will be our only other communication option. If anything happens to her while she's gone, I won't be notified, since I am not her next of kin and she still hasn't come out to her family. I simply have to trust that she will be fine, and that the universe will safely bring her back home.

I have had months to prepare for her departure, but I still can't wrap my head around the fact that it's happening. During those months, everything has stayed the same, with the exception of our mutual awareness that time is flying by and her exit date is right around the corner. We've gone to the beach. She's held my hand while cruising in my truck. She's flown into my office with the biggest grin and made me blush like a teenager with her first crush. My love for her has only gotten deeper during this time and I cherish every moment I have with her, just like I always have.

But the closer we get to the date, the harder I fight to stay in denial, drinking more and staying busier so I won't have to face my feelings about our looming separation. Silence becomes my ally, as I am not good at speaking about my pain.

Actually, neither of us is good at that.

■ ■ ■

To avoid long separations, the Navy works with straight married couples under a policy called "spouse co-location." This policy keeps couples in different commands, one at sea and one on shore duty, in the same geographical area to maintain stability in their relationships. But that option isn't open to us for obvious reasons. Gay sailors have to sacrifice one of two things: our careers or our relationship. Right now, it's my relationship with Sue that will be sacrificed. Not forever, but for now.

Separations and reunions with loved ones are a normal part of military culture, and both are difficult in their own way. All service members eventually learn the ins and outs of navigating this part of military life.

Separations are filled with grief, worry, and sorrow. Group farewells are the most common, with sailors either departing onboard ships or on chartered flights to overseas locations. In these instances, departing loved ones hold young toddlers as they tearfully say goodbye or gently try to break away from young children who clutch their uniformed legs, a gut-wrenching scene. Couples hold each other, cry, and kiss, not concerned about the Navy's policy against public displays of affection (PDA) in uniform. Farewell signs are visible in hands and lying on the ground. Uniformed sailors—husbands, wives, fathers, mothers, lovers— try their best to maintain their composure in this moment, because the split is unbearable.

Group reunions are a joyous experience, with signs, banners, balloons, streamers, and celebration whistles. Children and spouses rush into their loved ones' arms, full of PDAs and joy, overflowing with relief and, for the moment, forgetting the past six months where they counted down the days to when they would be a family reunited. A lot has occurred in what is usually a six-month-to-a-yearlong separation, however, and these families now begin the hard process of getting used to being with each other and finding a new rhythm.

Then there are separations such as the one Sue and I are about to endure: She is being transferred away from me because we are not considered a couple in the Navy's eyes. We will say goodbye at the airport—a personal goodbye, something that is only between us.

Being gay will create extra obstacles for us, of course. Our emotions can't be too obvious, and our true goodbyes and hellos will have to happen in private, behind closed doors. When we are alone at the airport, we'll have to make sure we don't know anyone around us. Even then, our interaction will be restrained. We will whisper a few words in each other's ears and give one another a quick hug—a hug that will leave us feeling cheated, like we can't fully express our pain, sadness, and grief . . . like we can't fully be human. Our military bearing will then take over, helping us to shove our grief as far down as possible, helping us get through the moment and put our minds on the task ahead. And the same will be true when she returns and we are reunited—we will have to hide our joy and relief until we are alone and safe from prying eyes.

So, either way you go, goodbyes and reunions are difficult. So difficult that, at some point, walls naturally go up. There's a disconnection and a reconnection period, sometimes lasting days and sometimes for months or longer, depending upon the experience.

Many relationships do not survive this cyclical process. But I am determined that our relationship will not be one of them.

The dreaded day finally arrives. When I wake up and realize that I will be sleeping alone tonight, I want to put my head back under the covers and reverse time.

Sue and I tiptoe around each other all morning, not knowing what to say and afraid to say anything that will open the cascade of emotions that sit just below the surface.

When it's time to take her to the airport, I carry her luggage to my truck. I return to find her saying goodbye to 6-Pac, which opens the floodgates. We hug, kiss, and hold each other, saying our true goodbye and trying to not completely lose it. We then get into my truck and hold hands while we silently drive to the airport.

We check her bags and walk to the gate, keeping a small distance between us, ever mindful of our presence in the world. This is our first goodbye ever, and I'm grateful to not be surrounded by my shipmates, as I'm not sure I can hide my pain. We sit next to each other at the gate in silence until her flight is called, then stand and share a hug.

"I'm going to miss you so much, Q," I whisper in her ear. "Get home soon. I love you, babe."

She holds me tight and whispers back, "I love you too, K . . . and I hate this . . ."

I remain in place as she walks toward the plane, not taking my eyes off her, searing that final moment in my mind where she is still in the same room with me.

She stops and looks back with her beautiful sky-blue eyes—and reality sinks in. I want so badly for this to be a dream, for her to turn around and walk back to me right now and for us to get in my truck together and go home. Instead, I give her a small smile and a little wave, thinking, *Fuck this . . .*

And then she disappears down the corridor and I move to the window, where I stay until she and her plane vanish from the sky.

My head drops. I turn away from the window, slowly walk out of the airport, and get into my truck.

As I drive home, I feel more alone than I can ever remember feeling before. I long for her to be sitting next to me—holding my hand, playing her favorite Fleetwood Mac song on repeat, and laughing at my stupid jokes. But she isn't. And I have already started the countdown in my head—*Only 364 more days.*

Chapter 19

ROCK BOTTOM

Dressed in my favorite red board shorts and white "Hang Loose" tank top, I'm sitting on a small aluminum lawn chair with blue-and-white interwoven webbing. A red cooler with a white top sits on the ground to my right, and my tan bare feet rest on a large white beach towel that conceals the orange linoleum living room floor. My chair is positioned in front of the couch in the center of the living room, and I vacantly stare ahead at a distorted black-and-green TV screen. A few days ago the picture tube blew out, and now it's just a fuzzy thing that distracts me.

The sliding glass door is open, and the vertical blinds keep slapping against each other. The nerves that sound activates in my spine beg me to walk over and tear them down, but I only look at them and will them to *please fucking stop*. I don't have an ounce of energy to get up and do anything about it.

6-Pac lies in front of the slider, ignoring the slapping sounds and intently searching for invading geckos.

It's Sunday afternoon, a day when I would normally be at the beach with Sue and my friends, but no one is here and I have no desire to do anything but sit alone at home on a lawn chair and get drunk.

I finish another beer, pry it out of my thick red koozie, drop the empty can on the floor, open the cooler, grab a new one, wrestle it into my koozie, crack it open, turn the tab 90 degrees clockwise to make it a Queer Beer, and in one gulp drain half of it.

The last few months have driven home the fact that I'm an alcoholic, and deep in my belly I know the jig is up. Somewhere in my grief and fog I am preparing to say goodbye to my other best friend, the only thing that has helped me emotionally check out since I was nine years old: booze.

I can't go to the Navy for help. In fact, no one from my command can know about my situation. I am reenlisting again next month and have been issued new orders to Patrol Squadron One, an aviation squadron based at Naval Air Station Barbers Point, seventeen miles west of Pearl Harbor. My priority is to keep those orders and be established at my new command when Sue returns to Hawaii nine months from now.

The Navy does provide addiction treatment at the Navy Alcohol Rehabilitation Center—ARC—but that's the last place I can go. The counselors at ARC would want me to be honest about my life, and I can't be. I can't say, "Actually, yes, I am incredibly sad. It's so tiring keeping silent about being gay, hiding my love for my partner, and trying to be a great Navy sailor all at the same time." If I were honest about my true feelings, ARC would not keep my confidentiality, so that's out of the question. I must find another solution.

It's not like I haven't been trying (if that's what you call it). A few months ago I called Alex, my drinking buddy from Georgia. She managed to climb out of this alcoholic hellhole and has been sober since 1988. She's gone on to become a successful chief and is now a detailer stationed in Washington, DC.

She cut right to the chase when I called her: "Just go to a meeting, Fred."

This only sent me to the kitchen for another beer, mumbling, *Right . . . just go to a fucking meeting.*

My next move was to call someone who didn't know me. The woman at the recovery program central office in town answered the phone. My meek voice asked her, "Can you send me some information on getting sober?"

"Well, we don't normally do that," she responded. "But I can have someone come pick you up and take you to a meeting if you want, or I can tell you where a meeting is at."

That felt like a herculean commitment; I declined the offer.

"All right, honey." Her voice was gentle. "Give me your address. I'll send you a meeting schedule and some pamphlets."

The days passed as I waited for the pamphlets. Unless I was at work, I drank around the clock. But something weird and totally out of character began to happen—for the first time in my life I started praying each morning when I woke up, "God, please don't let me drink today."

But by the end of the workday, muscle memory took over, and before I knew it I was heading to the Navy liquor store for a six-pack of beer.

And that's where I am now. I buy the beer. I pound three of them on the ten-minute drive home. Once I walk in my door, the routine is the same: hug 6-Pac and give him food, go straight to the couch, finish the six-pack of beer, drink more until I pass out, wake up sometime later in the evening, zombie-walk upstairs to my empty twin waterbed—the reminder of Sue's absence and my loneliness—pass out again, wake up hungover, and pray . . .

"God, please don't let me drink today."

■ ■ ■

I've done this for months, and I'm on track to continue when I receive a phone call one evening from a friend from my local Hash House Harriers (H3) club.

The motto of this club is "Drinkers with a running problem"; H3ers go on outrageous runs all over the world called Hash Dashes. Despite my state I went on a run with this crazy group a few nights ago. At the finish line, they christened me with a nickname—Tattoo—and we sang songs and guzzled full mugs of beer. When the festivities ended, another Hasher, Thud Stud, followed me in his car to make sure I got home safely . . . a totally useless designated driver.

Tonight he calls me.

"Hey, Karen, it's Ken."

"Who?" I chalk up my confusion to inebriation.

"Uhhh . . . Thud Stud." He laughs.

"Oh, hey!" I say, the pieces clicking together.

"Hey, listen, I want you to know that when I followed you home the other night you were all over the road," he says. "It scared the shit out of me."

This is the first time ever that someone has told me I'm a bad drunk driver, and it scares me. I suddenly realize it's a full-blown miracle that I've never been in an accident and hurt anyone before.

This phone call is the last bit of evidence I needed. My drinking has to end, and end soon.

Four days pass. I numbly stare ahead at the black-and-green TV and finish another beer, wishing that it wasn't coming to this. My chest feels like lead and I can't believe I've arrived at this moment, but I've tried every imaginable way to *not* stop drinking. Now I know there is only one way out. I'm not sure I can do it. Not sure I want to do it. But I can't go on living like this anymore because alcohol, the one thing that has always protected me from feeling my pain, is now creating more pain. At some point it will take me or someone else out, and the latter I couldn't live with.

I open the cooler, grab the last can of beer floating in the icy slush, and go through my routine until it meets my lips. I take my time, longing for *that feeling*—the one that makes everything okay, the one that has now eluded me for years. But it is nowhere to be found, so I savor each sip and stare at the empty can for a few moments—praying that it's my last drink and hoping that it isn't—before setting it next to the many others already lying on the ground. Then I crawl back to the couch, where I pass out.

The alarm set on my watch wakes me at 0330 the next morning. I find myself still on the couch. I smell stale beer and open my eyes to find a blue-and-white lawn chair two feet in front of me, sitting on a white beach towel next to a red-and-white cooler, surrounded by empty beer cans. The slider remains open, but the blinds are now silent. 6-Pac is nestled behind me on the back of the couch, and a black-and-green TV buzzes across the dark living room.

"God," I pray, "please don't let me drink today."

I zombie-walk to the kitchen and make a cup of coffee, then trudge upstairs and take a shower, put on my Summer Whites, and get to work by 0430.

I barely make it through the day without losing my shit. But I come straight home afterward—no Navy liquor store and no beer for the drive. I give 6-Pac a hug and feed him and then find my way to the couch, where I sleep reality away.

■ ■ ■

Tonight I pick up the meeting schedule pamphlet, still sitting unopened on the dining room table. I finally open it. I try to "just go to a meeting." But I can't find a meeting. Through my tears and fog, I drive in the dark, looking for a damn meeting, and the only thing I get is lost. Frustrated and feeling very alone, I turn around, go home, and inch my way up the stairs to my bedroom.

The day is Monday, August 24, 1992. It's my first day without a drink.

Chapter 20

A NEW BEGINNING

The following morning is my twenty-seventh birthday. I crawl out from under the covers and place my feet on the ground.

"God, please don't let me drink today."

Heavy and sluggish, I lumber through my morning routine and drive to work. This workday is one I survive but absolutely do not slay. Still, I manage not to go to the Navy liquor store on my way home.

I am shaking, exhausted, and numb. But I haven't had any booze.

This evening my meeting pamphlet guides me to a women's recovery meeting located in a church classroom between Pearl Harbor and the airport. I arrive at the church and sit in the parking lot, trying to muster the courage to enter the meeting room. I'm desperately afraid to cry and look like a fool, but this is do-or-die and I want to live, so I slowly make my way toward the building.

A half dozen women stand outside, smoking, laughing, and talking to each other. I quietly move past them, avoiding their eyes.

They stop talking and laughing to greet me, then feel my vibe and simply nod.

The meeting room has beige linoleum flooring and fluorescent lighting. Small wooden children's chairs of various colors line the walls. A round maroon area rug lies in the center of the room, and a woman with short blond hair is placing white folding chairs in a circle on the perimeter of the rug.

She smiles at me. "Hi, I'm Linda. Come in! What's your name?"

"Kaarrrennnn . . ." I choke back tears and immediately want to bolt.

Her eyes soften. "Hey, Karen. Is this your first meeting?"

I nod and she gives me an empathic *Girl, totally fuckin' been there* look and then gestures to a chair with a black binder and some paperwork on it. "That's my chair. You sit next to me tonight."

I walk over and sit down as Linda finishes setting up the room and then sits next to me and puts the binder on her lap. She gently nudges me with her upper arm and smiles. She's a complete stranger, yet her warm presence has already made me feel a little bit better.

One step down.

The other women stroll in at 7:00 p.m. and take a seat. They quiet down, smile, and nod at each other—just so damn happy, like they've known each other for years. But I keep up my avoiding eye contact approach, as I feel like a spotlight is right over my head and one look of love, pity, empathy, or concern is sure to send me over the edge.

The meeting starts with various readings. I try to pay attention, but it just isn't happening. They start sharing, one by one, and I occasionally hear a sentence or two that makes sense.

Eventually someone asks if I want to share; I look down and shake my head. I'm not even sure I'll survive this entire hour, as every time I glance at the clock only five minutes have passed. It takes everything in me to keep my butt planted next to protective Linda.

When the meeting ends, the women all stand and hug each other. I'm quietly making my way to the door when a few of them let out boisterous laughs.

I desperately want to laugh again.

Linda intercepts me at the door, hugs me, and hands me a small card with her phone number on it. "Call me any time, Karen. I mean it." She gives me a motherly look. "I'll see you here next week, right?"

"Sure, I'll be here," I say, as if I have any other option. "Thanks, Linda."

I numbly drive home, grateful that I made it through my second day without a drink.

Sue calls that evening from Diego Garcia. "Happy Birthday, K!"

"Thanks, Q," I say quietly.

"You sound tired. Are you okay?"

My eyes well up again. "I just got home from a meeting."

"A meeting? What kind of meeting?"

"A recovery meeting."

She's silent for a moment. "Wow. Are you okay?"

"I don't know. I think so." Tears begin to flow.

"That's a big step. I'm proud of you. It's gonna be okay."

"It's just been hard," I say, trying to catch my breath. "I miss you so much."

"I know. I miss you too. I wish I was with you, but we'll celebrate when I'm home on leave in November and I'll call you next week. Happy Birthday, K."

The next few days are the worst. I am capable only of working and coming home to the couch. My off-time creeps along;

in those unoccupied hours, I feel every bit of my raw, sensitive, exposed, and wounded existence. Fatigue and lethargy now rule me, so my biggest reprieve is sleeping, which I've been doing every chance I get.

I've somehow been spared cravings, an inexplicably divine intervention and gift of grace. Though my kitchen remains stocked with beer, gin, and wine, not once do I even reach for a drink.

Without work to distract me over the weekend, I'm crawling out of my skin, so I dial Linda. "Hey, Linda. It's Karen. The one from the meeting earlier this week."

"Hey, Karen!" Her voice is calm and comforting. "How are you doing?"

My throat tightens. "I guess I'm okay . . . I'm still sober . . . but this is really hard."

"God, I know that's right," she responds. "Want to come have coffee with me? I live in Aiea."

"I live in Aiea too. Thanks. I'd like that."

She gives me her address, which is only a few blocks away from my place. I head straight over. When she opens her door, she sees my panic and wraps me up in a hug, holding me until I relax.

"That's better," she says, and smiles. "Now how about that coffee?"

Linda has been clean for five years, a lifetime to less-than-a-week-sober me. She is a wise, funny, incredible, no-bullshit woman who loves kids and dogs but could mostly do without the rest of us. Her newly adopted toddler foster daughter is running up and down the hallway from the bedrooms to the living room and creating absolute havoc, which is overwhelming to my raw nerves but makes Linda sparkle and totally light up with joy.

We sit and talk and I start to feel better, if even for only a few minutes—but hey, a few minutes is an eternity right now. She asks me questions, and I answer them honestly. I tell her how alone I am without Sue, and now even more so without alcohol. She makes space for my pain. We talk while I cry, and she listens and relates and tells me how it was for her, and she laughs and hugs me.

Linda has the biggest heart and the kindest soul. As of today she becomes my guardian angel, my second mom, my friend, my confidant, my 100 percent go-to badass woman. She nicknames me "Kumquat" today and says I'm her new "favorite human gay fruitcake."

At this she snorts, clearly thinking that is the funniest thing ever. It isn't. But Linda can call me whatever she wants, as she helps me get my life back.

"Will I ever laugh again?" I ask her at one point, completely serious.

She puts her arms around me. "You will again someday, Kumquat. I promise."

My couch absorbs all of my detoxing cells and becomes my haven. To work, to my couch, to meetings. That is my mundane, just-try-to-keep-my-shit-together routine, as life without drinking doesn't resemble the life I've known. My home remains dark, the blinds closed, minimal lights on. Dark is where I am; I pray that light is where I'm headed.

My senses are distorted and my instincts have reverted to their very basic nature: survival. For weeks I stare at a fridge full of beer, trying to rewrite my habit—home, grab a beer, sit and drink, open another, sit and drink. My sense of smell doesn't register—not a fresh cup of coffee, not the plumeria flowers on my lanai, not even fresh-cut grass, my favorite smell of all. My appetite is all but gone and most food, with the exception of ramen noodles and Raisin Bran, makes me nauseous. Basic skills are no longer basic. Yellow stickies on my bathroom mirror remind me to do the things I need to do: shower, eat, make my bed, call Linda, go to a meeting, press my uniform, brush my teeth, sleep. Comfort is sinking into my couch, 6-Pac curled up behind me, and sleeping the slow and painful hours away.

Every now and again a dull ache erupts right in the center of my chest. Missing Sue, clear across the world. Wondering how she'll feel about the person she will someday return to. A stranger who was not here when she left. This is not a feeling that I allow to linger for very long, however; I make sure the ache disappears soon after it arises.

Anything not essential to survival—cleaning house, washing my truck, cooking anything that takes more effort than adding hot water—has been pushed aside. What little energy remains in my reserves I use for my two priorities: work and 6-Pac. He doesn't ask for much yet is seemingly never more than a few feet away, a comforting being with a loving heartbeat that keeps me connected to this world.

Others who have already been down this dark road take me under their wing. Linda is a constant presence; I also befriend "the two Kevins," one a naval submariner and the other an Air Force staff sergeant, both very active in recovery.

Submarine Kevin drives an old black thirty-foot stretch limousine Cadillac with peeling paint and pockmarks of rust. When he comes to pick me up for a meeting, he pulls up to my place with '70s classic rock music blaring, no horn necessary. His tinted window drops as I come out, and I half expect to see John Belushi in his fedora hat and Ray-Ban Wayfarers, but it's just skinny Kevin with his short light brown hair, wire-rimmed glasses, and quirky smile. Air Force Kevin, an avid scratch golfer with thick chestnut-brown hair and a wicked tan, kicks open the back door with his flip-flopped foot and I get in. Submarine Kevin opens the small sliding window between the lounge and the front seat, turns up the music, and chauffeurs us to our meeting.

Submarine Kevin drives like absolute shit, so Air Force Kevin and I stay low and lounge on our personal bench seats. We talk and do not look. Nine times out of ten, we get to a meeting safely. That tenth time, however, is a little sketchy: On top of his alcohol addiction, Submarine Kevin also has anger issues, and he is riding up the ass of the car in front of us. They eventually get fed up with his foolishness, and at the next stoplight they put their car in park and two big men and one much-bigger-than-me woman get out and rush us. Air Force Kevin and I fall into silent, scared shock. Submarine Kevin rolls down his window and apologizes profusely—"Dude, my bad. Seriously. I'm sorry."

Thankfully, they don't beat our scrawny asses. I'm pretty sure they feel bad for us.

I'm no longer in the mood to fight people. Now that I'm sober, I just want to live.

The fog slowly lifts, day by day. It's not a tangible *everything is fine*; it's more of a *I think I can make it through today* feeling. I notice moments of pleasure. A warm bubble bath, a funny movie, 6-Pac wrapping around my neck and shoulders—those things feel good again. My senses return, more vibrant and intense than before, and get my attention. Birds chirping in the palm trees, waves crashing on the beach, tropical flowers, fresh-cut grass, my favorite takeout sushi, the Pacific Ocean stretching to the horizon, and chiseled green mountain ranges towering over the middle of the island—all these things take my breath away.

With the help of others and simply by not drinking and fol-lowing suggestions, I've been given a chance at a new life in a world that since childhood I've been too numb to experience—a world I lost my connection to the moment I chose to disconnect with booze.

This new way of life is different, and hard, and amazing, and real. This new way of life is one giant step out of hiding. And although one of the toughest things I've ever done, this new way of life is the best gift I've ever given myself.

Chapter 21

MY WORLD

My legs get weak and my chest softens. *There's my girl.* Sue's curly brown hair bobs in the midst of other dazed passengers as they stream from the airplane tunnel. She slowly scans the room until her sleepy eyes find mine, and she tilts her head and offers a tired but sweet Sue smile.

I've been dreaming about this moment since what feels like forever. I walk to meet her, put a fragrant white lei around her neck, and put my arms around her. "Hey, babe," I whisper.

Her warm body melts into mine and she whispers back, "Hey, K. It's so good to see you."

Sue is home for a week of leave after being gone for six months. After traveling for nearly twenty-four hours to get here, she now stands next to me in a red T-shirt, jeans, and bright white New Balance tennis shoes, holding a dark blue zip-up hoodie.

"You're going to burn up in those jeans," I say. "Come on. Let's get you home. You look absolutely beat."

She sits in the passenger seat and holds my hand as we drive home, yesterday's habit that now feels like a different lifetime. Music plays and we make occasional random comments. The weather. The traffic. Her flight. But a noticeable awkwardness floats between us, and a nervousness fills my chest.

Sue is right here. Her smile, her eyes, her hand in mine, her sweet energy. The same Sue. But a different Karen. I squeeze her hand a little tighter, and the realization that we won't just pick up where we left off slowly starts to sink in.

We pull into the driveway. "Go in and see Sixers, babe," I say, releasing her hand. "I'll get your stuff."

"Thanks, K." She hops out. "I can't wait to see him."

I arrive at the door with her bags to find 6-Pac purring and nuzzling up to her face. "He looks great," she says, then puts him down and reaches for me.

We give each other a kiss and hold each other quietly for a long moment. Then she looks up at me and says, "So do you, K."

I smile self-consciously.

"That was such a long flight," she says. "Wanna sit for a bit?"

"Sure, babe."

We settle onto the couch, side by side, and I feel the familiar warmth of her body as we melt into each other, her fingers interlaced with mine, our hands on my lap.

"God, I missed you, Q. It's been really hard without you." Tears start rolling down my cheeks and I look down. "I'm afraid to get used to you only to watch you leave again."

She sighs. "I know. I'm afraid of that too." She pulls my chin toward her and wipes the tears from my cheeks with her thumbs before putting her forehead against mine and closing her eyes. "For now, I'm just so happy to be home with you. That's all I care about." She tenderly kisses me and half-smiles. "Everything is going to be okay, babe. I promise."

We sit back, she puts her head on my shoulder, and we allow ourselves to stay present together in silence, breathing the same air for the first time in a long time.

■ ■ ■

I was completely lost when Sue left. She was my everything.

But since she left, things have changed. She remains my love but is no longer my everything. My highest priority is now my sobriety, because without it I know I'll have nothing. No Sue. No job. No life.

Sue wasn't here for my ugly bottoming-out or my early days of insanity when I immersed myself into recovery with amazing people who took me under their wing. She doesn't know Linda, or the Kevins, or the jokes we share, or how they listen to me when I'm sad and hug me when I cry. While she and I have continued to serve in a system that keeps us separate from each other, they have naturally stepped into some of the space she left behind when she got on that plane six months ago.

Now she's home for a week, and I don't know how we fit together anymore. Because of time and distance. Because of our hidden lives. Because of too much change. The woman I couldn't wait to be with again doesn't yet have a place in my new life and hasn't absorbed all my changes, just as I can't begin to understand the changes that life on Diego Garcia has brought to her. And it is impossible to find a new rhythm together in a short week's worth of time.

We have done our best to maintain our relationship, but I mostly feel disconnected. Her snail mail letters take weeks to arrive; when they do, I lightly run my fingers over the grooves in the stationary to momentarily feel a place that she's touched. When she calls, it's from a monitored government phone, so our love for each other is a topic we avoid. We have impersonal conversations that solidify our closeted life and push us deeper into our role as roommates. I hang up feeling cheated, happy to hear her voice but wishing we could just be "us," wishing I could love her like I do when we are together.

We feel the distance this is creating in our relationship, but we are blind to the long-term effects it will have. It's all we know, after all. All these subtle—and not-so-subtle—forces are pulling us apart, and this will one day make reconnecting and being vulnerable with each other that much more difficult.

But we don't know this yet.

We call Sue's new detailer the day after she arrives home. She has six more months to go on Diego Garcia, and we're excited to get her back to Hawaii. I recall her detailer's words a year ago: *If you go to Diego Garcia, you will have the duty station of your choice when your year is up. You can go back to Hawaii then if you want to.* Those words have been my beacon, something to hold on to as I count the days until we are reunited.

We sit at the table and Sue pushes the speaker button and dials. She looks nervous.

When her detailer picks up, Sue says, "Hi, Chief. This is YN1 Susan Ramsey." She gives him her social security number. "I'm looking for orders back to Hawaii after my tour in Diego Garcia is up in May."

"Hey, YN1. No problem, let me see what I have." His keyboard clicks for a few beats; then he comes back on and says, "Unfortunately, I don't have anything in Hawaii."

Sue's eyes widen in disbelief and she lets out an exasperated, "But your predecessor told me I could return to Hawaii after my year was up."

Panic consumes my chest and I silently freak out, hoping he'll help her. Help us. I report to VP-1 next month, and if Sue can't get orders back to Hawaii, we will be apart for years.

He is very matter-of-fact. "Well, YN1, I don't see anything in the notes about that—and regardless, there aren't any open billets in Hawaii. You can go to Guam, Guam, or Guam. The shortest I have is a two-year tour onboard a USNS ship."

Sue's face reddens with fury, and I grit my teeth and clench my fists under the table. We've waited for so long to get to the point where we can even make this phone call, and I can't believe we've been deceived.

"Isn't there anything else, Chief?" she pleads.

"Not unless you want the East Coast."

Sue is angry now. She loudly exhales and puts her forehead in her hand. "Fine, Chief! I'll take the USNS ship." She hangs up as tears well in her eyes, and she stares at me. "Two more fucking years, babe."

I sit motionless and say nothing. This is our worst-case scenario. Sue will not be coming home to me. She will be heading to Guam, to a USNS ship owned by the Military Sealift Command that replenishes US Navy ships at sea. She will serve with a number of civilians and a small crew of active-duty sailors and will spend much of her time underway. And that's that. Another two years on top of the six months she still has left on Diego Garcia and most of that time she will be at sea, making our ability to connect almost nonexistent and our total separation a minimum of three and a half years, given my upcoming three-year commitment with VP-1.

A sinking feeling suddenly makes me realize that we might never catch a break.

We got home from the beach a few hours ago. We tried to shake off the bad news with a nice day out, but we're still shattered and reeling, and all I want is to stay home with Sue tonight. But I've committed to attending my meetings while she is home, and I'm forcing myself to keep that commitment.

I walk down the stairs to find Sue on the couch watching TV, 6-Pac curled against her leg.

I sit on her other side. "Hey, babe, I'm leaving soon for my meeting. The Kevins should be here any minute."

"No problem, babe," she says. "I'll hang with Sixers while you're gone."

Loud music booms from the driveway as a beat-up limousine pulls up. Sue raises her eyebrows and rises from the couch to look out. "*Those* are your friends?"

Dorky Kevin rolls down his window, a quirky grin on his face, and lounging Kevin's leg kicks open the back door.

"Yep, that's them." I smile. "They're a little crazy, but they've been great to me. See you after the meeting, babe." I give her a quick kiss and reluctantly head out the door.

It's nearly impossible to settle back in with each other. The thought of dropping back into the bliss of Sue's love knowing that she will soon be ripped away from me again feels cruel, and our last goodbye was so painful that I'm afraid to let myself fully fall again. My guard stays up to protect my heart; I hold back both physically and emotionally, knowing that another two and a half years is upon us and absolutely broken by that fact. We still love each other, though—that I know for certain. The rest is just going to have to work its way out, if and when we ever get the chance to reunite.

We do find wonderful moments together at our old spot, Makaha Beach. We go there almost daily. The beach naturally brings us joy and removes pressure and expectations; it's a place where we can just be "us."

On Sue's final full day, we drive to Makaha in silence, our fingers interlaced and both of us lost in our own thoughts—thoughts that we certainly can't share or begin to unravel right now.

We set out beach chairs. "You coming in, K?"

"You know I'm not." I chuckle, shake my head, and smile. "I'll be right here."

She shrugs with her *I tried* look, grabs her boogie board, and heads out; I grab a Diet Coke and settle in. I fight off tears behind my white-and-purple Oakley sunglasses and try not to imagine her gone again while I watch her get pummeled by whitewater waves. She comes up one final time and stumbles toward me—out of breath, sand in every crevice, and wearing her *Why the fuck didn't you rescue me?* look.

I put my game face on and force a laugh, though all I feel in this moment is devastation that this isn't my everyday life anymore.

The night before she leaves we are mostly silent. What is there to say? When we turn in, we hold each other for our final night together for I don't know how long. Tears fall on my pillow as I lie behind her and try not to disturb her until exhaustion finally allows me to sleep.

When morning comes, I wake early and peacefully watch her until she opens her eyes. We awkwardly stumble around each other through coffee and showers before she brings her suitcase down the stairs and says goodbye to 6-Pac before we share our own true goodbye at home.

At the airport we repeat our public goodbye of six months earlier, but this time is different. It will be so difficult to find our way back to each other after this and we both know it, even though we don't speak the words out loud. Three years of travel and deployments, career aspirations, new friends, and personal growth, all experienced separately from each other, is a lifetime. But the hardest obstacle we'll have to overcome is keeping our relationship hidden while also trying to keep it alive.

Two more fucking years. My heart explodes and my insides scream as she walks up the ramp toward the plane. She turns back and looks at me one last time, and I give her a slight wave and a small smile, because it's what I'm supposed to do. It's all I have.

Then she's out of sight, and soon her plane disappears from the sky. Just like that, she's gone again.

I leave the airport feeling lost and empty, wishing that we'd had the time during this visit to fall back into each other's lives and become who we are together, the magic that is "us." But that isn't my reality.

This is my reality: as quickly as she fell back into my world, she was just as quickly ripped right back out.

PART THREE

Chapter 22

A ONE-IN-A-MILLION
MENTOR

I report as a newly promoted YN1 (E-6) to Patrol Squadron One (VP-1), which is located at Naval Air Station Barbers Point, in a gigantic hangar that looks like a large LEGO airplane.

An ivory rectangular building is the body of the hangar and holds office spaces for multiple commands that utilize the hangar as their home base. Covered open-bay spaces connect and run down each side of the building and serve much like enormous carports: planes are towed underneath them when they require maintenance. Colorful logos painted on the side of the hangar inform the location of each squadron—VP-4 Skinny Dragons, VP-9 Golden Eagles, and my new squadron, VP-1 Screaming Eagles.

I'm thrilled to be joining a brown-shoe aviation squadron and excited to start my next Navy adventure.

I leave my truck in the large parking lot across the street and walk toward the hangar in my Summer Whites, which definitely make me stand out amongst the other sailors; they're all in blue coveralls or dungarees. As a YN1, I now wear three crows, an eagle, and yeoman crossed quills on my left sleeve. Before I departed CINCPACFLT, I was also awarded my first Navy and Marine Corps Commendation Medal (NCM), a coveted, fancy green ribbon with two white stripes that now tops the three rows of ribbons centered above my left shirt pocket. The days of my dragging my seabag down a pier in my Dress Blues while my cover slips down to my nose are long behind me. I'm sharp, poised, and confident. I carry a black canvas briefcase in my left hand, and my damn cover fits my head like a glove.

I approach the hangar. A few dozen P-3s, the singular reason that patrol squadrons exist, are parked outside on the tarmac, and inside I find maintenance workers from each squadron working on P-3C Orion airplanes. I ask a nearby sailor where VP-1 Admin is, and he directs me to a door at the top of a wooden staircase with the Screaming Eagles logo painted on it.

At the end of a long hallway I find a door that reads *VP-1 Admin Department LCPO*. Chief Booker, a petite Asian American woman with short, curly dark brown hair and black-rimmed glasses that rest comfortably on her perfectly round cheeks, sits in a room just big enough for her desk and chair, two other chairs, and a short metal bookshelf. She looks up as I arrive at her doorway.

"Hi, Chief," I say. "I'm YN1 Solt. I'm checking in today."

She stands and shakes my hand. "YN1! It's nice to finally meet you. Welcome aboard!"

"Thanks, Chief!" She seems kind. She is also very short, just like Sue. I already like her.

She gestures to an empty chair. "Take a seat. Let's talk for a minute before I introduce you to the rest of the yeomen. Also, congratulations on making first class!"

"Appreciate that, Chief!" I respond, and feel a sense of pride rise in my chest.

"Because of your new rank, I'd like to put you into a leadership position immediately," she says. "We do have a YN1, but she prefers to work independently with the squadron's classified communications material. Unless you have any reservations, you will be the LPO."

"Really?" I'm stoked. "That's perfect, Chief! Thank you."

"Great! Then let's go meet your sailors."

We enter the Admin Office, where Chief introduces me to three women: YN2 Manelli, the office supervisor, who has straight chestnut-brown hair and perfectly trimmed bangs; YN3 Taft, a tall Black woman; and YNSN Vance, a young blond woman.

"Hey, everyone," she says cheerfully, "this is YN1 Solt, your new LPO."

They all come to greet me at the front of the room and we shake hands.

As I'm meeting my new team, I hear a deep, "Morning, Admin!" and turn to see a crisp, confident, bald-headed master chief strutting into the office.

In unison, the office replies, "Good morning, Master Chief!"

My chief blushes. "Good morning, Master Chief! This is YN1 Solt, our new admin LPO." She turns to me. "YN1, this is Master Chief Halverson, the squadron command master chief."

He reaches out his hand, and we share a firm handshake. "Hello, Petty Officer Solt. Welcome aboard!"

"Thank you, Master Chief. It's great to be here."

And it is. I think I'm going to like this job.

Master Chief Henry Halverson is the top enlisted sailor in the squadron. As the squadron's command master chief (CMC), he is responsible for the welfare, morale, discipline, growth, and training of the squadron's enlisted personnel and reports solely to the top two officers in the squadron, the commanding officer

(CO) and the executive officer (XO). The chiefs and only the chiefs call him "H."

Master Chief Halverson is a black-shoe submariner in an aviation squadron. The squadron chiefs and officers strut around in their brown aviation shoes, but not him. He won't change his shoes to save his life—as I will soon learn, in his heart he is a stubborn nonconformist. The chiefs and officers constantly give him shit about it, but he just glares at them with a wicked eyebrow crease, which oddly reminds me of *The Look*.

Master Chief Halverson is "Joe Navy." He has been enlisted for twenty-seven years and this is his final command before he will retire, as thirty years is the maximum allowed without a waiver from the bigwigs in DC. You certainly wouldn't know it, as he acts like a young sailor who's just getting started. He has the sharpest and crispest uniform of anyone in the squadron—actually, of anyone I've ever met. His shoulders are wide and his waist fit and trim, the epitome of a squared-away sailor. He stays in tip-top shape by lifting weights and running at lunchtime each day with a conspicuous blue neoprene brace covering his right knee. His square jawline, bald head, thinning eyebrows, and five-foot-nine frame move boldly and swiftly through his world with precision.

Proudly from Alabama, his southern accent comes out direct and lacks any fluff. He throws a quick "YN1! How the heck are ya?" in my direction whenever he blows by me in the hangar. He drives a little dark red piece-of-shit Ford Ranger, and as he drives away from the hangar you can see his bald head, topped with his khaki garrison cover, through its always-open back sliding-glass window. Navy through and through, he even irons a front crease down the center of the jeans he wears as civilian attire.

He seems to have time for everyone. When he arrives in the morning, he greets the sailors in our office and then crosses his arms, glances around, and waits to see if anyone needs anything. If they do, he prioritizes them, listens, and renders some great tidbit of advice. But more often than not, whatever they tell him makes him put his hands on his hips, lean back, and roar out a deep, genuine belly laugh, because very little is a big deal to him. He's a no-bullshit sailor, and I immediately respect and like him.

Which is not to say that he isn't tough as nails. Master Chief Halverson is responsible for Disciplinary Review Boards (DRBs), where the command chiefs screen sailors who are in some sort of trouble. As the command legal yeoman, I complete the paperwork for DRBs, Executive Officer Inquiries (XOIs), and Captain's Masts (NJPs) and am in the room during XOIs and NJPs. Master Chief Halverson runs DRBs in a very unique way, and I've seen him counsel more than one "shithead."

It always begins the same way: "Petty Officer Smith, if I ever see you in my office for any more bullshit, I swear to God"—he puts his hands on his desk, slowly rises, and leans in till he's six inches from the offending sailor's eyes—"I will rip your head off and shit down your throat!" He won't break eye contact, and in that one moment, he sure as hell looks like he could pull off that threat. "Understood!?"

The sailor getting berated remains at attention, shaking in his boots, his eyes bigger than half-dollars, trying not to soil himself, and responds in a quivering voice, "Understood, Master Chief."

My new command master chief is a force of nature. The CO, XO, and officers respect him because he cares for his sailors and makes it his mission to truly know and mentor us. The chiefs love and idolize him because he is an amazing example of what a chief petty officer should be. And the junior sailors love and adore him because he really gives a shit about us, is concerned for our welfare, and is consistent and fair. In my entire career, I've never met another sailor like him.

Because of Master Chief Halverson—seeing service through his eyes and the way he leads and mentors—I will fall in love with the Navy in a way I never dreamed, and feel inspired to rise to a new level. The longer I work under his leadership, the more I'll want to be just like him.

Since it's only my first day at VP-1, however, I don't yet know the impact that this remarkable master chief is going to have on my life. He glances at my chief and then back at me and says, "Your arrival is good timing, YN1. We have a shitload of work ahead of us in the next few months."

My chief nods her head in agreement but does not interrupt.

"Understood, Master Chief," I say. "I'm looking forward to the challenge."

"Good, because we need you on point quickly," he says, putting his hands on his hips. "There's a two-day pre-deployment trip in February. You're on the short list to join the crew, so get your gear issue ASAP from Maintenance and get up to speed on all things Admin."

VP-1 is in workups for a six-month deployment to leave in May for Diego Garcia, the same island where Sue is stationed. I stand there, dumbfounded. Master Chief has just informed me that I will be joining a small crew that will fly on one of the squadron's P-3s—from Hawaii to Guam to Thailand to Diego Garcia—for a thirty-six-hour pre-deployment visit. The Navy creates an astonishingly small world at times, and this time it means I will be on the same island with Sue in the middle of the Indian Ocean for a little over a day in February and a few weeks in May before she transfers to Guam.

I can't believe my good luck. But my priority is to stay safe and in hiding, so I squash my elation, remain professional, and react to this news with only a nod.

"Got it, Master Chief. I'll be ready."

He reaches out his hand again. "That's what I like to hear. Welcome aboard again, YN1. I'm looking forward to working with you."

I shake his hand. "You as well, Master Chief."

Chapter 23

HER WORLD

Dressed in my freshly issued shiny green flight jacket and green flight suit, I board my first P-3 airplane. Both my flight jacket and flight suit—a long-sleeve onesie with a full-torso zipper, diagonal chest, and shoulder-, thigh-, and ankle-zippered pockets—have PATRON ONE Screaming Eagles patches Velcroed on the right chest, leather name tags Velcroed on the left chest, and small American flags sewn on the left shoulder. My "suitcase" is a spacious green canvas flight bag, packed halfway full, that will double as my pillow. My flight bag and my dark blue sleeping bag are wedged against the fuselage under some gear on the deck of the plane.

The pilots, flight crew, command master chief, maintenance master chief, and leaders from each of the squadron's departments are making this trip. Our objective is to touch base with the squadron currently on deployment, learn their challenges, and gain an understanding of what we will encounter when the entire squadron deploys in May.

It's been three months since I've seen Sue and I'm thrilled to spend a day with her, put my arms around her, and hear her infectious laugh. If we were a straight couple, my shipmates would know about my partner and they would be happy for me.

But that is obviously not my situation, so I suppress my excitement and talk shop with the crew like this is just another trip.

As soon as the wheels go up, some of us venture to the galley and others hit the deck in their sleeping bags. It's going to be long days of travel each way in this small four-propeller airplane.

The galley is an area in the back of the plane that has a small white table and two maroon bench seats. As I approach it, Master Chief Halverson breaks out a cribbage board.

"Whoa," I say. "I love cribbage!"

He cracks the side of the deck of cards on the table. "Well," he says, his deep voice booming over the airplane's vibration and loud humming, "let's see what you got, yeoman."

The master chief and I play for hours. Everyone stops by to talk to him, either to shoot the shit or get his opinion on a variety of issues, while we play game after game. Whatever question comes his way, including those about career decisions, he always has a direct but thoughtful answer.

We eventually take a break for crucial naps, as Diego Garcia is fourteen hours ahead of Hawaii and I'll need to hit the ground running when we finally arrive. Post-nap, I return to the galley to find the master chief already there with a few other chiefs. He breaks out the board and we reconvene for another round.

Travel continues for another agonizing two days. We make evening stops in Guam and Thailand, but I do not join the boys in town.

I'm just counting down the hours to Sue.

When the announcement is made that we will finally be touching down on Diego Garcia, the pilots let me sit in the cockpit. A beautiful, remote tropical island that resembles an outline of a footprint comes into view in the middle of the sea. My heart swells with excitement as, seconds later, the pilots nail a smooth landing.

Fierce, direct, and blinding sunshine hits me the moment I step off the plane, and within seconds the back of my flight suit is completely soaked. The radical shift in temperature and the fourteen-hour time-change jetlag from hell has me extremely disoriented.

Members from our sister squadron wait outside of the hangar to greet us. They are the main reason that I'm here, and I need to keep it together. There is an overwhelming push-pull between my heart and my reality, and I have to pretend to be cool (which I'm not) and stay closeted (which I totally will).

I scan the area for Sue as if she's just waiting to pop out from behind a bush and fly into my arms—a stupid move, obviously, but it's what my heart wants. Once I establish that she definitely isn't here, I shift my attention to my colleagues and join the others walking toward the hangar, figuring that she will eventually find me.

The crew and I spend the afternoon getting briefed by our sister squadron before we are driven the mile or so into town, where the barracks, a small store, the gym, and a few places to eat are located. I'm assigned a private room; I take a quick shower and am unpacking my flight bag when there's a knock at my door.

In a scene straight out of the *Twilight Zone*, I open the door to find my love standing before me—but not alone. She's with a very tan, taller woman with short, curly dark brown hair.

Sue and I maintain our composure and quickly hug. "K," she says, "this is Nancy, a good friend of mine."

Nancy and I shake hands.

"She's going to join us for dinner," Sue says.

My mouth drops open. This is the last thing I want; we haven't seen each other in *three months*. But I have zero fight in me.

"Uh, all right," I mumble—but what I'm thinking is, *What the hell?*

■ ■ ■

We take an island bus to the Expat Club, a not-good-but-the-best-you-can-do-in-a-place-like-this restaurant by the water that is lit by torch-like lights on tall posts. Nancy leads us to a dark wooden table near an open window. Stars fill the sky and the moon reflects off of the water, creating a beautiful golden streak of ripples that flow toward us.

Dinner with a stranger is awkward and uncomfortable, but I ignore her and try to connect with Sue. "God, I am so tired, Q."

She lets out a small chuckle and nods. "It's a long haul out here. Trust me, I know."

A small Filipino waitress arrives, and Sue greets her like a friend. "Hey, Lina. This is my friend Karen."

Lina nods brusquely, all business. "What can I get you to drink?"

They order beers.

"I'll take a Diet Coke," I say.

"We'll also take a large veggie pizza," Nancy says.

When did that get decided? I wonder.

Lina scoots away as quickly as she arrived.

I stay quiet and confused. Sue gives me a sheepish look and then puts her attention on Nancy. They laugh and talk about work and island life and I sip my Diet Coke, trying to stay awake and not understanding half of their discussion. I'm exhausted and am gazing out at the water when Nancy says, "We're going snorkeling tomorrow, Karen. Wanna come?"

My head spins toward Sue with an incredulous look. Has she really made plans on the only day I will be here?

Her face turns red. "Want to, K?" she asks awkwardly.

My heart sinks as I look into her eyes. I'm flabbergasted. Hell no, I don't want to go snorkeling. That is the last thing I want to do. But apparently that's where Sue is going to be.

"Sure," I finally say. "I guess so." I turn back toward the ocean and go silent.

The pizza arrives and, just like fried chicken in Thailand is definitely not fried chicken, this is *so not pizza*. Round and loaded with some kind of unidentifiable veggie matter, it is hard and chewy and tastes like stale bagels. They talk, laugh, and dig in, drinking and forgetting that I have just flown for three goddamn days to spend a few precious moments with Sue while I silently choke down stale bagel pizza with my Diet Coke.

We head back to town. I'm pissed and feel blindsided. Whatever this is, I don't like it, and my mind is reeling. We've been apart for nine months, and it's been beyond difficult to stay connected. But shit, if she found someone new, she could have told me before I flew out here.

We get out of the bus.

"I'm tired," I say to Sue. "I guess I'll see you tomorrow."

She avoids my eyes. "Okay. Night, K."

I walk away. This whole night was like being with a stranger.

After I complete turnover briefings the following morning, I return to my room and reluctantly change into a white tank top, blue board shorts, and flip-flops. As the sun is wicked strong here, I lather on sunblock and grab my blue VP-1 ballcap for extra protection.

Sue arrives in a white tank top and faded red board shorts, holding snorkeling gear in a red mesh bag. "Hey, K." She gives me a quick hug. "Ready to go?"

"Sure, I guess," I say, even though I want to say, *Uh no, babe. This is the last thing I want to do.* But I want to be where Sue is, so I'm going snorkeling.

Nancy waits in a small outboard motorboat at the dock

wearing pink shorts and a sun-faded pink bikini top. She beams at Sue as we join her. I'm amazed by their Diego Garcia tans, which blow my Hawaii tan out of the water.

Nancy drives and Sue stands up front with her as we leave the dock. They laugh and talk like they do this every day and I sit in the back with my hand on my ballcap, watching the wake cut through the crystal-clear water and listening to the hum of the engine.

We arrive at their favorite snorkeling site, and Nancy idles the boat while Sue tosses out the anchor. When we quit drifting, Nancy turns off the motor and small slapping sounds hit the side of the boat as they grab their mesh bags and put on their masks, fins, and snorkels. Sue turns to me. "You joining us, K? There's an extra set of gear."

"No, I'm gonna stay on the boat."

They glance at each other, shrug a *whatever*, sit on the edge of the boat, and fall off backwards.

I'm thinking, *Fuck snorkeling with you and your new friend. I'm not doing it. This will be quick, and then we can head back to shore.*

But I sit, and sit, and sit on that boat, and gradually it occurs to me that this is *not* going to be quick. My unsunblocked ears, sticking out from under my ballcap, are on fire. I am too. Each hour with Nancy is one less hour I can spend with Sue—and the longer I wait, the angrier I get. Does she give two shits that my time here with her is limited?

The boat rocks gently while they repeatedly dive down and resurface, occasionally dropping glossy, fist-size, brown-and-white-spotted shells over the edge of the boat with outstretched arms. I cup my hands over my ears, silently cursing and furious at myself for joining this outing. My heart was so set on being alone with Sue that the words *no thanks* eluded me entirely, and now I'm paying the price.

They eventually return to the boat invigorated and refreshed from their dive, but *I am absolutely done.* One look at me, and Sue sees it. Silent and fuming, I give her *The Look.* We head back to base.

The whir of the boat's motor competes with my raging thoughts and the hot wind hits my back as I stare over the wake, trying to calm myself and refusing to acknowledge either of them. Then a silver dolphin glides through our wake and effortlessly jumps out and over the water, and my heart leaps.

I point and yell, "Look!"

Sue joins me in the back as dozens of playful shiny dolphins slip in and out of the water, and my dark mood is momentarily forgotten. I relish this moment of pure joy, grateful to the universe for this reality check.

The dolphins eventually swim off. Sue smiles at me and returns to the front with Nancy.

After we dock, I storm off to my room. I've had enough.

Sue calls after me, "K, do you want to have dinner with me?"

I stop, turn, and glare at her.

She gazes at me with soft eyes. "Just you and me. In my room."

"Sure. Whatever." I head off to shower and inspect my burning ears.

An hour later, I knock on Sue's door.

She opens right away. "Hey, K." Her tone is gentle and inviting.

"Hey," I say, my jaw tight and my guard up.

Sue has a spacious two-person room all to herself with a four-foot-high twin bed, two tall wooden stand-up lockers, a small desk with a chair, a wooden entertainment stand with a 20-inch TV, and a russet love seat that faces the TV. In the far back left corner of the room is a small sink and a private bathroom.

"Wow," I say, surprised by her good fortune. "Nice room, Q."

"Yeah, I'm lucky, that's for sure. Come sit with me on the couch." She takes a look at my ears, which have turned a painful reddish purple since this afternoon, and winces. "Sorry about earlier. I didn't know your ears were so burnt."

With twelve hours left on the island, I'm afraid to be honest or vulnerable. We're also in her barracks room and others could hear us if our voices were raised, so I quash my feelings and keep it simple. "Yeah, I just wish I hadn't gone."

Sue says nothing. Regret is written all over her face, and the unease between us is palpable. "Anyway," she says, "pizza will be here any minute."

"Oh my God. Seriously? Pizza again?"

She shrugs and smiles. "They deliver."

The pizza arrives and we sit together on the couch and eat in silence. There is so much that I'm not brave enough to ask. I wonder if they're together. I wonder where *my Sue* has been for the last day. I wonder if we're okay. But I refuse to ask her any of that because I want to forget the last twenty-four hours, sit on this couch, and convince myself that she still loves me. If she tells me anything other than what I want to believe, I will have to swallow her words all the way back to Hawaii, and I can't be grieving on a military flight with my new shipmates who have no idea I'm gay. Keeping my shit together is top priority.

There is one thing I do know: I don't belong here. This is her world, her home, and her life without me. We don't know how to be us here because we *can't* be us here. And I don't know what I was thinking. Seeing her for two days is worse than not seeing her at all.

Sue seems to be thinking the same thing. So we keep it safe and make small talk—her work and upcoming transfer, my new job, 6-Pac, her anxiety about transferring to Guam and being underway all the time.

A heavy weight descends when there's no small talk left. I'm leaving early in the morning and have to go to my room and get some sleep, but I sure don't want to. I'd rather lie in bed and hold her and reassure myself that we're okay. But that's too risky, and we know it. We are both now first classes and have a lot to lose if we are caught. Neither of us is willing to take the chance.

Sue puts her hand on my knee. "I wish you could stay, but someone could see you leave my room."

I nod and stand. "I know."

We share a long hug and a kiss. This goodbye is confusing as hell.

"I love you, Q."

"I love you too. I'll see you back here in a few months."

And with that, I turn and walk the few hundred feet to my room—a similar setup, but minus Sue.

Early the next morning, I walk up the stairs to the P-3 in my green flight suit, recalling how excited I was when we arrived less than forty-eight hours ago and trying not to think about what a disaster this all was. I unroll my sleeping bag near the fuselage, crawl into it as deeply as I can, and cover my head as the plane rushes down the runway and takes off over the Indian Ocean, flying away from my girl and an experience I never saw coming. The hum of the propellors and the vibrating fuselage offers much-needed privacy as I lie in my sleeping bag and cry.

The obvious is not lost on me. Sue has created a life on her little island that doesn't include me—that can't include me. She has found someone who makes her smile and laugh, if even for a few months, so that she isn't alone and miserable. She didn't get to stay in Hawaii with me and 6-Pac in our apartment, with our bed and our shower and the freedom to go to our beach. Those little things are not little. That sort of freedom is indescribable. I wish things—*so many things*—were different, but she has had to find new friends, especially new gay friends, to be happy where she is. I was naive to think I could just interrupt her flow.

Military life is a lot to manage, especially on opposite sides of the world. How could our relationship not take a hit? How could we not lose "us" while hiding "us" at the same time? It is an impossible feat. If we stay together, the coming three years are going to test us. I hope we are up for it, because I can't imagine my life without her.

I crawl out of my sleeping bag an hour later and go to the head, where I splash cold water on my face and wait for the evidence of my emotions to vanish. When my eyes are less red and my face is no longer splotchy, I make my way to the galley, where a chief, an officer, and Master Chief Halverson, his pale bald head poking out of the top of his green flight suit, are talking.

The master chief smiles. "Ready to get your ass kicked, yeoman?"

I engage my military bearing and slide in next to the officer. Master Chief Halverson places the cribbage board between us and cracks the side of the deck on the table.

"Bring it, Master Chief," I say, thankful to be YN1 Solt again.

Chapter 24

SEASHELLS
AND SILENCE

Three months pass, and it comes time to make the return trip to Diego Garcia. I will be deployed there for six months, and with Sue also gone there is now officially no one left to be the *take care of all the shit at home* person in Hawaii, so I have enlisted outside help: Sue's good friend Jake will be my cat and house sitter while I'm gone.

I met Jake—a five-foot-nine bodybuilder with a large fore-head, thick neck, huge shoulders, and thinning light brown hair—a few years ago when he was on the island visiting Sue, and he expressed a desire to live in Hawaii then. Of course he knows nothing about my relationship with Sue, but they are close and she trusts him, so I trust him. I invited him to move to Hawaii from Michigan, stay in our apartment, and get settled on the island for free in return for his help taking care of 6-Pac and keeping an eye on things while I'm away, and he eagerly accepted.

After packing up and attending to last-minute details, I savor one last snuggle with 6-Pac on the morning of my departure. He wraps around my neck like always and purrs loudly as I reach back and rub his ears. "I'm sure going to miss you, little man," I tell him before reluctantly setting him down and heading out.

My two hundred support and maintenance shipmates are scheduled for a chartered flight from hell from Honolulu to Diego Garcia. Our eight P-3 airplanes with their eleven-man flight crews are currently on the three-day trip through Guam and Thailand. Although that way of doing it took longer, it was definitely more comfortable to be in a small plane where I could stretch my legs, play card games, and take naps. Flying halfway around the world on a chartered flight with my butt planted in an airplane seat while wearing my dungarees is definitely *not* on my list of favorite things to do.

At the Honolulu airport we file onto the plane and instinctively divide by rank. My sailors stream by me and sit in the back with the rest of the junior sailors. I have an aisle seat just over the wings with the rest of the first classes and sit next to a few of my gay peers. The officers and chiefs all sit in front of us.

As the plane leaves Oahu, I put on my headset, start my CD player, recline my seat its allotted inch, and close my eyes. My last trip to Diego Garcia feels like ages ago. The experience gutted me and, for better or worse, forced me to come to terms with the life that I do and don't have with Sue.

Our year of separation has now tripled, and we will never recover the time we've lost. Our intimacy and deep connection are all but gone, and as the months go by we are becoming more like the "roommates" everyone thinks we are. I will forever regret this. But I also have to be honest with myself about our new priorities. Sue's order of priority is: 1) her family, 2) her career, 3) me. My order is: 1) my sobriety, 2) my career, 3) her. And not only have our careers bumped "us" down a wrung, but she also prioritized another woman over me the last time we saw one another. The invisible forces we've been fighting against since the start of our relationship are winning, and I don't know how I'm going to feel seeing her again.

We have had little contact since that trip—only a few phone calls and letters. This doesn't bother me like it did after she first left, however. Now almost nine months sober, I have immersed myself in recovery and am growing up. I understand now that before Sue left, I was making my happiness entirely contingent upon my relationship—and that wasn't fair to Sue or to me.

I'm envious of my many sleeping shipmates. I am wide-awake and deeply uncomfortable in this seat. I continually flex my legs, twist my torso, and shift my stiff body, trying to find a more bearable position, my mind still racing.

My new expectations with Sue are different. I've discovered that I am okay without her, even though I don't like the idea of losing her and certainly wouldn't choose it. We will be on the same island again for two weeks before she departs for Guam, and I plan to relish my precious time with her. I will surrender to the split that is occurring between us, continue to focus on my work and myself, and hope things improve. With no other choice, I will love Sue from a distance and hope that we will someday reunite.

A few stops and a day later, I peer beyond my seatmates at the crystal-clear blue water and the footprint outline of Diego Garcia. My heart rate increases immediately. My gay peers pick up on my mood, and knowing that my partner is on the island, they beam at me with shit-eating grins. No one in my squadron knows what happened during my recent trip here, and I plan to keep it that way.

After we deplane, we pile our baggage in the back of an old school bus and I grab a seat for the ride into town, where I am assigned a private barracks room with a single bed, stand-up locker, dresser, and a small TV. I also have a full bath all to myself—a huge perk that's due to my newly acquired seniority and which I couldn't be happier about.

A soft knock interrupts my unpacking and I open my door to find Sue, all cheeks and stunning blue eyes, reminding me of someone I used to know. "Hey, K! How was the trip over?"

We shut the door before sharing a long hug and a quick kiss. I keep my arms around her waist, lean back, and roll my eyes. "Well, you know. It was horrible, and I thought my ass was going to fall off in that brick seat."

She shakes her head and laughs. "God, I know that's right. That trip is a nightmare." She takes my hand, and we walk over to sit on the bed.

As soon as we sit, my anxiety immediately rises and I get up. "You stay put," I say. "I have to keep moving or I'm going to fall out." Three months ago suddenly feels like yesterday, and I don't know where we stand. There is so much that I want to say, so much that needs to be said, but there is no way in hell I'm going there. Not right now.

She rests on my bed as I hang my uniforms in the stand-up locker.

"K?" she says softly.

I stop and turn to face her. "Yeah?"

"I love you," she says, tenderness in her eyes.

My heart rate eases and my legs go weak. Because *this* is my girl. My beachcomber, my love, the one who can avoid tough conversations even better than I can. This is her way of making up.

I walk over and put my arms around her. "I love you too, babe."

I have to put February in the past or we won't survive. Resolving issues with almost no time together while we are building our careers and have hundreds of eyes on us feels like an impossible feat. We have enough pain—the pain of separation, the pain of hiding our relationship, the pain of our escalating walls. The day to address even more pain beyond that is not today.

She settles into my arms. "I've missed you so much." Her voice is the sound of love.

I melt into her body. "Me too, babe. Me too."

The next morning my peers and I take the school bus back out to the hangar, where I head topside to the spacious Admin Office at the end of a long hallway. A half dozen dark wooden desks sit on white linoleum flooring under drop-down rectangular fluorescent light fixtures. The large windows lining the walls overlook the flight line and the squadron's P-3s.

My desk is situated just inside and to the left of the door, and my sailors each have their own desks in the middle of the office. Organized bookshelves full of the manuals we need to be proficient with in order to perform our jobs are located on the far-left wall.

YN2 Manelli is directing the organizing efforts to YN3 Taft and YNSN Vance. They look drained from the fourteen-hour time change but are working well as a team and seem content as they listen to music, deliriously joke with each other, unpack boxes, and set up the office.

I start arranging my desk and consider the assignments I've had so far—two ships, an overseas tour, and an Admiral's Staff—and how they have led me to this point, overseeing an entire Admin Department. My most fulfilling responsibility is supervising the yeomen and ensuring that they are not only doing well in the present but also on track for their future careers. Although leading sailors is a new step in my career and one that has taken time to settle into, I truly love how rewarding it is to work with junior sailors.

Chief Booker recently passed her admin responsibilities to me so that she could focus solely on being the command drug and alcohol program advisor (DAPA)—a full-time job, especially on deployment. This means that in addition to being the admin leading petty officer and the command legal yeoman, I also oversee and track all command action items using the command tickler, a bizarre word that translates to "administrative action item tracker." Incoming action items are routed to me, I assign them to the responsible department, and then I track them through to completion using the tickler. This includes three hundred monthly travel claims, officer fitness reports, enlisted evaluations, awards, officer transfers and receipts, and command directives due for periodic review and updating.

This all feels like a lot sometimes, but now that I'm sober, my focus is sharp, my days are full, and I'm thriving—enjoying the Navy more than I ever have before.

For the next two weeks, a sweet comfort returns to my and Sue's interactions. We have dinner with each other in the evenings, she meets my gay friends and introduces me to hers—Nancy, thankfully, is long gone—our subtle body language returns, and we talk and laugh and are quietly loving and affectionate when we're alone with one another in our rooms. We've rediscovered the easy rhythm that has always characterized our relationship, and it's wonderful.

But we never address the elephant in the room.

On her final day on the island, Sue acquires her command vehicle and takes me to the plantation.

Old, deteriorated buildings mark the spot that was the center of the island's population until the early 1970s. We park and Sue leads me on a path through dense, junglelike vegetation to the shoreline where she has beachcombed for the past year.

The plantation is isolated and far from town, so we have the freedom to loosen up. This is the first time I have ever beach-combed with Sue, and it is an amazingly peaceful and serene experience. Both lost in our own thoughts, we slowly scan the shoreline—walking barefoot in the sand, flip-flops in hand. Crystal blue ocean water to our right, a thick green jungle on our left, and the sun beating down on our bodies, we pick up flawless, glossy shells carried in by the high tide.

I make a secret promise to myself that I will keep this image of Sue in my memory until we can be together again. "It's beautiful here, babe," I say. "I'm glad we had this time together."

She sighs and a cloud of sadness passes over her face. "I know, K. I wish you could have been here the entire year. We would have had so much fun."

We manage to carve out a few quiet moments in my room to say our goodbyes the following evening. We hold each other close, not taking for granted the preciousness of the time we've been allowed to spend with one another these last two weeks. For the next two years, she will be farther away from me than halfway around the world was, because she'll be underway—out at sea and therefore even more out of touch than she was here.

I pull her closer and inhale her essence one last time. "I love you, babe. I can't wait for the day when we never have to say goodbye again."

"I love you too, K. It feels like that's all we do anymore," she says, starting to choke up. "I just hope that time will fly by." She leans her head back and half-smiles up at me before giving me one last small kiss and a deeper hug. And then she picks up her suitcase and heads out the door to the van that will take her to the airstrip.

I shut the door and sit down on my bed—my head down, tears streaming. I try to wrap my head around the fact that she is gone again, just when I was getting used to her, and wonder if we will ever truly be together again. Already another countdown has begun.

Only two and a half more years . . .

Chapter 25

GOALS
AND GOSSIP

plan to make the best of my six months on Diego Garcia, so
I set a few deployment goals. I want to advance to the position of chief petty officer, and that's something I will have to
work hard for over the course of the next few years. That work
will start here. I will also be celebrating my first sober anniver-
sary on the island; I commit myself to using this time to grow
personally.

I started my Enlisted Aviation Warfare Specialist (EAWS)
qualification—getting my wings—before leaving Hawaii. The
entire process typically takes a year, but I want to complete it
in six months so it will be mentioned in my November enlisted
evaluation. It is a voluntary and challenging program and will
teach me many things pertinent to the aviation community,
including the capabilities and maintenance requirements of all
Navy airplanes. My understanding in key areas will be required
before obtaining prerequisite signatures by EAWS-qualified
sailors within the squadron. A written exam and an in-person
review board are the final steps.

I have another, more personal, goal: to get fit. I start lifting weights at the gym in town, a short walk from my barracks room. As I'm a novice at this weight-lifting stuff, I go each day and watch others work out. Then I do what they do.

I'm doing lat pulldowns one day when Master Chief Halverson and the maintenance master chief pass by holding weight belts in their workout-gloved hands.

"Trying to get buff, yeoman?" the master chief ribs me.

He told me on our previous trip in February that he also no longer drinks and loves to work out, so I'm not surprised to see him at the gym.

"I'm already buff, Master Chief," I joke. "You guys need some help?"

They chuckle and move on.

After asking a few strangers to spot me, I learn pretty quickly that a workout buddy would be helpful, so I ask Amy, one of my peers who lives in the barracks room next to mine. Amy works in the squadron's Maintenance Department, is about my height and has big, brown deerlike eyes. She's funny and witty and has a deep, raspy voice and a laugh that I can often hear echoing up from the squadron smoke pit on the side of the hangar.

She looks sideways at me when I ask. "Um, sure," she says. "But don't kill me."

"Of course I won't," I say, but she doesn't know that I haven't a clue what I'm doing.

We do a leg workout that evening, loaded with squats and lunges.

When the bus arrives the following morning, I leave my room to find Amy struggling to board it.

She glares at me. "Murderer! Murderer!" she yells. "I can't pick up my legs!"

I'm still trying to not be a dummy, so I say nothing but do chuckle under my breath a bit.

■ ■ ■

Because Diego Garcia is the tiniest place on the planet, Amy and I regularly pass the two master chiefs in the gym. Even though we think we're killing it, we're definitely novices. The master chiefs cross their arms and shake their heads at our horrendously poor form until Master Chief Halverson can't take it anymore.

"Good God, you two!" he says one day. "You're gonna jack up your shoulders if you keep pulling that bar over your neck like that."

I feel like a complete idiot. "But that's how everyone else does it."

"Everyone else is stupid. You should know that by now." He shakes his head, grabs the bar, and models the correct form. "Now don't fuck it up again!"

After a few more corrections, the master chief has had enough. "Goddamn it . . . I give. I can't get a damn thing done watching over the three of you!" He glares at me and Amy. "You two meet us here tomorrow at 1700, and we'll turn this shit show around."

After that, he runs all three of us into the ground on a daily basis, and Amy isn't the only one screaming, "Murderer!" in the mornings. He's simply a natural leader.

"Okay, here's the plan," he says the first morning. "We have three routines. Day one is back and biceps, day two is chest and triceps, and day three is legs and shoulders. We do some core every day. Then we repeat. That way you work hard but give your muscles time to recover. Oh, and no days off on deployment. Got it?"

We all nod compliantly. Like, who's going to argue with him?

My favorite day is chest and triceps, as I love push-ups, bench press, skull-crushers, and bodyweight dips.

Master Chief stops by as I'm skull-crushing one day. "Keep your elbows in, add ten pounds, and quit being a wimp," he admonishes me, then straddles a bench next to me, grabs two dumbbells from the ground, and places them on his thighs before lying back and hoisting them for his next set of flies.

Keeping in line with my time-honored nickname tradition, Amy and I secretly nickname the master chiefs H-Bob and G-Bob. One day they overhear us, and after that we become K-Bob, A-Bob, H-Bob, and G-Bob—nicknames to be used strictly outside of working hours (during workouts, mostly, but also when A-Bob and I make fun of H-Bob and G-Bob behind their backs, which is often).

Ever the mentor, "H-Bob" takes every opportunity to instill his wisdom; he regularly checks on me and has me come to his office so he can give me advice. By this point, we've gotten to know one another well enough that I think of him as just "H" in my head, though it would still be inappropriate to call him that out loud.

One day in August, he pokes his head into my office. "YN1! In my office!"

"Roger that, Master Chief," I respond.

I arrive in his small, organized office, notebook in hand. He's sitting at his wooden desk, in front of a large window that shines on his bald head. As I walk in, he jots some notes in a folder and, without looking up, says, "Take a seat."

I place my open notebook on my lap and wait until he puts the folder in his outbox and leans back.

"Look, YN1," he says, "I want you to be in the best position you can be to make chief, so I have a collateral duty I'd like you to consider."

Being promoted to chief petty officer—E-7—is no easy process. Less than 10 percent of the Navy's enlisted sailors ever rise to that level. To be promoted to the ranks of E-4 through E-6, sailors take a Navy-wide exam and are selected based upon how well they do on the exam compared to their peers. To make chief, you first take an exam in January and must pass at an unspecified cutoff mark. Those who don't "make the cut" return the following January and restart the process. Those who do make the cut are then eligible for review by a Navy-wide Advancement Selection Board consisting of select master chiefs from throughout the Fleet.

The Advancement Selection Board undergoes weeks of sequestered sessions in Millington, Tennessee, where they review the records of all eligible sailors. They take into consideration duty stations (locations and how challenging they were), evaluations, collateral duties, awards, warfare qualifications (like EAWS), time in service and pay grade, community service, and any other factor that would set someone apart from their peers. Selection, therefore, is twofold: you must pass the exam *and* be chosen by the board. If both of those happen, you become a chief petty officer.

Fourteen years is the Navy's average to make chief, and I'll have a little over eleven when I first take the chief's exam in January of 1995.

I nod and say nothing as H interlaces his fingers on his desk and leans forward. "Since you're getting buff like me, I'd like you to run the Remedial PRT Program. The current coordinator transfers soon, and it would be great for your record."

The command Physical Readiness Test (PRT) is a semi-annual test that each sailor must pass to be physically "within standards." There are three fitness tests: a 1.5-mile run (optional swim), sit-ups, and push-ups. Body fat percentage is also measured. Minimum passing scores are based on standards that are broken down by age and gender. The higher your score, the better your remarks on your annual performance evaluation. If a sailor fails any portion of the PRT or does not meet the body fat standards, they get placed in the "Remedial PRT Program." Master Chief wants me to be the coordinator of this program, which would entail working with these sailors to get back to standards before they're administratively separated from the Navy for PRT failure.

"Hell yes, Master Chief," I say. "I'd love to run the remedial program."

His seriousness turns into a full smile. "Great. I knew you would. I'll have the current coordinator come see you. Keep me posted on your turnover."

"I will." I stand and move toward the door, but before I exit I glance back and say, "Thanks again, Master Chief."

My cribbage competition with H remains fierce; we have played countless games on this deployment. My typical day consists of work, exercise, working with the Remedial PRT folks, having shitty pizza delivered, working more, studying, and going to sleep. But on the weekends, I give myself a little reprieve from the hustle: I go beachcombing if I can find a vehicle, and if I can't I go to H's barracks room to see if he's up for a game or two.

When I show up at his door, he always greets me with his standard welcome: "Ready to get your ass kicked, yeoman?"

"We'll see whose ass gets kicked today, Master Chief," I say, "but I think it's going to be the guy you see in your mirror."

The chief lounging on H's couch laughs, and H grabs the cribbage board.

H has a system in all aspects of his life. This is also true at his barracks room, a few buildings away from mine, where he and the rest of the chiefs live on the second deck. When his door is open, he's available and anyone is welcome to enter. If a chief or officer needs advice, he shuts his door, a clear *do not disturb* sign. If a junior sailor needs counseling or advice, he asks them to bring their chief, as he is a firm believer in not only guiding sailors but also mentoring and keeping his chiefs in the loop.

A few chiefs are usually sitting on his couch chatting him up when I arrive, as he is everyone's mentor, not just mine, and they use his room like a lounge. He and I never discuss our personal lives. We sit and play and give each other shit and are never alone behind closed doors. Not ever.

What I will later know but have no awareness of now is that I don't have a clear understanding of the fine line we're walking. Too naive and green, I'm not aware of the perception others are developing. In my eyes, H is amazing. We have so much in common—our sobriety, weight lifting, cribbage, and our love for the Navy—that I want nothing more than to soak up every bit of wisdom I can from him. And I believe he sees a little bit of himself in me, with my hunger, drive, and determination.

But it's not lost on me that not everyone is okay with our relationship. Toward the end of deployment, H and I are back at it with cribbage when one of the squadron maintenance chiefs starts to enter H's room, then stops dead in his tracks when he sees me. He rolls his eyes, shakes his head, and loudly exhales before walking away.

H looks up but says nothing, nor does he look at me. He picks up his hand, slaps two cards down in the crib, and barks, "Well, you gonna play or just sit there lollygagging, yeoman?"

I'm surprised he's not even going to acknowledge what just happened. But he continues to stare at me, so I retort, "You're just mad because I'm kicking your ass, Master Chief," and then slap two cards on top of his.

A few minutes later, he seems even more frustrated, but that's probably because I'm absolutely kicking his ass.

I will later learn that this maintenance chief has been regularly complaining about our relationship to other sailors in the squadron on Diego Garcia, but right now, I'm oblivious.

On November 2, I complete my prerequisite signatures, take my EAWS qualification exam, pass the oral in-person review board, and am awarded my "wings"—silver wings that will be pinned and centered above my ribbons for the rest of my career. Mary, a newly pinned chief petty officer and a gay friend I met through Sue, pins my wings on me in a small ceremony on the beach. Three other people are also present: two first class friends and peers of mine and the squadron's command master chief—my mentor—H-Bob.

Chapter 26

BOMBSHELLS

A week before the end of deployment, I return from a two-day trip to Bahrain, where I finalized the squadron's end-of-deployment awards at the Admiral's Staff. This includes my second Navy and Marine Corps Achievement Medal (NAM), which is depicted by a gold star on my green-and-orange medal.

I exit the P-3 and head topside in my flight suit to find my sailors packing their desks into moving boxes. They wave and "YN1!!!" roars over the pop music playing from the boom box in the back of the office. I smile, set the two-inch stack of freshly signed awards on my desk, and wave back at them.

YN2 Manelli comes over to greet me. "How was the trip?"

"Busy—super busy—and damn, it is hot and dry as hell over there," I tell her. "It's good to be back. After you all get done packing, have everyone meet me at my desk and we'll get these awards organized and placed in awards folders. How have things been here?"

"All good," she says, an enormous smile on her face. "Just packing up to go home."

"Don't let me stop your progress," I respond, also beaming, as a roll of clear packing tape flies across the office, lobbed by newly promoted YN3 Vance to YN3 Taft.

The best time for a Navy sailor is returning to homeport, and just like everyone around me I'm excited to get home, go to my meetings, see my friends, and give 6-Pac a big squeeze. But what I am looking forward to more than anything is returning to something that's priceless: freedom. Sleeping in my bed, driving my truck, eating my favorite food, going to the beach, taking a bath, and cruising all over Hawaii. I also can't wait to be free to be gay again—as in, not having to look over my shoulder or watch every damn word I say. *That* I'm looking forward to like it's nobody's business, because it really isn't.

The enthusiasm in my office is contagious, so I grab an empty box from the flat stack in the center of the room and yell over the music, "Toss me the tape!"

It flies across the room to me and I unfold and flip the box, line up the bottom flaps, run a clear strip over them and another crossways, then flip it again and start filling it with the contents of my desk. When the box is full, I secure the top with two more strips of tape and write, "YN1 – ADMIN" on the side with a thick black Sharpie.

After my desk is relocated into three boxes, I note that it's evening time in Hawaii and decide to check in with Jake. I pick up the receiver on my phone, one of the few that dials off the island, push "9," hear another dial tone, then dial my home number.

"Yeah?" a voice on the other end snaps sharply.

Yikes! "Jake? Is that you?"

"Yeah . . . it's me."

"Cool," I say, caught off guard by his tone. "It doesn't sound like you. Hey, I'm just calling because I return in about a week."

A grunt and then silence.

My body tenses. "Is everything okay, Jake?"

He grumbles harshly into the phone, "The landlord found out about 6-Pac and said the cat has to go!"

I feel like I've been punched in the gut. I sit on my empty desk, put my feet on my chair and my elbows on my knees, and hold the receiver to my ear. *Shit.* The landlord didn't know about 6-Pac and, like most landlords in Hawaii, thinks animals are dirt-carrying, orange carpet–ruining, flea-attracting pests. "Damn it," I say. "Can you work with him until I get back?"

"Yeah, I don't know . . ."

"What do you mean you don't know?" Now I'm irritated. "Look, Jake, I need you to *know* that nothing can happen to 6-Pac. That was *your* part of the deal. Please ask him to wait until I get home next week. Then I'll figure something out."

"Whatever." I hear a *click* and then the dial tone.

Blown away that he just hung up on me, I put the receiver back in its cradle and my mind goes straight into fix-it mode. *Can Linda help? One of the Kevins?* I'm sure I can find someone to step in if I need to.

My thoughts are interrupted when an unsmiling and serious H calls to me from the doorway, "YN1, please come to my office."

Before I can respond, he's vanished.

I get off my desk, grab my notepad, and enter his office to find him standing with his back to me on the other side of his large wooden desk. His arms are crossed, and he's gazing out of the window.

He takes a deep breath, turns to face me, and points to the door. "Close the door."

I pause, raise my eyebrows, and tilt my head. We're never behind closed doors together. He tightens his lips together and nods his head in confirmation. I shut the door.

He clears his throat, and his thin eyebrows crease the bridge of his nose. When he opens his mouth, the words fall out like bombs: "I don't know how to tell you this, so I'm just going to tell you. One of the chiefs called my wife and told her that you and I are having an affair."

I'm stunned. "Holy shit!" I blurt out. "There's no way! She doesn't believe it, does she?"

He stares dead at me. "She does. It's not good."

"Fuck." I am absolutely mortified. And furious. First, we sure as hell are not having an affair. Second, I can't believe one of the chiefs would do that. Third, I have a pretty strong suspicion which eye-rolling, exhaling, lying chief made that call.

My heart pounds and I grit my teeth. I need a moment to center and calm myself, so I look beyond H's right shoulder and through the window, where a maintenance crew is preparing one of the P-3s for its return flight home. Then I take a breath and meet his level gaze.

"Man, that's so fucked up, Master Chief. I'm really sorry. Do you think she'll believe you when you get home?"

He shakes his ashen face, his eyes bloodshot and glassy from lack of sleep. "I doubt it. I've been on the phone with her all night. She's furious, and she has one hell of a temper."

I'm at a loss for words. His arms across his chest again, H turns and looks out the window again. When he turns back to me, he drops another bomb with the same broken bluntness as before: "But I need you to know that I do have feelings for you."

My knees wobble; I gulp an inhale and break eye contact. *Shit.*

How did I not see this? We spend so much time together; surely, I should have picked up on his feelings. But I didn't. I'm utterly floored.

Time stands still as I try to gather myself. His last statement suggests a possibility that is so far from my reality.

My mind is scrambling. I can't be honest with him. If I was permitted to be open about my life, he would already know that

I'm gay. I would have told him on the flight to Diego Garcia, just as a straight person would if she was getting to see her husband for a few days. But I don't have that kind of freedom. Being honest with him could ruin my career.

His telling me that he has feelings for me could also ruin his.

But I'm more worried about him exposing my secret than about me exposing his. His seniority alone makes him more credible, and on top of that, this is still the witch-hunting era and he is Joe Navy. I can't be honest with him.

This is a mess. I not only have to keep protecting my secret but will now also have to keep and protect his.

So I give him what truth I'm capable of, relying on my perfected skills of dodging and weaving and engaging the fine art of self-preservation to carry me through.

My eyes rise to meet his once again. "Master Chief, I'm so sorry that this has happened. I'm horrified that a chief called your wife and lied to her. That's a huge betrayal, and I really hope that she will see that it's a lie."

He nods and waits for me to acknowledge his other statement.

"But Master Chief," I say, more quietly now, "you're my mentor. I admire you so much and hope to be just like you." My twitchy legs urge me to flee, but I take a deep breath, exhale, and finish. "I'm really sorry"—I pause, steeling myself to deliver the words he does not want to hear—"but I don't have feelings for you."

His weary eyes stay steady on me for a moment before he turns back a third time to the window to gather his military bearing and try to regain his composure. A chief betrayed him, his wife doesn't believe him, and I've told him that I do not return the feelings he has for me.

"Are you going to be okay, Master Chief?"

His body expands with a full inhale. He uncrosses his arms

and turns back around. A different man—the one I know—has returned: his jawline square, face composed, military bearing back in check. He puts his hands on his hips, nods his head, and smiles his kind smile. "Thank you, YN1. I'll be fine."

I turn and slowly leave his office, feeling absolutely crushed.

Chapter 27

MAN PROBLEMS

H is on one of the first P-3s to return to Hawaii, and I leave a week later on another chartered flight from hell. Between our conversation and his departure, I don't see him again. I hope he is working things out with his wife—and I also have some important things of my own to work out: Where is Sue? Is 6-Pac okay? What's up with Jake? How did I get into this mess with H?

The back of the airplane is again packed with the junior sailors. It sounds like a cabin filled with children hyped up on too much candy, but it's simply the excitement of returning home. I have too much on my mind to feel the same elation, so I settle into my seat, put on my headphones, and try to rest, though I know the probability of my actually getting any sleep hovers somewhere around 0 percent.

But I need you to know that I do have feelings for you. His words replay in my mind, along with my incessant internal questioning: *How did I not see it? How did what seemed like a mentoring relationship come to this? What would make a chief call H's wife and tell her that we are having an affair? Did he really believe that? Do others?* Decades later, one of my closest friends and peers from this squadron will say to me, "It does beg the question: How did H not know you were gay?"

By the same token, however, how did I not know that H had feelings for me?

My recovery program dictates that "rigorous honesty" is necessary in all phases of my life to stay sober. But I simply can't remain in the Navy and be honest about being gay. If I'm going to be rigorously honest about anything, it is this: I'm choosing to remain in the Navy and serve within an oppressive system where I have to hide who I am. Nine years ago, when I figured out that I was gay, I could have found another career. I knew I was a target. But it's not like society's views are so much more progressive than the Navy's. In or out of the Navy, I would have remained closeted. I would still be hiding.

But one thing has become crystal clear: my choices are creating startling consequences that I have no idea how to resolve.

I arrive back in my apartment completely worn out from twenty-six hours of travel, delays, and a huge time change, but my exhaustion melts when I find my sweet gray-haired, blue-eyed 6-Pac in the front hallway of my apartment, looking up at me. I drop my bags and pick him up for a long-overdue cuddle.

As I'm saying hello to 6-Pac, Jake's heavy footsteps descend the stairs and I turn to find him with bulging eyes, a beet-red face, and sweat dotting his brawny body.

He shoves a framed picture in my chest of me and Sue. "So, you and Sue are lesbian lovers!"

6-Pac leaps from my arms to escape Jake's fury and I'm left frozen, bewildered, and speechless. Neither Sue nor I would ever tell him that we are partners, as she is not out to anyone in her family, which can only mean one thing: in my absence, Jake went nosing through our personal items and discovered our relationship. What that has to do with him and why it has provoked his rage I have no idea, but here we are, and I have to deal with this.

Even though my heart is exploding out of my chest and my mind is racing with confusion, I attempt to appear calm and unaffected. I walk past him, set the picture on the dining room table, and say, "Look, Jake, my personal life is none of your business." I hear the quiver in my voice.

He leans his demented face close to mine and hisses, "You lied to me, so I lied to you."

I blink. "You lied to me? About what?"

He smirks and glances at 6-Pac, and suddenly I understand that he made up that entire story to punish me. I am furious. "So, you're telling me the landlord doesn't know about 6-Pac?"

Jake says nothing but is unyielding, his eyes beyond intense. I'm mesmerized by the purple, wormlike veins bulging under his clenched jawline.

First H and now Jake? I'm done. "Look, Jake, you need to get your stuff and move out."

"I'm not going anywhere," he says, spit flying through his gritted teeth. He turns and storms back upstairs, where I hear a deadbolt—a lock that was not on his bedroom door before I left—turn behind him.

Jake lives in that room for the next three weeks. He listens to every phone call I make or receive on the phone line he had installed in his room, destroys some of my furniture, follows me in his truck whenever I leave the house, puts cat feces in my bed, and does other things too disturbing to mention. It takes three weeks of my calling the police (who can't help) and landlord before my landlord finally comes to my rescue and escorts Jake off the premises. Jake glares at me every step of the many trips he makes to collect his things and leave.

But my relief is short-lived. While Jake is no longer *in* the house, there is no end to his harassment. He leaves threatening notes on my front porch and repeatedly cuts the padlock off my garage door in the middle of the night. He also tries to upend my and Sue's careers by sending letters to both our commands, addressed from each other, with *MY LESBIAN BUDDY* typed under our names.

The final straw comes in early February, when I turn the corner a block from my apartment on my way home from work and see him sitting in his red truck, a demented grin on his face, waving at me with a slow open-and-closed finger gesture. My heart races as I try to ignore him and drive by—and then rush home, lock the door, and close the blinds. I have no idea if he is right behind me, but his constant and erratic harassment makes me feel like he is always close.

The fear I'm experiencing is beyond anything I have ever gone through. I feel so helpless, especially right now, sitting on my couch in the dark, knowing I can't stop him. Once again, my inability to be honest about who I am and whom I love has caused unnecessary pain and chaos. I have been secretly hunted behind my back for years by NCIS and the Navy, and now I am visibly being hunted and stalked by a homophobic madman who says he told his family that he and I were engaged to be married, who feels like I have done him wrong. This is beyond absurd. If I had known Jake had feelings for me, I never would have invited him to stay in our home and watch over 6-Pac.

I call Linda, who has listened to this terrifying drama since I returned home. "Hey, L. I need to move. I think he's going to kill me. He was right around the corner just now."

She exhales. "Oh, Kumquat. I'm so sorry. I'll call the Kevins. We'll make a plan."

The following Sunday, I quickly and secretly move to Makakilo to be closer to the squadron and to get away from Jake. My recovery buds swoop in with a beautiful and loving caravan: Linda in her minivan, Submarine Kevin in his limousine with his music blaring, Air Force Kevin looking cool in his white convertible with the top down, and one more friend of theirs who's driving a small U-Haul. With my truck, we have everything we need for a quick escape.

Linda arrives and wraps me up in her nurturing embrace. "Okay. Kumquat, let's get this show on the road!"

Everyone knows what I've been through with Jake, and this is a moving party with a mission. We carry load after load into our vehicles, until the apartment is empty. Then I lift 6-Pac onto my shoulders and we head off to Makakilo, the same town where Sue lived when we met.

I am grateful to have such loving people in my life and immediately feel a little safer.

Jake's letters to the squadron eventually stop. But it takes me a long time to remove him from my reasons for looking over my shoulder, and even decades later, he will never be fully gone from my mind.

Thankfully, I never see him again. I pray I never do.

Chapter 28

DON'T ASK,
DON'T TELL

One of my saving graces when Jake was sending those *MY LESBIAN BUDDY* letters to my command was that he did so in 1994—after Don't Ask, Don't Tell. Because of that policy, no one in my command could officially ask me if that line in the return address was true.

My very discreet and awesome squadron postal clerk also brought those letters directly to me, which was further protection for me. But since the letters were constant and he was concerned that I was in danger, he also notified H, who called me into his office to see if I was okay.

I explained that a man who was interested in me was harassing me because he had feelings for me and the feelings weren't mutual. H did not ask me if the wording on the envelopes was true, and if he had, I would have lied. It was bizarre to be discussing any of this with H after our own awkward conversation a few short months earlier, but he was still my command master chief, and my welfare was his responsibility.

It was during these years that I started to grasp how LGBTQ+ equality and civil rights were used as political ploys. Equal rights were fought for and progress appeared to inch along, only to be contested and even destroyed when new politicians, especially new commanders in chief—presidents—were elected to office, a cycle which continues to this day.

About the same time that I was deploying to Diego Garcia, Bill Clinton was campaigning for president of the United States. He specifically promised that he would end the ban on gays serving in the military and would also oppose laws that discriminated based on sexual orientation. Because of these promises, Clinton received huge support from the LGBTQ+ community and was inaugurated into office in January of 1993.

On April 23, 1993, President Clinton said, "I believe that this country's policies should be heavily biased in favor of non-discrimination. I believe when you tell people that they can't do certain things in this country that other people can do, there ought to be an overwhelming and compelling reason for it."

Although ending the homosexual military ban remained one of his top agenda items, Clinton faced overwhelming resistance from top military leaders and the Senate Armed Services Committee, who brought in witness after witness who claimed that allowing openly gay, lesbian, and bisexual service members would create problems within military units and upset morale. General Colin Powell, a Black man and the chairman of the joint chiefs of staff—the highest position in the military—probably had the most influence with regard to the policy. When he testified to the Senate Armed Services Committee, he said, "Skin color is a benign, nonbehavioral characteristic. Sexual orientation is perhaps the most profound of human behavioral characteristics. Comparison of the two is a convenient but invalid argument."

But Clinton was determined, so after all of the hearings were complete he reapproached General Powell. This time Powell proposed a different idea: "What if we just stop asking?"

This brought on Don't Ask, Don't Tell (DADT), a policy where gay, lesbian, and bisexual service members could serve in the military—as long as we remained closeted. We would no longer have to openly lie about our sexual orientation, but we were also not permitted to disclose it. This policy represented a supposed compromise between those who wanted gays to be able to openly serve and those who didn't.

Under DADT, the government could no longer ask us our sexual orientation. The question, "Have you ever engaged in homosexual activity (sexual relations with another person of the same sex)?" was removed from enlistment documents and security clearance forms, and we could no longer be witch-hunted by our commanders or NCIS. Dishonesty and hiding were still required, however, and all the same rules were still in place. As long as we stayed hidden in the closet, we could keep serving, but any disclosure of our sexual orientation would still result in being charged with "homosexual conduct" under the Uniform Code of Military Justice (UCMJ). Anyone found guilty would be immediately discharged from active duty, just like always.

When DADT first went into effect, I was relieved that I could no longer be witch-hunted, asked questions about my sexuality on security clearance documents, or be directly asked about those *MY LESBIAN BUDDY* letters Jake was sending to my command. But I was also dismayed that there was open acknowledgment from the very top of our government that gays were honorably serving our country, and yet we were still being prohibited from doing so openly. DADT continued to perpetuate harm. Our forced silence meant that we couldn't speak out against homophobic comments or abuse within our ranks, and it also created deeper internalized homophobia within ourselves, since DADT's underlying message was, *We are aware that you're serving. As long as you aren't your honest self, you can continue to serve—and even die for—your country. But if we do see (or hear) you, we will still prosecute you to the fullest.*

I believe that President Clinton genuinely wanted to end the ban; I also know that he wanted the gay vote. DADT gave outsiders the impression of progress, a little fluff to keep Clinton's promise and silence the critics. But it didn't solve much, as a different kind of witch-hunting took the NCIS investigations' place: far too many gay service members were still either rooted out by aggressive commanders or outed by homophobic coworkers in their commands or units post-DADT. In fact, by 2009, fifteen years after DADT was first enacted, the military had sought out and discharged close to 14,000 gays, lesbians, and bisexuals. These numbers were about a third less than the numbers that preceded DADT—this, under a policy that was intended to protect and allow us to keep serving.

DADT didn't outwardly change the world I lived and worked in. The biggest difference was an inner awareness that I was no longer under constant threat from NCIS—which, make no mistake, was an enormous relief unto itself. But I had no way of looking down the road into my future to see how this new reality would only amplify my deeply rooted internalized homophobia and constant expectation of some form of punishment for being gay.

The other area where LGBTQ+ rights were being contested in the 1990s was the beginning of the same-sex marriage debate. In 1993, the Hawaiian Supreme Court ruled (3-1) that the state could not ban same-sex marriages without "a compelling reason." However, Hawaiian voters approved a constitutional amendment to ban same-sex marriage, which gained national attention and prompted many other American states to subsequently pass acts defining marriage as a legal union between one man and one woman.

On September 21, 1996, almost four years into his term, President Clinton—the same guy who'd promised to make life better for the LGBTQ+ community—signed the Defense of Marriage Act (DOMA) into law. DOMA was the epitome of discrimination and prevented same-sex couples from receiving federal protections and benefits given to married heterosexual couples. It also allowed states to refuse to recognize same-sex marriage certificates from other states and would play a huge role in limiting the rights of the LGBTQ+ community for decades to come.

Between DADT and DOMA, Clinton failed the LGBTQ+ community. Even as he espoused his belief in equality for all, he signed policies in favor of discrimination.

Equality doesn't work unless it truly is equal. DADT especially had a huge impact on the lives of what I would guess to be hundreds of thousands of gay service members, mine included. Tens of thousands of those service members continue to pay the price for a policy and a government that betrayed and even persecuted them after they sacrificed for their country.

Chapter 29

PIECES FALLING INTO PLACE

At the end of the year, I am selected as the 1994 Command Senior Sailor of the Year, awarded annually to one E-6. Already chosen as the Sailor of the Quarter earlier in the year and ranked #1 among the forty first class petty officers in the squadron, I am thrilled to receive the following comment from my commanding officer on my performance evaluation: "The finest first class petty officer I have seen in eighteen years of service."

I'll be leaving in November for my final six-month deployment with VP-1 to Misawa, Japan, so my younger brother, Paul, has moved to Hawaii to be my *take care of all the shit at home* person. Now twenty-three years old—which is wild, since he was twelve when I joined the Navy—Paul is a slim five foot ten with thick, long blond ponytailed hair and a deep golden tan. In flip-flops and board shorts, he looks like he could have been born on the islands. It's a huge relief to know he'll take care my Hawaii life while I'm away.

After saying my goodbyes to Paul and 6-Pac, I climb onboard my next chartered flight from hell. Once I'm seated, I focus on what lies ahead.

I will soon be calling my detailer for orders. I'm hoping to reunite with Sue. She called me in July from some faraway port and first shared the awesome news that she'd been selected to chief petty officer. After a round of *woo-hoos* and *oh my God, Q*s, she calmly said, "One more thing, K. Before we get cut off, I got new orders. I'm being sent to an Admiral's Staff in San Diego."

Relief coursed through me and I exhaled. Our separation might finally be coming to an end. "Cool, no worries, babe!" I said. "I'll find a job in San Diego."

There's no question in my mind that I can also obtain orders to San Diego, as there's an enormous Navy presence there. Even if it means leaving Hawaii, the place I love so much, I'm all in. Sue has sacrificed enough.

The airplane is quiet and most of my shipmates are now asleep as I reflect on this last year. YN2 Manelli is the only yeoman from the previous trio who remains in the squadron; we have three new yeomen, YN2 Kimbrough, YN3 Tenley, and YNSN Lopez. YN2 Kimbrough is a bubbly and assertive Filipino American superstar, a single parent who skillfully handles her personal life and is hungry to move up the ranks. YN3 Tenley, a petite blond sailor, is professional, observant, and always smiling. She has latched onto YN2 Kimbrough, as has YNSN Lopez, a sweet, quiet, and very talented young Hispanic sailor. The three of them are joined at the hip, and though they take care of business and seem serious about learning the ropes from YN2 Manelli, they are also constantly glancing at each other and giggling at jokes I am not privy to.

What a roller-coaster ride it's been lately—the highs and lows of my personal and professional life. The Navy now owns a huge part of my heart, and I get tremendous satisfaction watching my sailors thrive. My initial challenges as a leader taught me many things, but mostly what I believe are the top keys to good leadership: always being there for my sailors, professionally and personally; training and helping them advance to their next level; and putting their needs above the mission when necessary. The last one is not something the Navy would have me do, but it's my rebel way, a secret I'm good with. The Navy will always survive, but it won't thrive unless sailors feel valued, respected, and cared for. They come first, no matter what. Once I fully grasped that, everything fell into place.

No one's leadership has impacted my growth like H's has, and I still have a tremendous amount of respect for him as my command master chief. He remains a constant presence in my work life and throughout the command, where his deep belly laugh can be heard bouncing off the high walls inside the hangar.

Nothing has changed and everything has changed since the day of his confession. A heaviness now resides between us; our old levity now exists only somewhere in the past. My military bearing comes in handy as I deflect, engage my humor, work hard, and hustle, and he continues to treat me as his protégé. I keep pressing forward, pretending our conversation last year never happened, knowing that every job in the Navy has a termination date and this will eventually pass. But until that day, I have one more deployment with the squadron and I will also get my first shot at making chief petty officer.

I place my headphones over my ears, close my eyes, and listen to my new favorite CD, Heather Nova's *Oyster*, hoping to get any amount of sleep for the remainder of the flight.

I'm reviewing and editing awards at my desk in March when H pokes his shiny bald head in the door. My office in Japan is amazingly large: an open, bright room that is perfect for me and my team. White linoleum floors, a half dozen spotless white desks, rectangular fluorescent lighting, and white bookshelves stocked with nicely organized manuals lining the back of the office. My desk is just in front of the bookshelves, where it's easy to stay out of the way, avoid distraction from customers, and supervise the office. My team doesn't see H, as they are hard at work, smiling and giggling amongst themselves, a daily scene that is more fulfilling to observe than they will ever know.

"YN1," he bellows, "your presence is requested in the XO's office ASAP." He has a stern look on his face.

My sailors jump and then turn to me with large, worried eyes—a silent, *Oh shit, YN1.*

I close the award folder, grab my notebook, and confidently smile at them as I stride through the office, letting them know I'll be just fine.

A few doors down the hallway I reach the XO's office, a spacious room with beige carpet and a large mahogany desk that sits catty-corner to the door. "Yes, sir!" I say to the XO as I stop a few feet inside his doorway.

He leans against the front of his desk, H a few feet to his right, both with arms crossed and brooding looks. An exceptionally tall, thin man with thinning sandy-brown hair, my XO is a badass pilot whom I enjoy tremendously. He is hardworking, polite, generous, professional, and has a wicked sense of humor. He's going to be a great commanding officer when he assumes that title later this year.

He maintains his ominous look, which is now starting to freak me out a bit—then shifts his eyes toward H, and they both relax and smile. He turns and grabs a sheet of paper from his desk and holds it up. "Chief's exam results are in, YN1," he says. "You made the cut!"

"I did!?" I exclaim. "Oh man, that's awesome, sir!"

I took the 175-question Navy-wide chief's exam in January, and the paper he's holding shows that I passed. This means my record will be reviewed by the 1995 Chief Petty Officer Selection Board; I've made it to the second phase. It's the first time I've been eligible, and I am aware that I'm competing against thousands of yeomen Navy-wide, many of whom are far senior to me, so I'm not holding my breath—but I sure as shit am crossing my fingers.

"One step down," my XO says, a sparkle in his eyes. "Good job, YN1. Hope to see your name on the final list in July. Now quit screwing around and get your ass back to work. We're off to inform the others on this list."

He and H grab their covers and high-five me on their way out.

One month later, I sit on my bed in the barracks one evening and make that long-awaited phone call to my detailer in DC.

I don't beat around the bush once I have her on the phone: "Hey, Chief, do you have anything in San Diego?"

I'm expecting her to tell me she has several available assignments in San Diego, but instead she responds, "Actually, I have some great news, YN1. I'd like you to come to Washington, DC, and screen to take my job. I've reviewed your record and think you'd be a great detailer."

My heart catches and my throat tightens. A detailer? There's no way in hell I can go to DC. "Um, thanks, Chief—I appreciate that—but I really need to go to San Diego," I say meekly.

She sounds shocked *and* offended as she clips back, "You *do know* that you might not have a choice, right, YN1?"

Becoming a detailer is an honor that very few sailors get screened or selected for; it's an amazing job that would probably shoot me through the roof with my career. But it won't put me back with Sue, which is my priority. Already schooled in the fact that I can't have it all, I am choosing my relationship.

It's a déjà vu moment; I feel like I'm right back in front of Chief Roll on the *Frank Cable* or the cheng on the *Canopus*. I try my best to smooth it over and get my way. "I understand, Chief, and am grateful that you would even consider me. But I really need to get to San Diego. I'm asking you to please choose someone else for your position."

She loudly exhales, and the phone goes silent for a few moments. Then her tone softens. "Fine, YN1. Let me see what I have."

After a few rounds of push and pull, I negotiate orders to SEAL Team Five, located at the Naval Amphibious Base Coronado. In San Diego. After three and a half long years, I will finally be reunited with my love—but not before taking a six-month detour to Whidbey Island, Washington, as the squadron was notified by the chief of naval operations that we are making a homeport change. We are to start the process immediately, and get the entire squadron to Whidbey Island by no later than mid-July.

One month later, I hop on my final charter flight from hell from Japan back to Hawaii. YN2 Manelli will not be joining us for the homeport change—her time in the squadron is up—so my badass yeomen trio will pack up their household goods and head to Washington first to establish our office. Although I transfer in December and could technically save the government money with the one move to San Diego, I am considered "essential personnel," so I will make two moves, spending the next six months with the squadron in Whidbey Island before finally making my way to Sue.

From the moment I arrived on Oahu six years ago and took my first inhale, I knew that this place was heaven. Though I can't wait to reunite with Sue, I'm heartbroken to leave this island that has changed my life and blessed me in so many ways: falling in love, getting sober, making wonderful friends, working for the best the Navy has to offer, becoming a solid sailor, and discovering the true meaning of leadership. Oh, and finding my way—the way that works best for me.

My twin-size waterbed and my couch, both reminders of the highs and the lows I encountered on this island, are carried out by two kind Hawaiian men. They effortlessly load them into a large white truck with wooden boards lining its sides and throw "hang loose" shaka signs out of their windows as they drive off. My truck has also been sold and Paul left a few days ago, returning to Arizona with 6-Pac. He'll care for him until I travel south to San Diego at the end of the year. My few remaining household items were packed out a few days ago and I am standing in my empty living room in Makakilo, grateful for the town that provided me refuge when I needed it. I lock up, place the key under the mat, and drive my rental car onto the H-1 east toward Waikiki, where I will spend two days in a hotel before my official departure.

My hotel phone rings later that afternoon, and I answer it to hear a familiar, deep, confident voice say, "Hey, Chief! Why aren't you here yet?"

"Chief?" I'm stunned. "Master Chief, don't mess with me."

"I'm not messing with you . . . Chief!"

I freak out. "No shit, Master Chief? It's for real!?"

"It is, Chief. It's for real." I feel his smile from across the ocean. Then he quickly shifts back to his usual gruff self. "Now quit fucking around and get your ass to the squadron ASAP. You've got some catching up to do, Chief!"

G-Bob laughs in the background as H hangs up.

I sit on my bed, totally beside myself. I can't even put what I'm feeling into words. Hawaii has just given me my final gift:

making chief. It's huge, but it isn't the biggest gift I've received here; sobriety and getting my life back are. Those two things will always ride the pinnacle of that list.

But making chief is pretty damn close.

After calling and informing an elated Sue, I call Linda.

"L, I made chief!"

Her excitement is *so* Linda. "Chief Kumquat! I knew you could do it!"

Man, I'm going to miss her. While I was in Japan, she was diagnosed with multiple sclerosis, news that has devastated her and her family and everyone who loves her—and that's a long list. She can't drive anymore and will probably be in a wheelchair in the next few years. Life has thrown a lot at this special woman, and I am heartbroken for her.

"Thanks, L. I could never have done any of this without you. I love you. Hey, move to San Diego with me." That thought makes me grin.

"Don't make me cry, you little Kumquat! And I love you too." She hangs up just as her voice starts to break.

The following evening, I have one final dinner at a fancy restaurant with a huge aquarium in its middle in downtown Waikiki with my buds: Linda, the Kevins, and a few other great friends who I met in recovery. Sitting at the head of a long table, I feel so loved as they toast me with soft drinks and bubble water.

"To Chief Kumquat!" Linda calls out. She gives me a tender look. "Really gonna miss you, K."

I'll never be able to repay how this crew helped me reclaim my life. There really aren't words that can do it justice. I fight back tears and a lump lands in my throat as I stand and hold up my glass. "I'm gonna miss you all too. Thanks for helping me get my life back. You have no idea what you've done for me. I love you and will be back someday." We tap our glasses together and I try to smile, though all I want to do is cry.

We walk a few blocks to the beach after dinner because Linda has a lei that she is adamant about putting in the waters of Waikiki, even though walking is harder for her these days. ("I don't give a shit how late it is," she said when I tried to talk her out of it. "We're going to the damn beach because I said so!")

When we make it to the shore, she tears up. "I can't believe you're leaving, you little shit. This lei will send you off with the spirit of aloha. It will also bring you home to us someday. I love you, and I will miss you a lot." She walks to the water's edge and tosses the lei in.

Full of so much of everything in this moment—profound love and deep sorrow—I am aware that I'm leaving not only these amazing souls but also an island that owns my heart. I watch the lei gently float out into the surf and say a little prayer that it really will bring me home again someday.

Chapter 30

BIRTH OF A CHIEF

The windshield wipers on my new (used) 1994 hunter-green Jeep Grand Cherokee work overtime as I drive up Interstate 5, elated to be heading to Whidbey Island to begin chief selectee training. The CD disk changer under my back seat shuffles through my favorite music and I sing along to every tune, overjoyed and thinking of what's ahead—the day that I'll put on khakis and then transfer to be reunited with my love.

Hawaiian sunshine and rainbows noticeably in my past, I've driven north for hours through steady rainfall with no end in sight. Deep green trees line both sides of the interstate, a stunning change of scenery. I'm excited to live in the magnificent Pacific Northwest and experience a part of the country I've never even visited.

An hour north of Seattle I exit the freeway at Burlington, cruise over Deception Pass, and head down the scenic, narrow, winding road that leads into Whidbey Island. My trip is complete when I arrive at Amy's—A-Bob's—house in Oak Harbor, a small town on Whidbey Island. Amy remains one of my closest friends in the squadron and is welcoming me into her home until my transfer to San Diego in December.

I pull into her gravel driveway and park next to her new 1996 hunter-green Jeep Grand Cherokee. She walks from her house wearing a baggy white T-shirt, jeans, and flip-flops, a lit cigarette in her hand. We give each other a hug and laugh—"Are you kidding me? We have the same car?"

Amy's home is beautiful, a two-story, cabin-style cedar house that she has been renting out for the past few years, patiently waiting for the day she could return. Her husband is also in the Navy and will be on Oahu another year before rejoining her and their sweet son, a blond-haired, blue-eyed toddler named Jason who is currently standing next to Amy and tugging on her pant leg.

She squats and says, "Jason, this is my friend Karen."

His cheeks turn bright pink, and he smushes his face into her leg.

"It's nice to meet you, Jason," I say.

He's shy right now, but soon Jason and I will become headbanging, drive-all-over-Whidbey-Island, Smashing Pumpkins rocker buds, something that will give me a great deal of joy.

I haven't even finished unpacking my Jeep when H and G-Bob pull into the driveway, as if they have a secret GPS on me.

"Chief!" they yell as they exit their car. "Where the hell have you been!?"

My mouth stays shut. Chief's initiation season, sort of a second boot camp for chief selects, has already commenced and I am well behind in the "festivities." I'm afraid that anything I say will be used against me in the coming months, and I'm still trying to not be a dummy.

They each shake my hand and give me hugs.

"Don't get used to this," H says. "This is the last time we'll be nice to you for the next two months."

G-Bob's eyebrows raise and he nods his head in agreement. It's great to see how pleased they are for me, and the realization that I've made chief petty officer sinks in a little bit more.

H then reaches into his pocket and pulls out a gold anchor chief's pendant. His eyes sparkle and his face beams as he hands it to me. "This is for you, Chief."

"Holy shit," I exclaim, "thanks, Master Chief! This is beautiful!"

Amy watches from a few feet away with a somber smile, saying nothing. She wasn't selected for chief this year, and I imagine this moment is bittersweet.

I turn to her. "Man, I wish you made it too, A-Bob."

"Don't you worry, K-Bob, I'll get there," she says. "You just have fun. You deserve it."

I arrive at work the following morning, head topside to check in with my team, and then go to the squadron training room, a large, open room where my fellow selectees are already standing at attention in front of a dozen squadron chiefs sitting on gray padded chairs. All eyes are on me as I enter the hushed room and one of the chiefs slowly mutters, "Well, well, well . . . look who the cat dragged in."

I bite my tongue and resist indulging in my famous eye roll as I join my peers. I know the chiefs are already primed to make me pay for missing the last few weeks of training while I closed out the squadron in Hawaii. It's going to be a rough ride.

Besides me, three of my peers were selected to chief, and the only thing not unusual about this moment is that I am the only female. Actually, I am one of two females out of ninety-six chief-selectees on the entire air base, which means I am under a particular kind of scrutiny—especially from some relentless female chiefs here on the base. From now until September 15, the day I will officially start wearing khakis, this training will be many things: challenging, fun, humbling, crazy, stupid, inspiring, humiliating, but also *really* special. I would endure an entire year of it if that's what I had to do in order to put on that uniform.

Until that special day, I—along with every other chief select Navy-wide—will carry a charge book, a conspicuously large, beautiful briefcase-like maple wood box with a precise nautical theme made up by secret chief laws, with me everywhere I go, letting every chief on base know that I am fair game. Stored within my charge book is all of my guidance and, more importantly, a signature page for each chief, senior chief, and master chief on the base. On these pages, they will write down their "charge"—what they expect of me as a chief petty officer—and how much the judge should charge, or fine, me on the day of initiation (that part has me a little worried).

Before I arrived in Whidbey Island, my three amazing fellow selectees made all our charge books, including mine, to the same specifications. The cover of mine has a gold plate that reads *YNC(AW) Karen Marie Solt*, under which is stamped *15 September 1995*. Under that plate my squadron patch, *PATRON ONE Screaming Eagles*, is glued to the wood. Pewter yeoman quills and air warfare wings are pressed into the wood under the squadron patch and a large chief's anchor engraved on a gold metal plate is centered at the bottom. The handle is a twisted beige nautical rope secured with brass fasteners, and a small brass lock hangs under the handle. One of my goals is to get as many signatures as I can, especially from all my squadron chiefs. The other is not to lose my charge book, as thievery and trickery are both real and the repercussions for falling prey to either one are severe.

My lessons are crucial and start with a few rules of the chief petty officer: Rule #1: The chief is always right. Rule #2: In the unlikely event that a subordinate is correct, refer to Rule #1. Rule #3: The chief does not sleep; the chief rests. Rule #4: The chief is never late; the chief is detained elsewhere. Rule #5: The chief never leaves work; the chief's presence is required elsewhere. Rule #6: The chief never reads the paper in her office; the chief studies. Rule #7: The chief never curses or swears at a subordinate; the chief educates. And Rule #8: Whoever should enter the chief's office with an idea of their own, shall depart with the chief's ideas. These I memorize and put into place immediately.

As the CMC, H is tasked with ensuring my fellow selectees and I are well trained and ready to be great chiefs. He oversees the squadron chiefs who sponsor each of us, and he assigns me the only female gay aviation chief in the squadron, a petite but larger-than-life Hispanic woman. Proudly from the Bronx, she has short, curly dark brown hair and deep brown eyes that shine behind her oval, tinted wire framed glasses. She is a watchful mama bear and constantly calls me down to her office in Maintenance—"Slug [my current affectionate nickname], get down here ASAP!"

I dash down, and when I enter her office she holds up her coffee cup and says with zero eye contact, "One cream, two sugars." She forever shakes her head at me and my shenanigans, especially the day I steal her brown shoes while she's working out and wear them around the hangar for an hour in my dungarees—which is fun and makes my shipmates laugh, but also leads to some not-so-fun push-ups and more runs to the coffee pot.

Amidst all the antics, there is one thing that casts a small cloud over the festivities. Once I am honored as a chief, I will wear my gold anchors on the collar points of my khaki uniform, and it is customary to ask important people—usually close friends, family, or mentors—to pin them at the ceremony.

A few days after I arrived in Whidbey Island, I went to H's office. He sat at his desk on a phone call but motioned me inside.

I stood, holding my heavy charge book, and waited.

He eventually hung up. "What the hell do you want, Slug?" he snapped, clearly struggling to keep a straight face.

I ignored his tone and asked my question: "Master Chief, would you do me the honor of pinning one of my anchors?" I wanted him to pin one and my parents, who would be coming from Arizona, to pin the other.

His face dropped and he looked down, shaking his head. "There's nothing that would make me happier, YN1. But I'm sorry. I just can't. I hope you understand."

"Oh. Sure. Yeah, no problem, Master Chief." Confused, I disappointedly left his office.

After training that day, I asked G-Bob about it and he told me that H's wife still believed we'd had an affair. "He comes to work all day while she sleeps and then he's up all night arguing with her," he said. "It's been like this since Diego Garcia, and he's worn out."

"Wow, I had no idea, G-Bob," I say, feeling heartbroken over the situation. "I can't believe it's been two years and this is still happening. I hope it gets better for him after I transfer."

H had been nothing but professional with me for the past few years, but it sounded like that hadn't helped things at home. I now understood why he couldn't pin one of my anchors: it would only make things worse for him.

At 0400 on September 15, 1995, I arrive in my designated costume as the Red Power Ranger at Naval Air Station Whidbey Island Chief's Mess, a large building with many rooms, an open dining hall, and one of the last active private Chief's Messes in the Navy.

On this day the first half of the chief selects, forty-eight of us, will endure a full day of time-honored initiation proceedings. This will be a day of trial, tests, and rewards, and my fellow selectees and I will rely on each other to transition into our khaki uniform together, into one of the biggest fraternities the military has to offer. This is a day I've been preparing for my entire life.

I'd love to tell you what happens, but I can't. Sorry, it's tradition. These are secrets that the chief petty officer community keeps guarded with tight lips. But eleven hours later, at 1500, I stand facing hundreds of chiefs who all stand, cheer, and applaud boisterously.

I'm exhausted and now known as "Special Case"—guess I'm still a dummy sometimes. I was the last person to go through trial that day, and my red Power Ranger costume is now more of a reddish–dark brown Power Ranger costume, but initiation is over and I have been accepted into the Chief's Mess.

I look to my left at H, my badass gay sponsor, and the rest of my squadron chiefs, who are all beaming and clapping, and tremendous relief and gratitude washes over me. I couldn't have done any of this without their guidance and support. Seeing their happy faces makes my achievement that much sweeter.

An hour later, I join my fellow selectees, already standing in formation for the pinning ceremony, and fall into ranks in height order in the front row in my fresh khakis. I am elated and surprised to see my smiley and supportive yeoman trio, YN2 Kimbrough, YN3 Tenley, and YNSN Lopez, decked out in their Dress Whites and sitting with my parents and Paul.

The ceremony begins. My sponsor walks over with a full grin on her face, places my new dress khaki cover on my head, and shakes my hand. My parents pin my anchors on my collar points, my dad on my left and my mom on my right, before giving me hugs.

I walk to the edge of a long red carpet, edged on each side by three "bullets"—three-foot wooden painted posts that resemble bullets—connected by rope. In front of both, three chief petty officers stand spaced between the bullets. Two bells are rung on the ship's bell, and I walk forward as I am "piped aboard" (the boatswain's mate blows his whistle and another chief announces, "Chief petty officer, arriving!").

Holding a salute, I walk down the red carpet past that line of six chiefs, who all stand at attention and salute back. At the end of the carpet, I stop and hold my salute until the boatswain's mate ends his piping. Then I drop my salute, as do they, and I fall back into my place in formation.

After my fellow selectees are back in ranks, a master chief stands at the podium and announces, "All chiefs rise for the reading of the Chief Petty Officer Creed."

All chiefs, active and retired, rise and stand at attention. The master chief reads the creed in a solemn tone. When he finishes, he nods and steps off the podium—and I am now officially a chief petty officer. The proudest achievement of my life.

After the ceremony, I receive hugs and shake hand after hand. I'm stoked to share this occasion with my family and my sailors—the only junior sailors who came to the ceremony, which only confirms for me how amazing they are and how blessed I am to work with them.

H joins us and meets my parents and brother, and we take photos together.

"It's a pleasure to meet you all," he tells my parents. "Your daughter is simply the best I've ever known."

His entry in my charge book reads simply, "K-Bob, you done good."

Chapter 31

WORLDS COLLIDE

It's Sunday evening, my parents and Paul have just departed, and I'm in my room preparing my uniform for work in the morning. I depress the button on the starch can and spray a line of starch down the center of the back of my new khaki shirt, then run the scorching hot iron up the freshly starched area, meticulously creating a centerline military crease. Pressing my uniform is second nature by now, but these are khakis and I'm pinching myself. Dungarees now a part of my past, I will wear this uniform for the rest of my career.

The second line of starch evaporates with a sizzle as I slowly inch my way from the shoulder line to the shirttail on the first lateral military crease. I reflect on this moment. It's mind-blowing when I think about what I've overcome to get here, especially when I take stock of my entire journey.

My love for the Navy far surpasses anything I could have ever imagined. My rise in rank—three short years after hitting an addiction bottom that forever changed me—is validating. Getting sober gave me a new life and the ability to be the person I'm meant to be. *But this?* I never expected my life to change so drastically—and so quickly—when I went to that first meeting. These last three years have been a whirlwind.

I press the final military crease into the back of my shirt and think back to who I was twelve years ago: a defiant, reckless, alcoholic teenager whose only ambition was to find her next party; a misfit who rolled her eyes at the Navy recruiter—a chief—who sat across from me in his sharp khaki uniform, remained professional, and ignored my shitty attitude. Could he see then that I had the potential to be a chief someday? I have to believe the answer to that question is a firm *hell no.*

Three last sprays of starch rendered, I press creases into my sleeves and collar, then place my shirt on a cedar hanger on the edge of my open closet door.

I lay my slacks on the ironing board and firmly inch the hot iron down the center of the pant legs, making sure to avoid dreaded "railroad tracks." Tomorrow morning I'll wear the same uniform my recruiter wore the day I turned my nose up at the thought of joining the US Navy. My only commitment back then was to my own selfish agenda. I knew nothing about the dedication and determination it would take to become a chief petty officer, to put on this uniform that I have come to respect so much.

My slacks complete, I drape them over another cedar hanger next to my shirt, fold the ironing board, and place it and the starch back in the closet.

I gather my ribbons and insignias from the top of my dresser, hold them in the palm of my hand, and think back to the naive, lost young sailor I started out as. I endured so much to get here—being completely overwhelmed in boot camp; chipping away rust and paint; suffering sexual harassment and a sexual assault that almost did me in, one that I have never spoken about since first reporting it; realizing that I'm gay, and then learning how to adapt in a Navy that hunted sailors like me; moving mountains to be with my first love and then going through a painful breakup; getting into bar fights and engaging in reckless alcoholic behavior; finding love again and then hiding that love within a system that condemns it as a crime; hitting bottom and getting sober. And now becoming a new chief petty officer, excelling in a profession that I love while separated from a partner I also love and miss tremendously.

I lay my shirt on my bed and pin my ribbons and insignias in their proper locations—gold anchors with silver USN letters on my collar points; four rows of colorful ribbons, topped with my green-and-white Navy and Marine Corps Commendation Medal and green-and-orange Navy and Marine Corps Achievement Medal with two gold stars, over my left shirt pocket; wings centered above my ribbons; and my gold name tag above my right shirt pocket. I double-check the exact placement of each insignia and wonder if the rewards have been worth the price. Even now, full of pride at having made chief, I don't know the answer to that question.

What I do know is this: my two realities—the proud sailor who loves the Navy, my sailors, and the people I work with; and the lesbian who loves my partner, my lifestyle, and my truth—do not coexist. My ability to land on my feet has served me well for the last eleven and a half years, but the conflict between these two worlds has taken a huge toll, one that I can't fully understand yet. I have sacrificed much of who I am to wear this uniform.

I hang my shirt back on the closet door and then stand back and gaze at it. The elation that consumed me two months ago when H told me I'd been selected as a chief has not dissipated one bit. Tomorrow morning I will go to work as "the chief" for the first time in my career; in less than three months, I will transfer from VP-1 and drive down to San Diego to report to SEAL Team Five and reunite with my love, the concept of which remains an inconceivable and far-off dream.

Will I then have it all? Will my two halves then make me whole?

I pray that they will, because if they don't, I have no idea where I'll turn from here.

I dim my lights as I approach the front gate sentry on my way to the VP hangar. A surge of pride rushes through me as I hand him my new ID card.

"Good morning, Chief!" he says. The tone of respect he uses will take time getting used to. But hearing the word "chief" feels just right.

"Good morning!" I say with a grin.

He quickly glances at both sides of my ID before handing it back, then steps back and waves me through. I proceed onto the Naval Air Station and make my way to my new CPO parking space, just in front of the huge sliding doors that open into the VP hangar.

Rain starts falling, so I quickly put on my khaki garrison cover, grab my black canvas briefcase, and hurry through the open sliding doors.

As I enter the enormous hangar, I'm bombarded with beaming smiles and greetings from shipmates I have worked with for the past three years. "Good morning, Chief!" echoes from all angles. My heart soars as I soak in their genuine happiness for me.

"Good morning," I respond over and over, trying my damnedest to stifle some of my elation and remain professional but knowing I'm absolutely gushing.

After a joy-filled celebration in my office with my sailors, H asks me to join him in his office. Moments later I stand across from him, speechless, holding a small red box in my hand that contains the master chief anchors he was pinned with years ago.

"Those were mine, the *nine* anchors that I was pinned with," he says. "They are now yours. I want you to have them for the day you make master chief."

My mind is blown. Every step that I have taken for the last few years was taken with the intention of getting me here, walking into my squadron as a new chief petty officer. By putting his coveted nine anchors in my hand, H is already putting his faith in me that I will far exceed that goal.

I stand tall and meet his kind gaze. "Wow, H, this is incredibly gracious of you. I promise I'll wear them proudly someday."

He smiles and nods. "You're welcome, Karen. I have no doubt you'll get there in no time." Then his eyebrows crease, his demeanor shifts, and he becomes serious. "Um"—he hesitates—"there's one other reason I needed to speak with you."

A sinking feeling lands in my gut. "Sure, what's up, H?" I ask cautiously.

"I'm leaving my marriage and am getting a divorce." He glances away and takes a few breaths before bringing his eyes back to mine. His voice softens, and a tenderness and desperation I've never before heard from him enters his tone. "And I want to be with you. I'm in love with you, Karen. As soon as I retire, we can be together. Will you be with me?"

Shit.

H's words don't shock me this time—they just frustrate and dismay me. I'm horrified that, again, I didn't see this coming. Just three days ago, I stood in front of hundreds of chief petty officers and was welcomed into the Chief's Mess, and I see now that H and I misread each other in that moment. Where I saw pride and joy, he was expressing love and affection, and where he saw love and affection, I was expressing pride and joy. He now wants me to tell him that I love him, while all I want is for him to tell me how proud he is of me.

It's as if I've been struck in the chest; the air is forced from

my lungs, and a crushing sadness overcomes me. The desperation and pain on H's face reminds me of a time not so long ago
when I wasn't sure I was going to get through the next moment
and Linda put her arms around me and held me until I could
breathe again and knew that I was going to be okay. But I can't
do that with H. He's my mentor. He's my boss. And he has feelings for me.

The toughest, strongest, kindest man I know is three feet in
front of me, broken and lost, searching for hope, and the awareness that I can't help him—that I'm in fact only going to pile
more pain onto him—is almost more than I can bear.

My gut tells me there's only one way out. This time I have
to take a leap and choose me. I'm not in love with H—never
have been and never will be—and for him to understand that, he
needs to hear my truth. The truth of my secret half, the beautiful
hidden half that makes me whole. But also the truth that could
end my career here and now.

I fill my lungs with one more deep breath and speak words
that I didn't prepare myself to speak. "H, there is something I
need to tell you," I begin. "I'm so sorry, but I can't be with you."

My two worlds are about to collide.

He exhales slowly as his eyes drop and a wave of disbelief
flashes across his face. He then attempts to stand tall and engage
his military bearing—which is when I realize that military bearing isn't a superpower after all. It's a thief. It serves its purpose
during combat, forcing troops to disregard their fight-or-flight
responses and keep pressing forward. But it is harmful in relationships, where vulnerability is invaluable. It robs you of feeling
and the courage to express crucial emotions. And all humans
have feelings, even Joe Navy.

My instincts implore me to protect myself and find another
way, but I'm already committed. No more déjà vu. Not this time.

"H . . . I'm gay. I'm in a relationship and have been with my partner for five years."

His eyes widen and his mouth drops open. I press on.

"I couldn't tell you because I could get kicked out for being gay, and you know I love the Navy." With each word I speak, confidence rises within me. I manage to meet his stare as my breath regulates. "I didn't tell you before because I didn't want to put you in a compromising position. But this is the truth. I had no idea you still cared for me in that way. You are so special to me. But I'm not in love with you, H, and I can't ever be with you."

He doesn't move. He glares at me for a moment, then shifts his stunned gaze beyond me, as if he can't bear to look at me.

I'm a new chief who wants to protect myself, but I care so much about this man, and he is so lost that I also want to protect him. I want to tell him that he can get through this—that he can get through *anything*. I want to tell him that life sometimes feels like pure hell, but day by day it gets better; that he'll laugh again; that he'll find a way to land on his feet. Because I know all of that to be true.

Before the squadron left Hawaii, H requested a waiver from the Navy to go beyond his thirty-year maximum so he could finish his tour in Whidbey Island and then be reassigned back in Hawaii to retire. The Navy denied his request, which I believe was his biggest heartbreak of all. That was strike one.

After two long years, he's hit a breaking point and is ending his marriage. Strike two.

And now I just threw the final curveball that he never saw coming. It's not just that he's in love with me. He also thought I was in love with him.

I do love him, of course. I absolutely cherish him. But I am not *in love* with him. And with my disclosure that I'm gay, he now knows that not only is there no hope for that to change but he was also wrong about me all along.

I am strike three.

He's obviously been holding on since his first two strikes, waiting for me to put on khakis so that he could again tell me how he feels. He needed something, or someone, to rescue him. He thought it would be me. But it won't ever be me. I simply can't be the one to save him.

A stranger now stands before me. H struggles with his composure and vacantly stares through me. I want so badly for him to smile his kind smile and say, *It's okay, K-Bob. I understand. All good.* But he doesn't understand and it's not good. Not at all.

If only he had heard me the first time.

This is excruciating, but I don't know what else I could have done here. For the first time in my career I've told a superior that I'm gay, and now I'll have to wait for any fallout. But living like this is absolutely exhausting; I can't keep dodging and weaving and betraying myself time and again. For so long, I have felt forced to hide my truth. But not this time. This time I chose me.

His eyes connect with mine one more time, hitting me with a heart-crushing glare that contains an eerie mixture of despair and disbelief. He purses his lips and shakes his head, then drops down into his chair, where he slumps and blankly stares at the top of his desk.

I wait for a moment—shaken by his last glare, hoping he'll regroup and act like the H I've always known. But he doesn't look back up, so I turn and walk back to my desk, where I sit numbly, still clutching a small red box in my hand. H's master chief anchors. They no longer hold the same honor they did just a few short minutes ago when he reached across his desk with a proud smile on his face and handed them to me.

That was lifetimes ago.

My first day as a chief petty officer, and the elation and pride I was buzzing with only moments ago, have now been completely extinguished. I am speechless. I don't know if I've just sealed my fate. I don't know if my time wearing my new chief's uniform will be short-lived. I don't know anything, other than the fact that my sorrow and regret about what just transpired with H is overwhelming.

Chapter 32

TAKE IT ALL BACK

H left the hangar after our conversation Monday morning and hasn't returned to work since.

At 3:00 a.m. on Thursday morning, the phone rings. Wakened out of a dead sleep, I pick up and groggily say, "Hello?"

"I need everything back I ever gave you." H's deep, weary voice sounds labored.

Irritation sets in. *Christ. And you had to call in the middle of the night to tell me this?* But I only exhale and say, "Okay. And what would that be?"

"The golf club and the gold chief's anchor."

"Sure. And how would you like me to get it to you?"

"I'll meet you at the front gate at 0700."

Over the years, H has given me a few gifts. One is the anchor pendant a few months ago when I arrived on Whidbey Island. The other is a golf club he left leaning against my desk last year so that I would hopefully quit excelling as a horrible golfer (it didn't work).

And then, of course, there are the master chief anchors he handed to me just days ago.

He didn't ask me for those, and in my early morning haze, I don't even think about them. Later, I'll assume that he let me keep them because he thought of them not as a gift but as an honored tradition—not something that could be taken back.

I arrive at the gate at 0700 and wait in the security parking lot in my Jeep. A minute later, a white sedan pulls in and parks. H's wife is in the passenger seat.

I get out and stand near my Jeep, holding the golf club and the anchor.

A man with H's body shape and bald head gets out of the car. But this isn't H. This man wears civilian clothes—jeans with a center crease and a dark blue windbreaker—has a gray complexion, sunken eyes, and drooping shoulders, and walks slowly and uncertainly as he crosses the twenty feet to where I stand.

I'm dumbfounded; he looks so broken down that I want to walk toward him to save him from using one more drop of his energy. It is heartbreakingly obvious that he is not okay.

It's the beginning of the workday, and cars are driving through the gate. How many of the people inside them know us? I assume many do.

H's eyes are downcast. I so badly want him to look at me so that I can snap him out of his trance and see if he's all right—just one look to show me he's still in there, even though I can tell he isn't—but I realize the time when I could have helped him or been his friend has passed. My words on Monday were the final blow; we can't come back from that.

He reaches me, and I hand him the golf club and the pendant. I desperately want him to look up. I take a chance.

"H," I say softly, trying to catch his eye. "Are you okay?"

He doesn't lift his head, just slowly shakes it side to side.

I frantically try to think of what to ask him next—*What can I do to help you? Who can I call for you? Why don't you leave her today?*—but where H has lost his fight, his wife is just getting started. She gets out of their car and rushes toward me like she's going to drive her body right through mine.

She thinks I'm a threat; she thinks I'm trying to steal away her man.

But I am not that woman. The only thing I am is a chief who cares deeply about her mentor and friend, who wants him to be okay and is bone-weary from being in the middle of his marital drama.

As she gets closer, she starts to open her mouth, but my own rage surges and I sharply cut her off: "Nothing is going on or has ever happened between us!" I snap. "If you're not careful, you're gonna kill him!"

H exhales, slowly puts himself between us, and, with his back to me, puts his hand up and says wearily to his wife, "Just stop. Get back in the car, Maya."

He remains between us until she turns and storms furiously back to their car. After she takes a dozen steps, he follows her, the anchor and golf club hanging from his hand, without looking back or saying another word. I stand, trembling, as they get into their car and drive off, wondering how it came to this.

I sit in my Jeep for a few minutes, trying to gather myself, before driving through the gate to the squadron to park in chief's parking. Now feeling some of the same loss of spark that I just witnessed in H, I enter the hangar for what should be a normal workday, my mind a tangled mess.

"Morning, Chief!" my shipmates greet me.

I engage my military bearing and nod. "Good morning," I respond, and methodically walk topside, now on autopilot.

Halfway down the hallway, a shiny object on the ground captures my attention. Another sailor is walking toward me and bends down to pick it up. It is a crushed gold anchor. It looks like it was pounded on with a rock—or, more likely, a golf club.

"Wow—what a shame, Chief," the sailor remarks. "This looks like it was a nice anchor."

I purse my lips and nod in agreement but just keep moving. I know what it is—she crushed it.

Just keep moving.

H doesn't come to work that day or the next.

The silence feels familiar. Impending doom. That feeling in my belly. Something bad is coming. I absolutely know it. But I don't know how to stop it.

The following evening, Amy and I are at a restaurant and Jason is screaming up a storm. My worry is plaguing me.

"Something bad is going to happen, A-Bob," I try to explain. "He's either gonna kill her or she's gonna kill him." The words sound absurd as I speak them, but I know them to be true.

Amy, busy trying to calm Jason, sends a vague look in my direction but says nothing. She thinks I'm overreacting, figures it's just another marital drama that will work itself out. It wasn't so long ago that I thought the same, but after yesterday morning, not anymore.

Jason keeps screaming. He gets a free pass because he is a toddler.

My gut is also screaming, telling me this isn't going to end well.

I rack my brain for solutions and find none. I can't call H or check on him. I can't go to his leadership, as they are the XO and CO and what would I tell them? *"Hey, sir, Master Chief Halverson told me he is in love with me. I told him that I'm gay. His wife is pissed. He's extremely depressed, and I have a really strong feeling that he's in trouble. He needs help, but since I'm the problem, I can't be the one to help him. Can you please check on him?"*

Nope. I cannot do that.

All I can do is sit in this very familiar spot—helpless to act and swallowing the truth.

Chapter 33

THE UNBEARABLE
AWAKENING

The following afternoon, the house is quiet and I'm napping on Amy's brown leather couch in the middle of her cozy living room, a high ceiling over my head, an unlit fireplace facing me. My red sweatshirt, jeans, and white jogging socks are enough to keep me warm, but the tan throw blanket I've wrapped around myself creates the perfect refuge.

It's now been eight days since chief's initiation. I was already exhausted going into this week—and now, with H's drama piled on top, I am totally wiped out.

Amy and Jason are here, either upstairs in the loft that includes her entire master bedroom suite or in the kitchen, but whatever they're doing, they're not making a sound. The house is peaceful and warm and there is nowhere I would rather be than on this couch.

I hear a distant doorbell ring just as I start to drift into a heavy slumber.

Amy walks swiftly to the door and I crack my eyes open, praying it's not for me. A few deep voices carry over the expanse from the door to where I lie on the couch, and Amy opens the door wider.

Half a dozen people in khakis stand on the front porch, an indication that they are either officers or chiefs. I fully open my eyes and realize that they are both. Confusion envelops me when they enter the room with solemn faces.

I sit up.

My XO, a tall, thin, and kind Black man, leads the way. A few other senior ranking officials from my squadron—a redheaded female lieutenant and a few chief petty officers—follow. They stop in the living room between the fireplace and where I now sit on the couch. The tension is palpable as they glance at one another and nervously avoid my eyes.

My XO lets out a deep exhale, walks over, and sits on the edge of the couch. You could hear a pin drop as he turns toward me with the compassionate look of a father who wants to protect his young daughter. His eyes meet mine and then disengage while I wait and try to keep myself from falling into an abyss, knowing that this is about H and that it is very, very bad.

He shakes his head and his eyes begin to water as he tenderly puts his hand on my forearm and says, "Chief, I have some really bad news. Something terrible has happened." His voice quivers and breaks. "Master Chief Halverson died this afternoon. He took his own life."

The abyss swallows me up. My unblinking eyes remain on his, replaying his words in my mind—*Master Chief Halverson died this afternoon*—and hoping that I've misunderstood, because the H I know would never take his own life. But my XO's hand gently squeezes my forearm, and he nods his head.

I heard him correctly.

Shock overcomes me. I put my head in my hands and stare at the ground. Other than my disbelief that H took his own life, I don't have any questions. I know why it happened. *I'm leaving my marriage and am getting a divorce . . . and I want to be with you. I'm in love with you, Karen. As soon as I retire, we can be together. Will you be with me?* Other than H himself, I know better than anyone what drove him to do this. As I stare downward, my mind reels and my soul wails, but nothing comes out. Just silence, and my heart bursting through my chest in a million exploding pieces.

I raise my head and see the others standing in front of me, each holding on to their last ounce of military bearing and struggling to keep it together. Pain fills the room; many of us just lost our hero, but all of us lost our brother. Their anguish is too much to absorb, as it connects me to my own broken heart and the horrible realization that he is really, irrevocably, gone. I force myself to disconnect and put my head down again.

They keep their concerned eyes on me, waiting for my next move—a level of attention that is simply more than I can endure. I'm being treated like a wife they are making a casualty call to— this is exactly like that knock on the door by service members in uniform, the call that every spouse dreads.

But I am not his wife. I am not even his girlfriend.

This is a total, never-ending nightmare.

Amy is grief-stricken, her eyes wide and face frozen in complete shock. She will tell me later that she is remembering my words the night before: *Something bad is going to happen . . .*

My mind is scattered, and I don't know what to say or do. What I really want is to get up from this fucking couch and run and never look back. There isn't any action I can take to fix this, and it feels like they're waiting for me to say, "I'll be okay. Thanks for telling me." But I'm not okay, because *Master Chief Halverson died this afternoon.* My mentor is gone.

Tears fall from my chin, reminding me that I'm not in a

dream—that he's dead and I did nothing to stop it, even though I knew that he was in trouble.

As I relive a moment I wish I could take back—*I'm so sorry . . . I'm gay . . . You are so special to me . . . But I'm not in love with you, H, and I can't ever be with you*—I press my lips together to avoid saying, "This is all my fault."

My belly knew all along. I felt deep down that something bad was going to happen, but I didn't know how to stop it. My telling him that I'm gay was his final straw. He was alone and had been pushed too far and I wasn't there to catch him. No one was there to catch him. This is all my fault.

None of my thoughts can be spoken out loud. His reputation is on the line—*I'm in love with you, Karen.* My career is on the line—*I'm gay.* I have to protect both, swallow my thoughts, and keep my wits, despite the fact that everything around me has just shattered.

My XO gently squeezes my arm again and says in a hushed tone, "Chief, I know this is incredibly hard. He was amazing and we all loved him. Is there anything I can do for you? Anything any of us can do for you?"

I shake my head, keep my eyes on the ground, and force out the first words I've said aloud since they entered the room. "No, sir," I say, my voice quivering. "Thanks for coming to tell me."

One of my squadronmates—an extremely sharp chief with perfect posture and blond hair cut high and tight—stands at the front of the group in full military bearing, watching over me like only a loving brother can. This is Aaron, one of my closest friends.

"Aaron," I say, "will you stay for a while?"

He nods. "Of course I will."

The XO gets up, as do I, and he and some of the others give me a hug and then leave.

I'm crawling out of my skin. "I have to walk," I tell Aaron. Then I turn to Amy. "Can I have a cigarette?"

She knows I quit smoking five years ago, but she just nods and hands one over.

She stays home with Jason while Aaron and I walk up and down her street, back and forth. I desperately want to get in my Jeep and speed away, never to return. I light the cigarette, but it tastes like shit and doesn't help, so after three drags I toss it. No drinking, no smoking, no drugging. No escaping.

The only words I can manage I keep repeating: "It's all my fault . . . It's all my fault."

Aaron keeps responding, "It's not your fault, Karen." But he doesn't know everything. No one does. *I'm gay . . . I'm not in love with you.* I feel responsible for *all* of it.

I eventually wear myself out. Aaron gives me a hug and leaves, and Amy and I sit on the couch and cry together. There aren't any words and there isn't any way to reverse this one. So we sit there until we can't sit there any longer, and then we both go to our rooms.

I sit on my bed and call Sue. "H died today," I say, and start to sob.

"What!? Oh my God, K. What happened?"

"He killed himself. I can't talk about it," I say, choking on my tears. "I just needed to hear your voice."

"I'm so sorry, K. I love you. Call me tomorrow, babe."

"I will . . . Love you too." I hang up.

My head drops to my hands and, as my emotions overcome me, I curl up on my side and fully sob into my pillow, finally letting myself lose total control. My chest heaves while my lungs fight to catch breath and I release muted, guttural wails into my soaked pillow.

In an instant, the past three years have exploded into one horrible tragedy—one that can never ever be undone. I wish this was merely the worst dream of my lifetime and I cry for us both, believing that H would still be alive if it wasn't for me and not knowing how I will live with the guilt. I wish he knew how much he meant to me. I wish that would have mattered.

Stay in the closet with Don't Ask, Don't Tell or tell my truth. Two impossible choices with severe consequences either way. I felt trapped. There seemed to be no way out.

But this time—oh my God, *this time*—I finally tell the truth. Take a chance. Risk my career. And *this*, this devastating outcome, is the result.

It is worse than anything I ever could have imagined.

Chapter 34

THE AFTERMATH

The morning of H's death, his wife called the wife of another chief in my squadron to tell her that H was having an affair—with me. When she started that conversation, H rose from where he was seated, went into their bedroom, closed the door, sat down with his back against it, and shot himself. He was forty-eight years old.

This is why my squadron leadership came to my door to notify me of his death. They believed we were having an affair. And when H died that day, I was left holding that story, unable to refute it and tell the truth without hurting his reputation and losing my career.

Given this, I don't attend the memorial service. The entire squadron goes while I sit outside on the driveway at Amy's house on a lawn chair.

Another lawn chair. Another bottom.

Clearly, I'm not welcome at the service, but even if I was, I know my presence there would be problematic. I am doubly crushed: not only have I just lost a man I cherished, I also now have to face people every day who believe his affair with me is the reason he died. All of this together is beyond anything I can manage. My hiding has knotted me up to a point that even I can't unravel the threads.

It is just too much.

So I stay on this lawn chair and stare vacantly across the street at a forest of tall pine trees—wishing I could be anywhere but here, wishing I could escape, wishing I never met H in the first place.

H's brother has come to Whidbey Island to attend the service and escort his body back to Alabama, where he will be buried. While he's here, he calls and asks to meet me.

I'm hesitant, to say the least. I can't fathom what he could want with me, and I'm not sure I can handle another person piling more blame on top of my own. But he is H's brother, so I agree to meet him in a local grocery store parking lot.

Rain streaks down my windshield and the overhead lights reflect off of dark wet asphalt as I wait in my Jeep. I think about all that has transpired since that chief made that horrible phone call to H's wife from Diego Garcia. Told the lie that H and I were having an affair. I wonder if he knows what he put in motion that day. I wonder if he would have made the same decision if he'd known that it would ruin lives. He transferred from the command when we returned from Diego Garcia. Is he aware of the fallout? Does he care?

My thoughts are interrupted when a car pulls up and a man with thick, short brown hair gets out wearing a heavy brown all-weather coat.

He comes over to my window, already dripping. "Hi, Karen. I'm Terry."

"Hi, Terry," I say. "Please, come get out of the rain."

He flicks the rain off of his shoulders before getting into my passenger seat.

H's brother, a man with a gentle face and light brown eyes with dark, puffy circles under them, is two feet from me, sitting next to me in my car. A composed and somber man, he is here to do the heartbreaking task of escorting his deceased brother home.

He stares out of the windshield, then takes a deep breath and turns toward me with a sad smile. "I know this is unusual and I promise not to take too much of your time, but I wanted to meet the woman my brother was in love with."

"H talked to you about me?" I ask, struck dumb by just how far this all went without my understanding.

He nods. "He did. He called me last week and told me that he was in love with you and that he was going to end his marriage. He told me how wonderful you are, and he sounded excited. I was happy for him. It's hard to believe he went from that excitement to now being gone." He glances out of the windshield, then meets my gaze again. "I just wanted to meet you, Karen. I hoped it would help me make some sense of it all."

He stops and waits, clearly searching my eyes for something that will help him "make some sense of it all." I'm not sure I can do that for him.

I look through him for a moment as my military bearing, a shield from more pain, takes over. I take a breath and struggle to find the right words, hoping for something that will help him. But I am also cautious, as he could leak my truth to his family or even to the squadron leadership, and I've just learned my lesson about truth-telling.

I tell him what I can without jeopardizing my safety.

"Terry, your brother was amazing, and I admired and respected him so much. I have never met anyone like him, and he helped me become a better sailor and chief. A better person. Truly, I wanted to be just like him. But I wasn't in love with him. I told him that the week before he died, and it hurt him. I wish so badly that things could have turned out differently. I'm so sorry."

He listens and nods. The sadness penetrating his eyes, his thoughtfulness, and his southern politeness all reminded me of H. "I understand. Thank you for sharing that with me and agreeing to meet with me, Karen. I will sure miss my big brother." Tears well up in his eyes. "I'll miss him a lot. But somehow meeting you helps." He looks down for a moment. "My mother is, clearly, a wreck. Would it be okay if she contacts you?"

"Of course she can." The words speak themselves, though I am not so sure I mean them.

"Thank you. She'll appreciate that." He extends his right hand, which I take in mine. He holds it for a second before placing his left hand over it and holding my gaze with his kind eyes. "I can see why my brother loved you, Karen, and I wish you the best."

I force myself to stay present and try to not lose it completely. "Thank you, Terry. He was an amazing man. I will truly miss him and I'm so sorry for your loss."

As the red of his taillights fades in the distance, I sit in my car and weep, trying to absorb the depth of the nightmare from which I simply cannot wake.

The beloved man that he was, H is remembered at two different memorial services, one in Hawaii and one in Whidbey. There is also a funeral in his hometown in Alabama, after which his mother calls me. Like his brother, she is distraught and wants someone to help her make some sense of it all—and wants to meet the woman her son was in love with.

She has the kindest southern accent. "I just can't believe my Henry is gone," she says mournfully.

She calls more than once. Every time I talk to her, a little more of me dies, but I also feel a deep obligation to comfort her. I don't have the answers anyone is looking for, and I'm trying to put my own pieces back together—but I can still be caring and compassionate, and doing so feels like I'm honoring H.

His mom asks for my address. A few days later, I receive a package in the mail: three casing shells from his 21-gun salute, as he was buried with full military honors, and some pictures of the gravesite, her and other family members, and him. It is strange to be treated as if I am a part of his family, but I have no idea how to remove myself from the middle of it. It seems kinder to simply allow it to happen.

My first attempt at returning to work is in early October. As soon as I park in a CPO parking spot, put on my cover, and step out of my Jeep, a petite, pretty Latina woman storms my way. It's the woman H's wife called that fateful day.

Her pace is quick, her face enraged.

I wait, bracing myself.

"How could you!?" she screams, an inch from my face. "You're a horrible person!"

I look down. "I know. I'm so sorry." I leave her standing there and walk, keeping my head down, into the hangar, avoiding eye contact with my shipmates who just witnessed our exchange.

Sailors still greet me, but more reservedly than before. "Morning, Chief," comes my way in somber voices.

"Morning," I say with a nod, and I make my way to Admin, where my team is huddled around Petty Officer Kimbrough's desk.

"Hey, everyone." I'm grateful for their familiar faces.

No high fives, no hoopla. Just "Hey, Chief," and then hugs and tears all around.

H's death has been unimaginably hard on everyone, including these incredible young sailors. I'm so sorry I couldn't protect them from this grief. They loved him too.

Sitting at my desk a half hour later, I wait for H to poke his head out of his now empty office and ask me a question, give me shit, or call me a slug. My heart sinks at the inconceivable realization that he'll never do that again.

The last words he ever said to me were, "I'll meet you at the front gate at 0700." What I would give to be able to turn back the clock.

The following two months are completely wiped from my memory, except for one moment. A few weeks after H's death, YN2 Kimbrough is briefing me when she suddenly stops, turns to YN3 Tenley, and says, "Do you see that look on Chief's face? She isn't hearing a thing I'm saying."

And it's true. Staying present is excruciating. Dissociating is helping me get through each moment. I'm as checked out as I've ever been.

My next memory is from December 1, the day I transfer from the squadron, drive back up the narrow, winding road up and over Deception Pass, and leave VP-1 and Whidbey Island behind.

My windshield wipers slap back and forth and tears stream down my face all the way down the West Coast. I have maintained a dam around my emotions for the past two months, terrified that I would completely fall apart if I allowed myself to feel anything at all. Now that I finally have space to let down my guard, they're all coming out in a flood.

Six months ago, the radio was filled with nothing but songs

of hope and anticipation. Now only songs filled with sorrow blare out of my speakers. Everything—the rain, the trees, the freeway—are the same. But not me. No singing this time. No joy. Nothing about me is the same.

I'm not sure it ever will be.

For the first time in my career I am taking a full month of leave. I drive directly to San Diego because I need to see Sue—need to know that she and I are still solid. One more day without seeing my love would be one day too many.

The hectic freeways of Los Angeles greet me with warmth and sunshine as they guide me southward to San Diego and Tierra Santa, a small, beautiful community where Sue has rented a two-bedroom home. When I exit onto Tierra Santa Boulevard, a four-lane street lined with large, fragrant eucalyptus trees, I feel my grip on the steering wheel relax for the first time in over 1,300 miles.

Relief hits me when I pull into the driveway and Sue comes out with a loving smile on her face and reaches for me with a comforting hug. Then she brings me inside to meet Missy, a small, beautiful, feisty-as-hell Siamese cat who is now a part of our family, just waiting for 6-Pac's return from Arizona at the end of the month.

We make our way to the couch and sit side by side in silence, once again breathing the same air. All the while, I fight back tears—over H, over the time Sue and I have lost, over the uncertainty of our future.

An entire lifetime has occurred in the three and a half years we've spent apart. We have both changed tremendously. We still love each other, and that in itself is a miracle. But we will still need to find "us" again—and now we will have to do so while I work through the deepest grief I've ever known.

I will always wonder how my relationship with Sue would have evolved if we'd never had to separate. Would we have been caught for being gay? Would we have stayed together? Would I have gotten sober? Would we both have made chief? Would H be alive?

Sue has an amazing ability to be present with heartbreak and grief. Just sitting there on the couch with her body next to mine, I soften, comforted by her silent, empathetic, and calming presence. *Sue is here. Still my girl. Her hand on my back. Her head leaning into mine.* She has no way of fully understanding everything I'm feeling, but she listens, tears also falling down her cheeks, and she puts her arms around me as I mourn.

This weekend we stay at a secluded bed-and-breakfast in Julian, a small mountain town an hour from San Diego. We take quiet walks in the pines, a reminder of my childhood in the forest. As we sit on the deck in the chilly mountain air, wrapped together in a warm blanket, the clear, starlit night sky above us allows me some perspective. It's hard to know how to start again, but the time we're spending together here, though our words are few, feels like a good beginning.

Our new beginning is filled with just being with each other, feeling the same air on our skin, sitting close on the couch, eating meals together, and taking naps. I lay myself on her lap, and she massages my head and strokes my hair. Tears roll across the bridge of my nose and onto her lap, and I fall asleep.

My sorrow is unbearable and depleting, leaving me very little to give to Sue. But she is patient. She loves and watches over me, giving me the time and space I need to stop feeling so broken, to slowly climb my way out from the abyss I wasn't sure just a couple of weeks ago that I could ever return from.

As I grieve the end of one life, I am also starting a new one here with Sue. It's a second chance I am not taking for granted. My hope is that her world and my world will eventually merge back into our world—that we will once more become the "us" we used to be.

Only time will tell if we are capable of getting there again.

Chapter 35

TAKING OFF
THE ARMOR

I spent another eleven years in the Navy, seeing the world and loving my time as a chief and then a senior chief. The day I became a chief petty officer and put on my khakis my life changed forever, and those changes were beautiful. Being a chief was everything it promised to be, and more. I was blessed to mentor and work with the most wonderful sailors a closeted senior chief could ever ask for.

My three goals for the remainder of my career were: 1) to never be separated from Sue again; 2) to not get caught for being gay; and 3) to someday put on H's nine anchors and become a command master chief. The first two I accomplished. The third never happened, in part because of my decision to prioritize my relationship and remain co-located with Sue.

Getting promoted to the rank of E-9 is so difficult that only approximately 1 percent of the Navy's enlisted ranks ever achieve that pinnacle. One of the reasons I did so well in my early career was that I transferred to so many locations all over the world. I proved that I was "worldwide assignable." But when Sue and I reunited after our three-and-a-half-year separation, I wasn't willing to transfer away from her again if I could help it. So every time I called for orders, I asked my detailer to give me any assignment available in San Diego. One after the other I turned down challenging billets in far-off locations and accepted less-challenging local billets in order to remain with my love, as did Sue. It was a trade-off, and it's one that I would make again and again. But it came at a cost: it hindered my, and Sue's, opportunity to advance.

In January of 1996, I reported to my next duty station, SEAL Team Five, where I was assigned for four years, the longest in my career.

Once I started there, I never wanted to leave. SEAL Team Five was the medicine I needed to help me get back on my feet. The SEALs, the yeomen, and my other shipmates there taught me more than I ever could have imagined, but two major things top the list: First, that precision and expertise are life-and-death skills that are continually practiced, honed, and perfected, moment by critical moment. Second, to chill the hell out. Life, I learned, is meant to be enjoyed, and playfulness is a crucial, if not *the* most crucial, part of life. Navy SEALs are much more than the Navy's greatest warriors. They are incredibly kind and strong and compassionate and humble, and they treated me as a part of their family.

I'll always be grateful that Team Five was my landing place after VP-1. I left there at the end of 1999 answering to a new nickname, Señorita Jefe, and my favorite title, Senior Chief Solt.

A week after the terrorist strikes on September 11, 2001, I reported as the leading administrative chief to Shore Intermediate Maintenance Activity (SIMA), the largest shore command in San Diego, to find that almost half of my office—five of us—were gay. Young, proud, flaming, and professional, this

quartet—three gay men and one lesbian—brought the underground gay community to the surface, a sharp contrast to the
deeply-closeted-always-looking-over-your-shoulder gayness I
had been conditioned with. After my many years of dodging
witch hunts and Don't Ask, Don't Tell, and then my tragedy
with H, it was a beautiful thing to experience the joy, love, and
camaraderie that filled that room, gay and straight. Of course,
the actual words "I'm gay" were never spoken out loud, but this
was a new generation of sailors, one that was more blended and
openly accepting than anything I had ever before experienced.
This was a modern breed of gayness, beautiful humans who were
comfortable in their skin. Their comfort with who they were
ultimately helped me feel far more comfortable in my own skin.

It was at SIMA when I walked into my office one afternoon
and immediately realized something was different. As I stopped
and looked around, trying to figure out what it was, the office
went silent and all my sailors sheepishly smiled, giggled, and
refused to meet my eyes. Then it hit me. The gay sailors had
organized all their administrative supplies—stickies, highlight-
ers, and markers—in rainbow patterns on their desks.

They watched my face carefully, clearly not sure what my
reaction would be. I just laughed and shook my head. With that
permission, the entire office burst into laughter, like they were
getting one over on the Navy.

Young and bold, fearless and fierce in a way I hadn't been in
a very long time, these young sailors showed me how it might
look if the Navy were to someday allow gay sailors to have it all.

After I transferred from SIMA, I was given the opportunity
to deploy onboard an aircraft carrier—something I'd always
wanted to do before I retired. So, in 2004, at thirty-eight years
old—my twenty-year retirement-eligible mark—I deployed to

the Western Pacific with my new aviation squadron, Sea Control Squadron 35 (VS-35), onboard the USS *John C. Stennis.*

Sue and I said our goodbyes behind closed doors, just as we always had. By this point, we were both seasoned senior chiefs, very focused on our careers and both trying to make master chief. I would certainly miss her, 6-Pac, and Missy, but we were now experts at time apart and had spent many months, weeks, and days away from each other throughout the years. We could do six months standing on our heads by now.

We were still very committed to each other, but our relationship had never been the same since our separation in Hawaii. We shared a deep bond, and a lot of laughter and fun, and we were amazing companions. But we each knew the cost of letting our guard down, and it was constant work to remain vulnerable and open with each other.

As I said goodbye to her before that deployment in my tan flight jacket, brown flight boots, and working khakis, Sue remained the center of my heart and it didn't seem possible that we would *never* get back to "us." I knew that it was in us, and I was just waiting for that day to arrive.

My deployment onboard the *Stennis* was in theory everything I wanted: I was the most senior enlisted female in the squadron, and the sailors in the five work centers I was supervising were incredibly professional and hardworking. But very soon after the ship left the dock, my gut spoke to tell me, *Karen, this isn't you anymore.* I didn't yet know where I did belong, but in my heart I knew that I no longer belonged in the Navy. I was retirement-eligible and still closeted under Don't Ask, Don't Tell. My environment and my identity—my two worlds—remained at odds, and it seemed they always would. I had to choose between letting go of the Navy or continuing to betray myself.

For the first time since coming out to H, I chose myself over self-betrayal: I submitted my request to retire. I would finish my obligation, and in early 2006 I would swap my uniform for civilian attire.

Six months later, I stood on the flight deck in my Dress Blues—*with slacks*—as the carrier returned to San Diego. We were a squadron in grief: our deployment had been unsuccessful, as VS-35 had experienced the tragic loss of four shipmates. We wore yellow ribbons representing Blue Wolf 704, the plane that had crashed—our plane, which had held four of the Navy's finest—pinned to our uniforms.

As the ship rounded Point Loma for North Island Naval Air Station, I scanned the sea of family members, children, balloons, and signs, looking for my love. My breath skipped a beat and my chest softened when I saw her—stunning blue eyes, warm smile, and cheeks for days—jumping and waving her arms wildly in the air so I could see her short self. Our eyes met, and we held each other in suspended time, the last six months instantly melting away. In my pocket were two champagne-diamond rings that I'd purchased in Australia. In my heart, I held renewed hope. In my head, I reminded myself that this wasn't a dream. Because in her eyes, I knew it was real. I was home again.

The carrier was tied up to the pier an hour later and I entered the quarterdeck, faced the officer of the deck, stood at attention, saluted, and asked, "Permission to go ashore?"

He saluted back. "Permission granted, Senior Chief."

We dropped our salutes, and then I took a few steps off the quarterdeck and turned and raised mine again, saluting the American flag waving in the San Diego sunshine on the stern of the ship. Then I walked down the gangway and descended the metal stairs, carrying my large green flight bag, a completely different sailor than the one who'd stumbled up the gangway twenty years earlier on the USS *Frank Cable* in her skirt and heels.

As I stepped off the brow and made my way to Sue, I didn't look back. One thing I knew for sure: The Navy had done what it promised it would do. It had grown me up.

Retiring from the Navy is a big achievement, and most celebrate with a ceremony. But I didn't want a ceremony. So much had happened in my career, and there was no way that I could stand on a stage, looking at my proud parents, my other close friends and shipmates, and Sue—and pretend that my love was just my friend. Sailors—from E-1 to E-7—would pass a folded American flag to me, while "God Bless the USA" played softly in the background. The flag would then be ceremoniously handed from me to my parents, since I couldn't hand it to Sue. I would listen to a guest speaker say the nicest things about my career, all the while thinking about H and how he didn't stick around long enough to see this day. Then I would have to give a speech. And that final hoop was the one I just couldn't see myself jump through. Without a doubt I would stand on that stage with my military bearing engaged, looking through everyone, and trying desperately to stay disconnected from my feelings so that I didn't choke on my words. That spotlight would be torturous.

I didn't want any of it.

So, instead of a ceremony, on my final day in uniform in January of 2006 I numbly drove off Naval Station San Diego—no fanfare—and headed home. Sue wasn't home yet, so I petted Missy and hoisted 6-Pac onto my shoulders before walking up the stairs to my bedroom. Feeling disembodied, I sat on the bed and took off my brown shoes and tan socks, and then my uniform. I removed my ribbons, my warfare pin, my name badge, and my anchors from my shirt. I rolled up my belt with my attached brushed-gold senior chief anchor belt buckle. I neatly placed my insignias, my belt, and my garrison hat—senior chief anchor still attached—in a keepsake box. It was a funeral for one; it was time to put Senior Chief Solt to rest.

I sat for a moment, holding the keepsake box in my hands, and then stood and placed it neatly on the back edge of my dresser.

Then I laid my khaki uniform on the bed, rolled my brown shoes and tan socks up in it, and walked back downstairs to the outside trash cans, where I tossed everything inside.

Not because I was mad.

Just because I was done.

Epilogue

COMING HOME

Wen I took my uniform off that last time, what I thought I would experience—freedom—is not what I experienced, at least not as easily and instantaneously as I'd expected. I was blindsided when my hiding followed me into retirement. I had somehow assumed that I would be able to close my Navy chapter, put it all behind me, and start fresh as a free civilian. But I quickly realized that I felt naked without my uniform—even more exposed and less safe. I didn't know what it was like to live without habitually looking over my shoulder. My identity was wrapped up in my many years in the Navy—and faulty as that identity was, I was lost without it. Wearing that uniform had altered every aspect of my life and of my sense of self.

Sue and I also continued to struggle. I had fought so hard to reunite with her that I hoped our second chance would last forever and we would eventually return to the fairy-tale love that I expected would arrive when we were both retired. But that wasn't the case.

We took a stab at couples counseling at one point, but when our counselor helped us identify our hurdles and encouraged us to proactively face our demons, we both offered firm resistance to different issues. The distance between us seemed insurmountable.

Looking back, it's easy to see why it was such a struggle for us to let one another fully in again. The odds were constantly stacked against us, and we still weren't truly free to love each other the way I wanted.

In the end, our second chance lasted until 2009. I simply didn't know how to free myself from my own struggles when doing so involved a relationship infused with fear, shame, and internalized homophobia. Although I still deeply loved Sue— because that kind of love never goes away—we weren't "us" anymore, and I finally had to accept that we never would be again. In one of the darkest periods of my life, we released each other with the same love and deep friendship that had sustained us for nineteen years.

There was one big win a few years later, however. Five years after I left the service to be true to myself, President Barack Obama did what should have been done decades earlier: he repealed Don't Ask, Don't Tell, giving gay service members the right to openly serve.

This was the end of an era of deep discrimination against the gay community. From World War II to the official repeal of DADT, 114,000 service members were discharged under the military's discriminatory service bans and never received compensation or acknowledgment for their service. This is a deep wound in our veteran community, and far too many gay veterans still fight for their less-than-honorable discharges to be upgraded.

Today's gay service members are not witch-hunted. They can get married, list their spouses as their next of kin, create families, even share their true feelings during separations and reunions. They don't have to change pronouns to avoid detection, and married same-sex couples are co-located, keeping them with the person they love. All told, they have more of the world that I dreamed of for so many years.

Despite these positive changes, however, military life can still be hard for gay service members. I wouldn't go so far as to say that they don't have to look over their shoulder. Many are still harassed and even assaulted. Our country and its politicians, the overseers of our military, set the tone for the equal treatment of its citizens, and the LGBTQ+ community—in and out of the military—remains under constant attack.

Still, the positive changes I saw occurring within the military kept my hope that the little girl who'd just wanted to play Little League with the boys would one day live in a world of true equality—a hope that seems insurmountable, but one I continue to keep.

Over the years, life normalized. I was out to everyone in my life. I had a great job, a sweet girlfriend, two wonderful dogs, a nice home, and decades of recovery under my belt. Heck, I even had a master's degree. I believed my days of looking over my shoulder were behind me and I was getting this hiding stuff figured out.

That belief came crashing down in March of 2017. I was participating in a large online forum when a coworker and friend who was also participating—someone who knew I was gay— jokingly called me out for the rainbow emoji I'd included next to my name with a sly, "Karen, why the rainbow?"

Instead of seizing the opportunity to respond by simply saying, "It's because I'm gay," I froze and then sidestepped: "Oh, I just love the colors of the rainbow."

We were in a public forum, and I didn't feel safe. His question caught me off guard, so I did what my long-cultivated instincts told me to do: I lied.

Not telling the truth was painful, but the shame that followed that self-betrayal was excruciating. I berated myself incessantly for hours. Within a day, chills, body aches, and a high fever forced me into bed, where I nursed my emotional and physical wounds and wondered if I would ever have the courage to fully come out.

I stayed in bed until my fever broke and my aches and pains subsided a week later. It was mid-morning when I finally started to feel better, and I sluggishly inched out from under my covers and got into the shower. Natural light streamed in through the long, narrow window next to me as hot water fell over my head. I closed my eyes, my mind spinning. I desperately wanted answers to the questions whirling through my head: *How did I get to this place where hiding is my norm? Where did I lose myself? Will I ever be okay just being myself? Will I ever be free?*

The universe responded when a vision of a helpless dog lying down in a crate flashed through my mind and a bolt of energy surged through my body. The dog looked like he had given up on life, the helplessness in his eyes unmistakable. I knew that look.

Like that, he was gone. And I understood. I opened my eyes, turned off the water, dried off, dressed, and went to my office, where I sat in front of my open laptop and let thousands of words flow from my fingertips.

The helpless dog image was one I had seen in my post-graduate studies. In the mid-1960s, a psychologist named Martin Seligman studied classical conditioning and assessed the psychological reactions dogs displayed under certain conditions. In the first part of the experiment, Seligman rang a bell before administering a horribly cruel electrical shock to the dogs. This conditioned the dogs to brace for and expect the shock anytime they heard the bell. He then put those same dogs in a crate with a small fence running through the middle, one that could easily be jumped over. Seligman could electrify the side that the dog was on, but the other side was normal. There was no bell this time; he simply electrified the floor.

He was surprised when, instead of jumping to the other side when he turned the electricity on, they instead simply lay down—gave up without even trying. But he realized that it was because they had been conditioned to expect pain. They had been conditioned to be helpless.

Seligman termed this reaction—*not trying* to get out of a negative situation because the past has taught you that you can't—"learned helplessness." A similar scenario occurs in India when elephant trainers catch baby elephants and cruelly restrain them by tying a rope around one of their legs and anchoring it. The captured baby elephant is not strong enough to break free. Any adult elephant could easily do so. But they don't. Because they have been conditioned by their past experiences to believe they are stuck.

In that one moment in the shower I realized, *This is me. I've been bracing my entire life.*

I had been conditioned into hiding. Being honest about being gay had always felt like a life-or-death confession to my body—especially since I told my truth to H.

With this realization, I could clearly see how it had all unfolded. When I was a little girl, my form of "self" didn't match society's image of who little girls are supposed to be. I learned to stuff down my feelings and escape my reality by going into hiding with my drinking and my misfit ways. This continued for twenty-two years in the Navy, where I stayed closeted in order to stay safe. The one time I did finally speak my truth to someone, that person took his own life, and I believed my coming out was the reason for it. Just like the past taught those dogs that a bell preceded a shock, my past taught me that coming out, just being myself, preceded danger. The belief that I hurt H, that being who I am resulted in his death, only reinforced my inability to feel safe in my truth.

This was my "hiding" bottom. I was completely spent from all of my attempts to dodge and weave and escape my inner demons. I had no choice but to finally face them. I stopped running, sat still in meditation, and, through a steady stream of tears, stayed present as a flood of insights rushed through me. I reconnected with the tough little blond-haired girl, barefoot with suntanned shoulders, I began my life as. I understood why I shut down, why I needed to escape. I clearly saw how I betrayed myself by going into hiding and becoming a rebel, an addict, a clown, a liar. I understood that every bottom I hit was the universe putting an end to that form of self-betrayal, bringing me home to my true self.

Knowing this about myself, I started a practice for myself. Similar to exposure therapy, where a person who has a deep fear or phobia has to do the actual thing that scares them, I started challenging myself to be honest and come out every time I was in a situation where I had the opportunity to hide. Though it had been years since I'd retired from the Navy by this point, I still had to acknowledge my trepidation around this admission. My heartbeat and temperature would increase as my insides braced, waiting for repercussions, every single time I said the words "I'm gay." But I made myself do it anyway.

The day of my vision was also the day I started writing this book. But not *this* book. The first version was a how-to book about the stages of hiding and how to stop. It didn't include anything about H. I feared writing about him might break me. When I finally had no choice but to include him on the page, it felt like that very thing might happen. This book and the inner work that has coincided with writing it have put me face-to-face with him. H's suicide was a painful tragedy, has been the biggest wound of my life, and has brought me to my knees more times than I care to count. He was such a special person. I loved him. I respected him. I spent the remainder of my career trying to make him proud. And I still miss him.

Over the years I have replayed it over and over thousands of times, wondering what I could have done differently. But today I know that H based his actions on a number of factors, and I am not responsible for the choice that he ultimately made. As much as I would love to make some sense of his death, I will never fully understand the depth of his despair.

I write these final words from my cozy home in the mountains. I have returned to my mile-high conservative hometown, four hundred miles from the Pacific Ocean. I have just lost my soulmate dog, Paco, who spent the last thirteen-and a half years with me and laid quietly by my side as I wrote these words. I'm finding my way without him, soaking in quiet days and four seasons while surrounded by ponderosa pines, granite boulders, new friends, and thoughtful neighbors. My father has now passed, and I'm watching over my aging mother, who lives four miles down the road. I am experiencing a state of mind that has always eluded me—contentedness—and deep in my soul, I know I am truly blessed. I've traveled the world. I've lost and have rediscovered myself. I've hit bottoms and have climbed my way back out again and again. And I've finally made my way home, because I now know that home is wherever I am honestly living my life.

When I look back at that girl I was in high school, drinking and drugging and rolling her eyes at the chief who came to speak to my class, it's easy to see the universe knew what she was doing all along. She threw me into a profession that placed a uniform on my body. She knew I would hide underneath it for as long as I needed its protection, for it to keep me safe. Until it no longer could. Then she knew I would shed that layer and trust myself to land on my feet and take things the rest of the way.

Serving my country was the greatest privilege of my life, and I'm so grateful for all the devotion and respect and honor and pride that came along with wearing that uniform. It gave me a home, a new family, a purpose, and a place to hide for many years. But it was ultimately in taking it off that I learned my greatest lesson: being vulnerable, naked, and exposed is where true courage resides.

ACKNOWLEDGMENTS

This was not a book I intended to write. I kept waiting for our collective story to be written by someone else because it was a story I needed to read so that I could heal. I had been in hiding for so long, it was painful to expose my truth, my vulnerability—my secrets—but what I learned through this process is that facing all of it has given me a level of freedom I've never before experienced.

First, to my fellow gay veterans, especially those appearing in these pages, thank you. It's not lost on me that my hiding helped me make it to retirement when tens of thousands of you were hunted and discharged and never received compensation or acknowledgment for your service. My hope is that, by uncovering and sharing my truth, my words will validate that your journey was not only difficult but also harmful and unjust. One of the greatest joys of my life was serving with you, and I'd like to thank you for finding me and leading me to my special underground family. I'm honored to call you my sisters and brothers.

To the many straight veterans I served with who knew I was gay and protected my truth, thank you. I am fully aware that this world is much more loving and accepting than we are conditioned to believe that it is, and I have hope for a better, more equal, world because of you. I'm blessed that my shady recruiter tricked me into joining the Navy; without his sneakiness, I never would have met and served with people as incredible as you.

If the Navy taught me anything, it's that we accomplish nothing important alone and are better together. Writing this book was a team project, and I could not have done it without the love and support of many incredible humans. At the tippy top of that list is MY Coach, the incredible Kristin Kaye—aka the "Book Shaman." Thank you for being much more than my writing coach—you have become one of my dearest friends. Your guidance and support and belief in my story gave me the courage to "just keep writing," even in my darkest moments. You kept me focused on my truth—the golden thread within me—and helped my story come to life on the page. I don't know how you do it, but I'll give it up to three things: the universe, your larger-than-life heart, and a secret, magic, intuitive potion that was specifically gifted to you.

Having kindhearted friends listen to my first pages or read my early drafts was an exercise in deep vulnerability, and I am grateful to the following friends for their support, gentle feedback, and patience, especially with my challenges in using proper tense: Tressa Yonekawa Bundren, Maura Conlon, Team Literary Alchemy, Rosemary and Carol Badgett, Christy Long, Robyn Sharier, John Tewksbury, Holly Masterson, Janice Marshall, Pegi Deitz Shea, Rick & Sylvia Seares, Amanda Hodgson, Laurie Temple, Cindy Yurkovich, and Madeleine Ferbal.

To Col. Grethe Cammermeyer, words cannot express my respect for the way you have served this world. Thank you for leading the way many years ago with your truth and for writing *Serving in Silence*. You are a champion for gay veterans and a hero of mine.

To Master Chief Petty Officer of the Navy Joe Campa, thank you for your open mind, big heart, and willingness to learn about an experience that was mostly hidden from you while you served.

ACKNOWLEDGMENTS

Having you endorse this memoir gives me hope that this wound can and will heal for our LGBTQ+ veteran community.

To my industry-disrupting publisher Brooke Warner, project manager Shannon Green, editor Krissa Lagos, art director Julie Metz, and to the entire She Writes Press team—thank you! I found the perfect house, and you all are amazing. I'm very grateful for all of your support, detail, and care with "my baby."

To my publicist, Lauren Cerand, thank you for the way you navigate the publishing world, for championing my story, and for helping me bring *Hiding for My Life* to the finish line. Your honesty, kindness, and boldness in this industry is beyond refreshing and is something I am very grateful for.

To Gabra Zackman and Julia Motyka. I simply adore the hell out of both of you and trust the universe knew what she was doing when she placed you in my path. Thank you for your love, support, and generosity, and for helping me get *Hiding for My Life* into Audiobookland.

My healing journey began decades ago, and a number of people have helped me simply focus on taking the next step. It started in 1992 with Linda, the one who called me Kumquat— I will always be grateful for you and your love and I miss you more than I can ever express. Thanks to Kim Bushong (my kindred latte companion) for your love, support, big heart, tough spirit, and for always laughing at my jokes. Thanks to Dr. Frantonia Pollins (Unapologetic First Lady) for teaching me to prioritize my inner hippie warrior. To my Astro Girls for always having my back. To John McMullin, Leigh Randolph, and all of my JOW peeps—thank you for teaching me that there are always three sides to every coin. To Dr. Dawn Brock, aka "The Guru," thank you for being a consistent lifeline for the past four years, for helping me face the depth of my sorrow, for helping me find perspective, and for giving me the tools to write my next chapter.

Kathy Hansen, thank you for being much more than a great friend. You are not only one of the kindest people I know, you are also the sister I never had. Thank you for listening to me as I read you these words through my tears, for your compassion, your understanding, and for always having my back. We've come a long way since our bar-fighting days, and having you on my side has always meant that I'm never alone.

Sue, we had quite a ride. Thank you. I'll always be grateful that I slipped on that tile in my jeans and made you fall in love with me (it's a bonus that I didn't break my leg doing it). I hope you always keep your head above the white water, that the beachcomber in you finds the shiniest shells, and that all of your days from here on out are full of sweet dogs, sunshine, and smooth sailing.

H, I'm not sure any one person has had more of an impact on my life. Thank you for helping me see the Navy through your eyes, for teaching me to be a great chief petty officer, and for giving me an experience that would force me to someday come out from hiding. I carried the knowledge I learned from you with me for the rest of my career, and even to this day I hope to always make you proud.

Mom and Dad (currently experiencing his next life as an astronaut), thank you for always loving and believing in me. Because of you, I'm resilient, tough, witty, loving, smart, and compassionate—the best qualities of both of you. I'm blessed to be your daughter, and I love you.

Lastly, to Paco. For many wonderful years, you were my family, my best friend, the one who lovingly greeted me at the door, the very sniffy pup who took me for slow walks around the neighborhood, the one who let me carry him up the hills as he aged. You have been the one being in my lifetime who truly loved me without conditions—here through it all, a peaceful, calm, and loving heartbeat just inches away as I navigated this life of mine. It was such a gift to ride this ride with you. Thank you for rescuing me and showing me the path to a softer and more open heart. I could not be more grateful for every bit of the life we shared together, and I hope you're screaming out "wheeeeeee" as you do backflips over the moon. When you've had enough of that, please find your way back to me. I'll be waiting right here.

ABOUT THE AUTHOR

Photo credit: Miranda Remington

Karen Solt is a retired US Navy senior chief petty officer who served as a gay sailor from 1984 to 2006, prior to and during Don't Ask, Don't Tell. After hiding her sexuality from the world for most of her life, Karen considers herself a "Combat Hideologist," and believes the way back to personal and global peace and freedom is for every human to come out from hiding and commit to living the truth of who they are. She holds a master's degree in psychology (counseling), is an emotional health coach, and loves to help others discover and heal their own hiding places. Karen currently resides in her small hometown, Prescott, Arizona, where she and her new, young dog, Kai, chase squirrels, drink lattes, and watch over her feisty mother.

To learn more, please visit Karen's website at:
www.hideology.com.

SELECTED TITLES FROM SHE WRITES PRESS

She Writes Press is an independent publishing company
founded to serve women writers everywhere.
Visit us at www.shewritespress.com.

Making the Rounds: Defying Norms in Love and Medicine. $17.95, 978-1-64742-273-8. In the late 1960s, Patricia Grayhall defies societal norms by coming out as a lesbian and dreaming of becoming a doctor—but the free-wheeling sexual revolution and the demands of her medical training complicate her search for the equal, loving relationship with a woman she so desires. Can she have both love and career?

Handsome: Stories of an Awkward Girl Boy Human by Holly Lorka. $16.95, 978-1-63152-783-8. As a horny little kid, Holly Lorka had no idea why God had put her in the wrong body and made her want to kiss girls. She had questions: Was she a monster? Would she ever be able to grow sideburns? And most importantly, where was her penis? Here, she tells the story of her romp through the first fifty years of her life searching for sex, love, acceptance, and answers to her questions.

You Can't Buy Love Like That: Growing Up Gay in the Sixties by Carol E. Anderson. $16.95, 978-1631523144. A young lesbian girl grows beyond fear to fearlessness as she comes of age in the '60s amid religious, social, and legal barriers.

Affliction: Growing Up With a Closeted Gay Dad by Laura Hall. $16.95, 978-1-64742-124-3. Laura Hall was born in a small city on the San Francisco peninsula to a straight mother and a gay father who lived in the shadows. This is her tender, frank account of how her father's secret became her inheritance and, ultimately, the path to her own healing.

Queerspawn in Love by Kellen Kaiser. $16.95, 978-1-63152-020-4. When the daughter of a quartet of lesbians falls in love with a man serving in the Israeli Defense Forces, she is forced to examine her own values and beliefs.

In Search of Pure Lust: A Memoir by Lise Weil. $16.95, 978-1-63152-385-4. Through the lens of her personal experiences as a lesbian coming of age in the '70s and '80s, Lise Weil documents an important chapter in lesbian history, her own long and difficult relationship history, and how her eventual dive into Zen practice became a turning point in her quest for love.